ACCENT, RHYTHM AND MEANING IN

LEGENDA

LEGENDA is the Modern Humanities Research Association's book imprint for new research in the Humanities. Founded in 1995 by Malcolm Bowie and others within the University of Oxford, Legenda has always been a collaborative publishing enterprise, directly governed by scholars. The Modern Humanities Research Association (MHRA) joined this collaboration in 1998, became half-owner in 2004, in partnership with Maney Publishing and then Routledge, and has since 2016 been sole owner. Titles range from medieval texts to contemporary cinema and form a widely comparative view of the modern humanities, including works on Arabic, Catalan, English, French, German, Greek, Italian, Portuguese, Russian, Spanish, and Yiddish literature. Editorial boards and committees of more than 60 leading academic specialists work in collaboration with bodies such as the Society for French Studies, the British Comparative Literature Association and the Association of Hispanists of Great Britain & Ireland.

The MHRA encourages and promotes advanced study and research in the field of the modern humanities, especially modern European languages and literature, including English, and also cinema. It aims to break down the barriers between scholars working in different disciplines and to maintain the unity of humanistic scholarship. The Association fulfils this purpose through the publication of journals, bibliographies, monographs, critical editions, and the MHRA Style Guide, and by making grants in support of research. Membership is open to all who work in the Humanities, whether independent or in a University post, and the participation of younger colleagues entering the field is especially welcomed.

ALSO PUBLISHED BY THE ASSOCIATION

Critical Texts
Tudor and Stuart Translations • *New Translations* • *European Translations*
MHRA Library of Medieval Welsh Literature

MHRA Bibliographies
Publications of the Modern Humanities Research Association

The Annual Bibliography of English Language & Literature
Austrian Studies
Modern Language Review
Portuguese Studies
The Slavonic and East European Review
Working Papers in the Humanities
The Yearbook of English Studies

www.mhra.org.uk
www.legendabooks.com

RESEARCH MONOGRAPHS IN FRENCH STUDIES

The *Research Monographs in French Studies* (RMFS) form a separate series within the Legenda programme and are published in association with the Society for French Studies. Individual members of the Society are entitled to purchase all RMFS titles at a discount.

The series seeks to publish the best new work in all areas of the literature, thought, theory, culture, film and language of the French-speaking world. Its distinctiveness lies in the relative brevity of its publications (50,000–60,000 words). As innovation is a priority of the series, volumes should predominantly consist of new material, although, subject to appropriate modification, previously published research may form up to one third of the whole. Proposals may include critical editions as well as critical studies. They should be sent with one or two sample chapters for consideration to Professor Diana Knight, Department of French and Francophone Studies, University of Nottingham, University Park, Nottingham NG7 2RD.

Editorial Committee
Diana Knight, University of Nottingham (General Editor)
Robert Blackwood, University of Liverpool
Jane Gilbert, University College London
Shirley Jordan, Newcastle University
Neil Kenny, All Souls College, Oxford
Max Silverman, University of Leeds

Advisory Committee
Wendy Ayres-Bennett, Murray Edwards College, Cambridge
Celia Britton, University College London
Ann Jefferson, New College, Oxford
Sarah Kay, New York University
Michael Moriarty, University of Cambridge
Keith Reader, University of Glasgow

ALSO IN THIS SERIES

www.rmfs.mhra.org.uk

Accent, Rhythm and Meaning
in French Verse

ROGER PENSOM

LEGENDA

Research Monographs in French Studies 44
Modern Humanities Research Association
2018

Published by Legenda
an imprint of the Modern Humanities Research Association
Salisbury House, Station Road, Cambridge CB1 2LA

ISBN 978-1-78188-697-7 (HB)
ISBN 978-1-78188-384-6 (PB)

First published 2018

Copy-Editor: Charlotte Brown

CONTENTS

In memoriam
PAUL VERRIER

ACKNOWLEDGEMENTS

Without the encouragement and constant oversight of my friend and colleague David Kuhn, this project would not have got off the ground. Whenever difficulty threatened to become obscurity, he was there with red ink and patient advice, through endless re-drafts, to keep the road open and the argument clear. All remaining shortcomings are mine alone.

The librarians of the Oxford University Faculty of Music are renowned for their courtesy and expertise. To them my thanks are due for help and advice in making the best use of their invaluable collection.

Thanks go also to Legenda's anonymous external reader, whose intervention sharpened the shape and direction of my argument. And to Charlotte Brown, for her hawk-eyed critique of my punctuation, notes and bibliography.

Closer to home, thanks for the tolerant support of my wife Barbara, who has lived uncomplainingly with this book for four years. She has found the time and patience to repeatedly proof-read it while remedying my incompetent management of a word-processor.

R.P., Finstock, April 2018

* * * * *

Roger Pensom very sadly died soon after this monograph went to press. The General Editor is extremely grateful to Adrian Armstrong for his willingness to provide academic oversight of the crucial last stages of production; his specialist knowledge, attention to detail and respect for the author's text and intentions have been invaluable. She also thanks Charlotte Brown, the copy-editor of this volume, for agreeing to take on the additional work of proof-reading and preparation of the index.

Diana Knight, September 2018

INTRODUCTION

What Is Verse and Why Do Poets Write It?

Shall I compare thee to a summer's day?	3 accents
Thou art more lovely and more temperate.	2 accents
Rough winds do shake the darling buds of May	6 accents
And summer's lease hath all too short a date.[1]	5 accents

Allowing for historical change this scansion will strike any English native speaker as more or less what the author intended. English has rule-governed word-accent and this accent tells the reader which words are important to the sense. This importance depends on how frequently a given word occurs generally in the language; a particular noun, adjective, verb will occur less frequently than a given pronoun, article or preposition and will thus carry an accent.[2]

Each line of this Shakespeare sonnet having ten syllables and a normal maximum of five accents, the poet's art arranges these accents in ways which contribute to the sense. The poem's form and sense emerge in part from the tension between the unchanging syllable-count and the shifting pattern of accents. Over these first four lines, the accent-count rises steeply. The balanced syntax and restrained accent-distribution of l. 2 is followed by a line with *six* accents which sets against the *lovely, temperate, thou*, the relatively 'intemperate' qualities of a possible *summer's day*. This 'intemperateness' hits us in the shock of the line-initial accent on *Rough winds* with its collision of accents, followed by the congruence of sense and accent in *shake*. We have to wait till l. 4 for the reflective calm of the first regular iambic pentameter with its alternation of five accented with five unaccented syllables. As the frequency of accents increases, so does the amount of articulatory and expiratory effort in the reciter. The vowels of the accented syllables are thus higher in pitch and intensity:

> Rough winds do shake the darling buds of May;

while the voiced consonants forming the onsets to the colliding accents also gain in intensity:

> *R*ough *w*inds do shake the darling buds of May.

This increased effort, involving diaphragm and the organs of articulation, tongue, lips and jaw, not only suggests 'stress' but also induces it. The passage from the initial calm of ll. 1 and 2 to what follows is not just semantically ('temperate' ≠ 'intemperate') but also physiologically a shock. Poets write verse because it gives them the raw materials for creating meaning outside language.

Where ordinary language is concerned, speakers of Italian and Spanish, for example, are spontaneously aware of the accentual patterning of their languages. Like English, each has word-accent that can be distinctive. In Italian *mando* [I send] is contrasted with *mando* [he sent], while in Spanish *compro* [I buy] contrasts with *compro* [he bought]. Compare the English 'refuse'/'refuse' or 'content'/'content'. French apparently presents a baffling exception. Students of English or Italian have little difficulty scanning their favourite poems, but for a French candidate for the literary *baccalauréat*, this can be a nightmare.

While linguists are in general agreement over the accentual structures of English, Italian and Spanish, the nature and role of accent in the French language is the object of ongoing controversy.[3] In the absence of a clear idea of the rhythms of French verse, the traditional approach to interpreting the verse-line has bored and confused generations of readers. The French ten-syllable and twelve-syllable verse-lines have canonically two fixed accents: one at the cesura ('#') and another on the final accentuable vowel of the line: 'D'un jeune audacieux # punissez l'insolence'. Having checked the syllable-count, we have to locate the cesura: in the ten-syllable line this is normally an accent on the fourth syllable followed by a pause/syntactical boundary/word-boundary (4 + 6), while in the twelve-syllable line it is after the accented sixth (6 + 6).[4] When for example Corneille punctuates, this is plain sailing:

> Levez-vous l'un et l'**autre**, # et parlez à loisir.[5]

But compare this to Rimbaud's line:

> — *Au Cabaret-Vert*: je #? demandai des tartines.[6]

Here the sixth syllable is an unaccented personal pronoun that cannot carry a word-accent, and what is more, no pause/syntactical boundary is possible between a personal pronoun and its verb. In the absence of accent and syntactical boundary, there only remains a word-boundary which is no more distinctive than that of any other word in the line.

And this is not the end of our woes. While looking for the cesura, we will be wondering what kind it is going to be. Will it be 'epic'? This worryingly inserts a rogue fifth syllable, a 'mute e' (ə), after the accented cesural syllable of the decasyllable, thus lengthening the line by one syllable:

> De vassela # gə fut assez chevalier.[7]

But also, in the twentieth century, Apollinaire's alexandrine:

> Les enfants de l'éco # lə viennent avec fracas.[8]

Then again, the cesura might be 'lyric'. This, in a ten-syllable line places an unaccented syllable (ə) in fourth position:

> Et fromagəs # est fors a digerer.[9]

Here the word-accent is on the *third* syllable and since there can be no pause/syntactical boundary between subject and verb, there is only a word-boundary to mark the '#', and even this is weakened by the *liaison*.

Or perhaps it is 'féminine ou enjambante', in which the accented cesural syllable is followed by an 'ə' in the same word:

> Rote guite # rnə, flauste, chalemie.[10]

Here of course there can be no pause, no syntactical boundary and no word-boundary following the accented fourth syllable. Unlike the 'epic', this does not add a syllable to the line.

Now, all this may keep us busy, but what is it for? Why do poets do these funny things? This zoo of aberrant cesural types corrals a class of moves known in the trade as 'poetic licence'. In other words, when for example a poet writes in an extra syllable he or she is breaking the rules.

This ad hoc account of cesural types is clearly unsatisfactory. What is needed is a theory that shows how these apparently exceptional instances are part of coherent poetic practice. The aim of this book is to follow through the implications of our previous studies to frame and test a theory which will point to a clear and continuing tradition in the writing of French verse over a thousand years. We aim to show that such verse, be it iso- or heterosyllabic, is built on patterns of alternating accent.[11] Against the current consensus that accent is irrelevant to metre, we will defend the view that accent is indispensable for the perception of metricality.[12] Further, denying that metre is unrelated to the poem's semantic dimension, we will find that in the work of justly renowned poets the patterning of accent contributes to the creation of meaning.[13]

Also intent on clearing the terrain, Benoît de Cornulier has published a theory of French Romantic verse in which, by analysing a large corpus of verse, he managed to show conclusively that poets follow rules that they *never* break.[14] His survey examined the distribution of syllable-types over syllable-positions in the verse of three nineteenth-century poets. Seeking rules for segmenting any Romantic alexandrine, he shows that in those verses lacking a clear 6 + 6 structure, there are nevertheless certain syllable-types that never occupy certain syllable positions. Take the following line:

> Qui courais, taché də lunules électriques.[15]

A twelve-syllable line such as this, with an atonic 'mute e' (ə) in sixth position, never has one in eighth position, thus permitting an 8 + 4 segmenting of the verse-line. His argument is technical and complex, using for example a posited distinction between an 'ə' *masculin* and an 'ə' *féminin*, which, he shows, occur in rule-governed distributions in his corpus. These ideas are criticised and developed by Jean-Michel Gouvard who discerns further unexpected regularities in the apparent metrical chaos of the Romantic alexandrine.[16]

What strikes the reader toiling through these dense and demanding critical texts is the apparent irrelevance of these formal phenomena to the semantic values of the poetry. If poets continue writing in verse because verse provides raw material for the creation of meaning, what exactly are Rimbaud, Verlaine, Mallarmé and others doing with those formal features identified by our critics? Yes, [ə] in French is a striking example of such raw material and Cornulier has shown that its behaviour in a large corpus of verse-lines is different from its behaviour in ordinary language. But what is the relevance of these properties to the interpretation of say a poem of Rimbaud? So far no answer.

It was then with eager anticipation that readers took up Cornulier's new book on the poetry of Rimbaud which promised to take us *De la métrique à l'interprétation*. But again we are disappointed. In spite of the title's promise, the analyses of 'Jeune ménage' and 'La Chanson de la plus haute tour', among others, proceed without reference to the author's metrical theory. A long essay on 'Qu'est-ce pour nous...' refers only in passing to the 'propriétés métricométriques' of his theory, which appear in full only in a general analysis of Rimbaud's versification on pp. 319–501.

The metrical and the semantic are thus by implication completely independent of each other: there is no way of getting from the one to the other and so the study of metre can tell us nothing about meaning. What then is the function of metre when it has lost its historical association with dance and music? Why do poets persist in being metrical?

There is an answer to this question: it takes the form of a theory which competes with that of Cornulier and which incidentally proposes a solution to the problem of the prosodic oddness of French among her Romance sisters. It finds in the study of Old, Middle, and modern French evidence for the continued existence in the language of an accentual prosody which permits an accentual interpretation of French metre. This is no eccentricity: since the eighteenth century, scholars, poets and amateurs have been proposing that French is less peculiar than is generally thought. In 1922 Édouard Dujardin, poet and author of *Les Lauriers sont coupés*, wrote: 'Comme le vers latin, comme le vers grec, comme les vers des grandes littératures modernes, le vers français est donc essentiellement constitué par la succession d'un certain nombre de pieds métriques'.[17] Although the proponents of the currently accepted model reject this idea, there is hard evidence to support the accentual thesis. A distributional analysis of ten- and twelve-syllable French verse-texts from the twelfth and the seventeenth centuries showed the continued operation of strong constraints on the distribution of accents within the verse-line.[18] This clear result challenged the prevalent view that French verse was simply a matter of recurring syllabic count and that the distribution of accents within the verse-line, other than those at the cesura and line-end, were either aleatory or just those of the language generally.[19] Arguments backed by both diachronic and experimental evidence pointed also to the presence in modern French of rule-governed accent within both the word and the phrase.[20] Valérie Beaudouin has found in her analysis of a large corpus of classical dramatic alexandrines that a statistically significant proportion of both hemistichs of the verse-line showed iambic (010101) or anapestic (001001) rhythm.[21] These studies open the way to a conception of accent-patterning in French verse which has a double function: it is indispensable to the measuring function of metre while secondly it serves the poet as raw material for the creation of poetic meaning. The disjunction of metre and meaning is thus closed with the restoration of metre to the semantic universe of the text.

It is not exactly news that French can accommodate accentual verse. Take for example the following lines by André Van Hasselt, from *Le Livre des paraboles*:

Ma montagne, mon chaste royaume,	001001001
Où je vis dans l'azur,	001001
Où les brises répandent leur baume,	001001001
Leur parfum le plus pur.	001001
Oh! que j'aime à gravir sur tes cimes	101001001
A marcher sur tes crêtes sublimes	001001001

Où le bruit de la terre finit,	001001001
Mais où l'aigle a son nid![22]	001001

If all French verse were like this, there would be no need for our argument. Like his eighteenth-century predecessor François Benoît Hoffman,[23] Van Hasselt arranges oxytonic French word-accent to produce verse of narcotic monotony.[24] Such verse is nevertheless legitimately French. Though Romance verse has, unlike the English pentameter, no fixed accents, Hugo Blank reminds us that 'this does not mean that the four basic rhythmic units, "iambus", "trochee", "dactyl" and "anapaest" are foreign to it. On the contrary, these rhythms are found everywhere'.[25] And French is no exception. But what Corneille and Racine preferred, as Beaudouin shows, was the alexandrine whose 6 + 6 structure allows for accentual contrast:

Pourquoi veux-tu, cruelle, irriter mes ennuis?[26]	010101 # 001001

This helps us to understand why the decasyllable, 4 + 6, and the alexandrine have been the dominant metres in French, each thus allowing for accentual contrast between the hemistichs. We shall see that poets of all periods have profited from the potential variety offered by these metres.

It may then be the very rhythmic variety of French verse which has discouraged some recent theorists from considering its accentual structures. The failure to model adequately the distribution of accents within the verse-line is due to the prevailing view that the rhythm of French verse is either simply that of the language generally,[27] or that it is 'aléatoire', a result of chance.[28] If this view is valid, then it follows that accent-distribution in French verse plays no part in the stylistic organisation of the poetry: its rhythm is, stylistically speaking, simply noise, playing no part in the creation of meaning.

Our reader should not be discouraged by the apparent force of this currently infl-uential idea. Against it, we shall argue that accent-patterning in French verse plays an indispensable role in the work of the great poets. This in turn implies that existing criticism of this poetry and the pedagogy associated with it must be based on an incomplete understanding of how the poem produces its meaning: the very source of the poem's life, its rhythm, has been generally ignored. Contrary to standard pedagogy, our accentual theory will claim to describe what is really happening when a French speaker reads French verse aloud. The natural accents of the language furnish the material from which the poet creates patterns unique to the poem and constitutive of its sense. Patterned accent in French verse thus has a double function: (a) it facilitates perception of invariant syllable-count; and (b) it is available to the poet for the creation of meaning.

The General Problem

The word 'verse' implies etymologically 'something that returns'; for most French verse, this is line-length, as in these lines by Alfred de Musset, from 'La Nuit d'octobre':

Le mal dont j'ai souffert s'est enfui comme un rêve;	12 syllables
Je n'en puis comparer le lointain souvenir	12

> Qu'à ces brouillards légers que l'aurore soulève,   12
> Et qu'avec la rosée on voit s'évanouir.[29]   12

Since for the currently prevailing view, recurring syllabic count is the necessary and sufficient condition for the description of French verse, the first question to confront the enquirer is: how does the writer/reader of syllabic verse recognise that the verse-line has the requisite number of syllables? How is line-length regulated? Do poets count on their fingers? It is agreed that counting is a non-linguistic activity. Is then the recognition of metricity an abstract and general ability of the human mind?

Fabb and Halle have published a theory of metre designed to account for this ability, which is evident across cultures and languages from Biblical Hebrew to Keats and Tennyson.[30] Their idea is that a given line is defined as metrically well-formed (or not) by the output of a formal grid which 'controls primarily the number of groups in the line and only secondarily the number of syllables'.[31] This grid is derived by the application of formal rules to an underlying accentual schema, which can be, for example, uniformly iambic (010101) or anapestic (001001). These rules arrange formal representations of the syllables of the line into groups. It is by the re-grouping of the heads of successive re-groupings of these representations that the well-formedness of the verse-line is affirmed.[32] It is an implication of the Fabb-Halle model that rhythm is secondary to metre, that well-formed metre itself makes rhythm possible.

This model is clearly interesting for a language like English whose accentual structure lends itself for example to iambic or dactylic metres, but is it applicable to French? Yes, the authors positively assert that 'all metrical verse in French from the *Chanson de Roland* down to the poetry of the 20th century is based on iambic groups'.[33] Our authors acknowledge the advice of a leading French metrician on these matters, but it seems not to have struck them that his position is very much at odds with theirs. His stance is uncompromising: 'C'est une caractéristique de la poésie littéraire française classique que l'équivalence métrique *repose uniquement sur des équivalences en nombre syllabique*'.[34] For Cornulier, the idea of an underlying iambic schema for French verse is without foundation. Denying the structuring role of accent in French verse, the current consensus view founds its idea of such verse on a single dogma: that the necessary and sufficient definition of French verse is the recurrence of a fixed syllabic count.

Cornulier then would identify French as an exception to the Fabb-Halle thesis that all metres have an underlying accentual structure. And the stand-off between him and them is not just technical, it is ideological too. The latter proclaim their allegiance to the generative programme of Noam Chomsky,[35] whose *Syntactic Structures* proposed a revolution in linguistic method.[36] In contrast to his empirically-minded American predecessors, he was a Cartesian rationalist who sought to show that linguistic universals determined the forms of all human language. Cornulier's definition of the metric of French as purely syllabic — i.e. non-accentual — presents a challenge to such generativists since recognition of a constant syllabic count is non-linguistic.[37] A purely syllabic metre would need some means of verse-length control, which for the Fabb-Halle theory is provided by underlying iambic schema. The Cornulier-Gouvard account of French metre which sees the distribution of accent within the verse-unit as *aléatoire* thus questions the generativist thesis by proposing French verse as an exception to the Fabb-Halle would-be universal theory of metre.

Though Fabb and Halle claim an underlying iambic schema for the French verse-line, they seem unaware of the the prevailing uncertainty surrounding the nature of accent in French.[38] On the other hand, Cornulier's very conservative definition of the French verse-line suggests that he is all too aware of it. For him, 'le vers français n'est pas accentuel', a formula which excludes accent from the domain of metre.[39] His judgement is seconded by Gasparov: 'all variations of stress-placement in lines and hemistichs occur here with a frequency dictated by the natural rhythm of the French language and nothing else'.[40] And Gouvard: 'Les accents à l'intérieur du vers sont distribués de manière aléatoire, sur n'importe quelle voyelle numéraire'.[41] Now this view of French verse is not new. It is simply that of the seventeenth-century grammarians of Port-Royal. Claude Lancelot, Antoine Arnaud, and Pierre Nicole wrote: 'Nos vers ne consistent qu'en deux choses: en la structure et la rime. La structure ne consiste qu'en un certain nombre de syllabes [...] non pas en pieds comme les vers des Grecs et des Romains'.[42]

Although Cornulier's theory is currently the standard point of reference for scholars working on French verse, I can find no examples of his model being applied consistently to the segmentation of the Romantic alexandrine. Steve Murphy's metrical analyses of Baudelaire use Cornulier's model with the following results:

> Cette fois, l'énumération d'exemples *ne conduit pas à trancher nettement* en faveur d'une seule solution globale [...]; *Nous serions tentés de supposer* que... (p. 281, my emphasis)

> Le caractère consistant de son second hémistiche *encourage cependant à favoriser également* l'hypothèse d'un 6–6 à effet suspensif. (p. 285, my emphasis)

> Cette fois, *il ne semble abusif* de voir [...]; Le vers C6 des 'Sept Vieillards' produit *peut-être* un nouveau cas d'ambivalence rythmique, *permettant* une analyse 6–6 [...] *ou éventuellement* une analyse en 4–4 = 4 [...]; Pour 24°, le rapport syntaxique [...] *renforce l'hypothèse* d'une superposition *possible* des schémas 6–6 et 4–4–4. (p. 286, my emphasis)[43]

Here my emphases mark the besetting hesitation which attends Murphy's attempt to put Cornulier's theory into practice. This theory is criticised and developed by Jean-Michel Gouvard who seeks further unexpected regularities in the apparent metrical chaos of the Romantic alexandrine. While Gouvard's intention is to elicit 'une structure qui indique non pas directement les "accents" du vers mais les positions syllabiques qui n'excluent pas une coupe métrique subséquente', his criteria for defining such positions are neither clear nor consistent.[44] His aim is to find criteria for more regularly segmenting the 'irregular' alexandrine, for example 4 + 4 + 4 or 8 + 4,[45] but a consistent application of his criteria generates counter-examples such as 3 + 5 + 4.[46] Gouvard expresses his intention to be useful to the metrical researcher, but, despite the abundance of ingredients, he fails to provide a recipe for the metrical cake.

Although the distributional approach taken by both Cornulier and Gouvard sets aside all semantic considerations, it is clear that the discovery of possible constraints on the segmentation of the Romantic verse-line would have stylistic implications. But Cornulier's *De la métrique à l'interprétation* defines the metrical and the semantic as completely independent of each other: there is no way of getting from *métrique* to *interprétation*, since it seems that the study of metre can tell us nothing about the meaning of a verse-text.[47]

The notion of verse was born of the close relationship between the steps of the dance and the accompanying song.[48] In Greek tragedy, the song and choreography of the chorus were intimately related to the metrical patterning of the verse. The to-and-fro of the dance required that the number of steps from the dancer's point of departure in a figure must equal those needed to get him back to it.[49] The persistence of isosyllabism, long after verse had parted company with dance and song, left verse with an echo of the physical movement of dance. It is hard to disassociate the idea of dance-steps from the duple or triple rhythms of the song that always accompanied them, that is to say the rhythms that actually measured the dance-unit and allowed the dancer to follow the figure; yet the Cornulier-Gouvard theory allows rhythm no part in the measuring of the verse-line. Whatever rhythm the verse-line may have is unrelated to its metre. What then could be the function of metre in French now that it has lost its historical association with song, dance and bodily movement? Why have poets remained incurably metrical?[50]

An answer to this question has been put forward. A theory in competition with the exclusive isosyllabism of Port-Royal proposed a solution to the problem of the apparent oddness of French among her Romance sisters. In 1814 a foreigner published a book challenging the verdict of Port-Royal. In it, the Abbé Scoppa, an Italian, argued for the kinship of French and Italian where accent was concerned. He proposed analysing the metre of both Italian and French verse via a system of recurring accentual feet. For example:

> Iambic ('˘' = unaccented; '–' = accented)
> Toujours aimer, toujours — souffrir, toujours mourir.[51]

This may look convincing, but proponents of isosyllabism have not found it difficult to find the flaws in the Abbé's system. The following scansion proposed by Scoppa himself shows why:

> Cependant sur le dos — de la plaine liquide.[52]

Here the accenting of a penult, a preposition, a definite article and a 'ə' produces a verse-line which contradicts what we know about the history of word-accent in French and which would sound bizarre to any native speaker.

These weaknesses did not however affect the general enthusiasm for Scoppa's proposal. As late as 1916, Hugo Thieme noted that: 'presque tous les ouvrages qui traitent de la versification française prennent Scoppa comme point de départ, qu'ils approuvent ou qu'ils désapprouvent la théorie de l'accent'.[53] So the intuition persisted that there must be some relation between the rhythm of the verse-line and its metricity. Everyone knew that there must be a fixed number of syllables per line, but they also felt that there was a lot more going on besides. In 1974 Lusson and Roubaud published a new theory defending the idea of a functional relation between rhythm and metre in French. They aimed to free the description of accentual metre from the prevailing dependence on semantic and stylistic considerations, but their theory ultimately showed internal incoherences and a marginal reliance on semantic values.[54] Overall, the shortcomings of accentual theories of French metre have led inevitably to the current reinstatement of isosyllabism as its necessary and sufficient definition. So much for the weaknesses of the accentual approach: what about those of isosyllabic theory?

In 1913, Georges Lote published a study of the alexandrine using the latest technology for automatic analysis of the spoken word.[55] Almost a decade in preparation, it featured recordings made, among others, of a substantial passage of alexandrines from Racine's *Phèdre*, read by Sarah Bernhardt, and the 'Ballade du duel' from Rostand's *Cyrano de Bergerac*, read by Constant Coquelin of the Comédie française, who had created the role.[56] Electronic analysis of these recited texts must have surprised those who had learned at school that French verse was defined by a recurring syllabic count.[57] The printout of one of the passages read by Bernhardt revealed that of the twenty-nine Racinian alexandrines recorded, only eleven had the expected twelve syllables, the remaining eighteen having ten, eleven, thirteen or fourteen. Coquelin's score was no better with only ten lines out of twenty-eight respecting the poet's isosyllabic intentions. Lote's judgement on the isosyllabists was categorical:

> Envisagée comme durée totale de l'alexandrin, ou comme durée des fragments rythmiques qui le constituent, ou bien encore au point de vue des nombres en invoquant une arithmétique aussi fallacieuse que vaine, la régularité métrique est un mythe dont il serait temps de débarrasser les manuels où l'on s'occupe de formuler et de définir les lois de la versification française.[58]

For Cornulier, Lote's view was based on a misconception: since Lote's analyses had shown that in verse, syllables varied in both length and quality, he concluded that adding up unalikes was incompatible with the idea of recurring regularity. But Cornulier points out that long or short, a syllable is still a syllable and that quality and length are irrelevant.[59] While this rejoinder annuls Lote's objection, there remains a lot for Cornulier to explain.

How was it that connoisseurs of the alexandrine such as Bernhardt, Coquelin, and Lote himself had not been instinctively aware of the metrical derelictions committed under their very noses while the recordings were being made? Surely someone present would have stiffened with astonishment on hearing those ten-, eleven-, thirteen- and fourteen-syllable alexandrines uttered by these thespian notables?

Cornulier is himself a connoisseur of the *vers boiteux*, having used it in his 1982 study as a diagnostic tool for testing the isosyllabic competence of his experimental subjects. The test material he used was *Les Djinns*, by Victor Hugo, written in strophes of progressively increasing and then decreasing line-lengths: strophe 1 has lines of one syllable, strophe 2, two and so on. Cornulier asked his subjects to listen to a text of the poem which he had doctored, each strophe having one Cornulian line which was syllabically irregular. For example, the seven-syllable strophe was booby-trapped with a line of six syllables. The experiment was designed to find out if a sample of French listeners could readily spot the aberrant lines.[60]

Cornulier concluded that his subjects had an innate ability to spot the syllabically irregular lines and his belief in this ability among francophones generally is fundamental to his theory of French verse. Now, there is something mystical about this ability and Cornulier himself, as we have noted, is reduced to calling it 'instinctive'.

What Cornulier has not spotted is that Lote, at the end of the nineteenth century, was unwittingly anticipating the experiment carried out by Cornulier himself in 1982. Unlike the *vers boiteux* apparently identified by Cornulier's discerning subjects, the aberrant alexandrines that infest Lote's printouts seem to have gone completely unnoticed by the specialist reciters and any amateurs present while the recording was in progress. Lote's unconditional rejection of isosyllabism may be naïve, yet his experiments incidentally demonstrated the insensitivity of a representative group of eighteen francophone poetry-lovers to breaches of isosyllabic recurrence — a result strikingly at odds with that claimed by Cornulier in his experiment of 1982.[61]

And not even poets were exempt from this metrical deafness. Koschwitz recorded in phonetic script a reading by his contemporary, the Parnassian and Nobel laureate Sully-Prudhomme (1839–1907), of his own verse 'Le Lever du soleil':

Flamboyant, invisible à force de splendeur,	12
Il est pèr(e) des blés, qui sont pèr(es) des races,	10
Mais il ne peuple point son immense rondeur	12
D'un troupeau de mortels turbulents et voraces.	12
Parmi les glob(es) noirs qu'il empourpre et conduit	11
Aux blêm(es) profondeurs que l'air léger fait bleues,	11
La terr(e) lui soumet la courbe qu'elle suit	11
Et cherche sa caresse à d'innombrables lieues.[62]	12

Though these eight printed lines all have the regulation twelve syllables, one of them has ten recorded, and three eleven.

Elsewhere, again in direct opposition to the findings of Lote, Cornulier and Gouvard agree with Fabb-Halle that rhythm is irrelevant to metre, albeit for reasons that imply the fundamental incompatibilities of the two theories. As for the measuring function of metre, Cornulier argued for an instinctive ability to recognise the recurring syllabic regularity of French verse-units which are no longer than eight syllables.[63] Gouvard states the position as follows:

> En effet, ce n'est pas en ayant conscience d'une identité comptable entre 8 et 8 et 8 et 8 syllabes qu'un quatrain d'octosyllabes sera perçu comme 'métrique', mais en sentant que, vers après vers, un nombre identique de *n* syllabes est répété. Ce nombre, en tant que tel, peut très bien ne pas être clairement identifié, puisque seul importe la perception de l'équivalence et non le nombre de syllabes qui assure cette équivalence, tout comme je peux reconnaître que deux octogones sont identiques sans avoir à compter le nombre de côtés qui composent chacune des deux figures.[64]

A closer look shows that Gouvard is comparing unalikes. If his contention is to be accepted, it would imply that the twin octagons are perceived instantly as a single configuration in space. The perception of line-length in verse however happens in time through the agency of memory: the six syllables of an alexandrine hemistich are not perceived simultaneously, but one at a time, whether the hearer counts them or not. The perception of the identity of line-lengths takes the time needed to read or to hear each of at least a pair of lines.[65] This is not analogous to perception of the equivalence of geometrical figures grasped instantaneously as a configuration in space.

So, while this latter is an immediate perception, the recognition of the equivalence of line-lengths is the outcome of a sustained if pre-conscious mental process. Experimental work by cognitive psychologists is relevant here. John Hurford's researches show that though, where perception of number is concerned, 'two can be perceived without counting, [...] the direct perception of numerosity without counting or analysis [...] only seems capable of taking human/numerical abilities to around three'.[66] He continues: 'Such an ability is only firmly established for very low numbers, such as two or perhaps three, so it is not plausible to claim that, say, six or seven are differentially accessible to a significant degree'.[67] Thus any explanation of immediate recognition of syllabic recurrence must accept that such recognition implies awareness that the verse-line is composed of groups of two and possibly three syllables. However, for Cornulier's 'loi des 8 syllabes', sequences of verse-units whose lengths are eight syllables or fewer are recognised instinctively by the reader as metrical.[68] Which is incompatible with Hurford's experimental findings. And as we have seen, Gouvard's attempt to rescue the idea of an extra-linguistic competence proves incoherent.

These shortcomings apart, serious drawbacks afflict the general application of the Cornulier-Gouvard theory. Does all French poetry presented to the reader as verse conform in fact to the stringent conditions of this theory? Take for example the following lines from Racine's 'Le Lundi, à Matines', in *Hymnes traduites du Bréviaire Romain*:

Tandis que le sommeil, réparant la nature,	12
Tient enchaînés le travail et le bruit,	10
Nous rompons ses liens, ô clarté toujours pure!	12
Pour te louer dans la profonde nuit.[69]	10

This text is destined to be set to music, and our isosyllabist has argued that such metrically 'irregular' texts constitute an exception to the isosyllabic norm as 'une sorte de modulation en marge de la métrique classique'.[70] But consider this, from La Fontaine's 'Le Corbeau et le renard' (Book I, 2, of the *Fables*):

Maître Corbeau, sur un arbre perché,	10
Tenait en son bec un fromage.	8
Maître Renard par l'odeur alléché,	10
Lui tint à peu près ce langage.	8

It continues:

Le Renard s'en saisit, et dit: Mon bon Monsieur,	12
Apprenez que tout flatteur	7
Vit au dépens de celui qui l'écoute;	10
Cette leçon vaut bien un fromage, sans doute.[71]	12

Of these four lines, not one has the same syllable-count as the line that follows it. And La Fontaine's verse is made to be spoken not sung.[72] As surely was that of Malherbe, the reformer of French classical verse:

Que n'êtes-vous lassées,	6
Mes tristes pensées,	5
De troubler ma raison?	6
Et faire avecque blâme	6

Rebeller mon âme   5
Contre sa guérison?[73]   6

Though all these pieces are irreproachably French and indubitably 'classical', none of them qualifies as verse by the criteria of Cornulier and Gouvard: both Racine and La Fontaine, more flagrantly, have written verses which do not meet the condition of 'un nombre identique de n syllabes répété'. Poets writing anisosyllabic verse like this are not the norm, yet they and their readers clearly believed they were writing verse and equally clearly had an idea of it not limited to a recurring syllabic count. If La Fontaine's anisosyllabic verse is metrically well-formed then the properties that enable readers/listeners to recognise such well-formedness should also be present in isosyllabic verse.

Perception of the metricity of these anisosyllabic texts derives from something other than a recurrent syllabic count, and the only possible candidate is the accentual rhythm of the verse, to which our critics deny any measuring role. Granted its measuring role in anisosyllabic verse, we may think that accent also plays a part in our recognition of a constant syllabic count.

But how does this measuring take place? We may find an answer by considering Paul Verrier's speculation in the context of the experimental work cited by Hurford fifty years later. Verrier was convinced that the metre of French was based on the 'alternation of accent'.[74] He shows what he means by noting without comment the accentual structure of an old popular song:

Le **bon** roi Dagobert   6
Av**ait** sa culotte à l'envers.   8

In the first line, the alternation of accented and unaccented syllables is binary (010101); in the second it is mainly ternary (01001001). For Verrier, the *alternance fixe* of French verse is not, like the English iambic pentameter, based on a recurring and fixed accentual scheme. Rather it moves freely between binary and ternary units. On the vexed question of how French readers/listeners recognise the metricity of isosyllabic verse, Hurford's response would have been that, in any verse-unit, they perceive a series of sub-units, each one containing either two or three syllables, with accent marking the boundary of each sub-unit. Although we have seen that Van Hasselt and others have no trouble writing fixed-metre verse in French, this French cousin of English fixed metre would appear deeply 'un-French' to any lover of French poetry. This is because the accentual structure of classic French poetry, unlike that of the English pentameter, is not tied to marked positions in the verse-line. The characteristic freedom of the relation between rhythmic unit and verse-unit banishes the monotony which dogs Van Hasselt's verse.

But the question now arises: how aware are francophone readers/listeners of the accentual structures of French verse? We will follow the example of Benoît de Cornulier, who tested his 'loi des 8' with an experiment.

An Experiment

The Cornulier-Gouvard theory attributes the recognition of metricity in French to an upper limit imposed on the syllable-count of the verse-unit. If one assumes, with Gasparov, that the distribution of accent within the verse-unit is simply that of the language generally, and that isosyllabism is the necessary and sufficient condition for the metricity of French verse, as does Cornulier, it follows that any series of six-syllable phrases, with or without rhyme, will be perceived as metrically well-formed.[75] Taking a register in which word-final [ə] is not pronounced, let us read aloud the following passages:

> (a) Parce qu'il n'a pas revu ce qu'il avait refait, une promesse vide de sens, pour dire vrai, ne vaut rien. Mais en vrai bon ami, à cause de ma vieille mère, il était enfin prêt à me faire faire la pose.

> (b) Gérard Dumarsais a bien de la chance. Sa femme bien-aimée, Marguerite, ne quitte presque plus l'endroit où elle vit en paix depuis bien des années. Une rencontre bienheureuse apportait un bonheur innocent.

> (c) Ce brave homme-là tient à ce que j'en parle. Sa belle jeune femme, quoique très maigre, ne déteste pas Port-au-Prince où elle habite depuis plus de vingt-deux ans. Un tel choc, bien que cruel, ne peut pas nuire à un bonheur doux.

Which of these passages, read aloud, triggers most readily an impression of metricity? If passage (a), then my hypothesis is instantly disproved, since it conforms exactly to the standard definition of the alexandrine as stated by Beaudouin: it is made up of four twelve-syllable lines each made up of two hemistichs of six syllables, of which the sixth and the twelfth are accented.[76]

Parce qu'il n'a pas revu # ce qu'il avait refait,	12	000001 # 000001
Une promesse vide de sens, # pour dire vrai, ne vaut rien.	12	001101 # 011011
Mais en vrai bon ami, # à cause de ma vieille mère,	12	001101 # 010011
Il était enfin prêt # à me faire faire la pose.	12	000011 # 001101[77]

These alexandrines show two sequences of five atonic syllables and one of four, all of which Milner finds are banished from French classical verse:

> La langue, laissée à elle-même, pourrait en proposer de nombreux exemples: les relatives en 'ce que je', 'ce que tu', etc, les conjonctives en 'ce que', en 'de ce que', les comparatives du type 'que je ne te le dis', 'que je ne le suis'; tout cela peut produire aisément les structures ordinaires de la langue. Or elles sont absolument exclues du vers.[78]

All of which may cause us to doubt Gasparov's claim that the rhythm of French verse is simply that of the language generally. Along with these runs of atonic syllables, there are in passage (a) seven instances of juxtaposed accents. The consequent distribution of accented and unaccented syllables in this passage may thus cause us to perceive it as 'unmetrical'. On the other hand, the choice of passage (b) commits us to accepting the metricity of verses which are anything but isosyllabic:

Gérard Dumarsais a bien de la chance.	10	0100101001
Sa femme bien-aimée, Marguérite,	8	01001001

Ne quitte presque plus l'endroit	7	0100101
Où elle vit en paix depuis bien des années.	11	00101001001
Une rencontre bienheureuse	7	0010101
Apportait un bonheur innocent.	9	001001001

Since the syllable-count here is so 'irregular', a sense of the metricity of the passage may, conversely to passage (a), be explained by another feature: the total absence of juxtaposed accents and of runs of more than two atonic syllables, that is, by 'alternation of accent' as envisaged by Verrier. That a sense of verse can exist in the absence of a regular syllable-count opens the way to a re-examination of the relation between isosyllabic verse and *vers libres* of the kind written by Racine and La Fontaine. Any sense of the metricity of these anisosyllabic lines is dissipated in passage (c) by a series of substitutions which, while they maintain the syllabic profile, eradicate alternation of accent:

Ce brave homme-là tient à ce que j'en parle.	10	0111100001
Sa belle jeune femme, quoique très maigre,	8	01110011
Ne déteste pas Port-au-Prince	7	0011101
Où elle habite depuis plus de vingt-deux ans.	11	00010000111
Un tel choc, bien que cruel,	7	0111001
Ne peut pas nuire à un bonheur doux.	9	000100011

All three of these passages are credible modern French, exemplifying Gasparov's 'natural rhythm of the French language'. While (a) and (c) show the language's characteristic freedom in that juxtaposed accents and runs of atonic syllables are subject to no formal ordering, (b) brings this 'natural rhythm' into accord with the principle of alternating accent.

Rhythm and Sense

As our reading of the Shakespeare sonnet showed, scanning seems relatively straightforward for readers of English syllabo-tonic verse, since readers and critics know where the accents are. Not so in French, where the lack of a generally accepted theory of accent leaves careful readers at a loss. If accent in French too can serve as a raw material for the creation of meaning, then a theory of such accent will be indispensable for an understanding of the poetic text.

As Chapter 1 will show, texts from the twelfth to the seventeenth century exhibit strong constraints on the distribution of accents within the verse-line. Arguments backed by evidence both diachronic and experimental will point to the presence in modern French verse of rule-governed accent within both the word and the phrase. Beaudouin has already found in her analysis of the classical alexandrine that a statistically significant proportion of both hemistichs showed either iambic or anapestic rhythm.[79]

As we have seen, modern French can readily accommodate accentual verse. After our earlier example from Van Hasselt, here is another by Édouard Wacken:

Tout aime et soupire:	01001
La brise et l'oiseau,	01001

La fleur qui se mire	01001
Et le clair ruisseau.	00101
La rose amoureuse	01001
Déjà tend, heureuse	00101
Ses lèvres de miel.[80]	01001

Modest stuff, agreed, but more interesting than our earlier example. It shows the potential of Verrier's *alternance de l'accent* in its more varied combination of 01 and 001. And it anticipates Verlaine's experiments with five-syllable verse-lines. These impose rhythmic variety since it is impossible to repeat the same foot in the line: 001 + 001? is too long and 01 + 01(0?) too short.

These poets are no exception, as Martin Duffell reminds us: a number of poets across the centuries had been writing syllabo-tonic verse in French, for example John Gower in the fourteenth century, Bonaventure des Périers in the sixteenth, and Victor Hugo in the nineteenth.[81] If all French verse were like this, there would be no need for our argument. But the anapestic monotony of Van Hasselt's poem made it easy to see why verse like his repelled good poets. What they preferred, as Verrier judged and Beaudouin shows, was the alexandrine whose 6 + 6 structure allows for metrical contrast:

Déja, selon la loi, le grand-prêtre mon père.[82]   010101 # 001001

Indeed, here the six-syllable series of each hemistich accommodates exactly Hurford's maximal groups, twos and threes: each hemistich lending itself to either a three-times-two or a two-times-three rhythmic structure. Hence the preponderance of the decasyllable and the alexandrine, each allowing for accentual contrast between hemistichs.[83] An important difference appears here between the metre of English and that of French: in English the verse-unit is the line, while in the French decasyllable and alexandrine, it is a sub-unit of the line, consisting of either four or six syllables. The English iambic pentameter, exemplified above in our Shakespeare sonnet, has, in its ideal form, a continuous structure of alternating positions marked for accent: 0101010101. In the Racine alexandrine just quoted, the verse-line as a whole does not show an overall accentual structure, each hemistich having a different number of accents.

We have seen that this absence of marked accentual positions has led some critics to assert that accent in French verse is unordered.[84] Accounts which see it as *aléatoire* or following 'the natural rhythm of the French language' obscure the fact that there is currently no generally accepted theory of this 'rhythm'. This question certainly agitated the minds of earlier students of French verse. In his chapter 'De la cadence', Louis Quicherat cites the objection levelled by Voltaire against a verse-line of Corneille:

Vous le mieux révéler qu'il ne me le révèle.

Quicherat comments:

L'oreille délicate de Voltaire a été choquée de *qu'il ne me le*. Il n'a pas expliqué d'où venait cette dureté; c'est qu'il manque un accent dans cet hémistiche, lequel retrouverait ses deux temps forts si on mettait: Vous le mieux révéler qu'il ne *vous* le révèle.[85]

A hundred and forty years later Jean-Claude Milner confirmed this censure of a string of five unaccented syllables in Corneille's verse with his pronouncement that such strings are 'absolument exclues des vers'.[86] Not only does this conversation across time show a lively sense of the role of accent in the perception of metricality, it also once more calls into question Gasparov's serene conviction that the accentual patterning of French verse is simply 'the natural rhythm of the language'.

The present writer is a native speaker of English who, like others brought up on accentual verse, may well be foisting his native accentual prejudices on French verse. The Romanian metrician, Mihai Dinu, has been equally wary of the influence of his mother-tongue on his views of the nature and role of accent in French verse.[87] What is needed, and what the following chapters will seek to provide, is not the justification of a prejudice, but arguments which, had they been available more than a century ago, might have been deployed by native francophones such as Louis Dumur and Edouard Dujardin in support of their accentualist intuitions. These intuitions, however apposite, leave questions to be answered. Quicherat unwittingly invites some of these by forcibly pressing the accentualist case:

> Nous sommes arrivés à une conclusion que nous trouvons toute formulée dans M. Mablin: 'Malgré le peu de fixité de la prosodie française, on peut faire dans cette langue des vers héxamètres, pentamètres, saphiques etc., comme les autres langues modernes en font. En effet, si par le mot prosodie, on a voulu désigner les accents, les accents de la langue française sont aussi fixés que ceux des autres langues modernes, et ceux des langues grecque et latine: on sait que tous les mots français ont l'accent sur la dernière, à l'exception des mots terminés par un e muet, qui l'ont sur la pénultième'.[88]

But alas, the devil, as always, is in the detail. What is meant by 'tous les mots français'? Quicherat's re-write of Corneille's alexandrine quoted above instinctively accents the indirect pronoun *vous*:

> Vous le mieux révéler qu'il ne *vous* le révèle.[89]

But he is just replacing one indirect pronoun, *me*, by another, *vous*; why then does he accent the latter but not the former? Is this simply a personal preference, a feature of *parole* rather than of *langue*?[90] No, here we have a francophone informant giving us a rare and precious clue to the prosodic structure of modern French. What exactly is it that distinguishes *vous* from *me* since both are indirect pronouns? We know that any French sentence ending with a full stop will have an accent on the final full vowel of the last word:

> Je suis Romaine, hélas! puisque Horace est Rom**ain**.[91]

But even a brief survey will disclose words that we never find in phrase-final position: *me, te, se, que, à, mon, sa, de, puis*, and so on. As above, the telegram test showed that words like these occurring frequently in the language have a lesser informational value than those occurring more rarely; which means that only words with significant informational value can end a phrase.[92] This is just another way of saying that such words are free to appear either within or at the end of a phrase. If then word-accent within the phrase needs justifying it can be done thus: only if a word can occur in accented phrase-final position, will it maintain its accentual identity within the phrase. Now, is the *vous* which Quicherat substitutes for *me* such a word? What distinguishes it from *me* is that it has a dual grammatical identity: it can either appear before the verb: 'je vous le donne', or after it as a disjunctive pronoun: 'je le donne à **vou**s', in which *vous* is phrase-final and thus accented. Is it not this second function which leads Quicherat to accord *vous* an accent within the phrase? *Me* is different since its distinct disjunctive form must always replace it in phrase-final position: 'Tu me le donnes' ≠ 'Tu le donnes à *moi*'.

This, like other similar cases one might cite, shows the need for a fuller account of accent in French generally. Unlike direct pronouns, indirect pronouns in French appear in accented form in phrase-final position (*moi, toi, lui, nous, vous*): did Corneille, when he read his verse aloud, distinguish indirect pronouns from direct ones by marking the former with what may be a linguistic accent?

> **Vou**s le mi**eu**x révéler qu'il ne **me** le révèle.

Is the order of direct and indirect pronouns in French related to their accentual status?[93] Why in standard French is 'je le vous promets'* instantly perceived as a solecism?[94] Elsewhere, is 'accent on the last vowel', e.g. 'conversa**tion**', the only one in this word? What happens when two word-accents collide, e.g. 'vo**isin pau**vre'? What is the relation between group-accent and word-accent?

Just as the study of English grammar owes a debt of gratitude to Scandinavian linguists such as Jespersen, so is France indebted to nineteenth-century German scholars for a deeper understanding of the history and structure of the French language. The aim of the anglophone writer of this book is to make in detail a case for the measuring role of accent in French verse by proposing a fuller account of the accentual prosody of French. The first chapter will present the evidence available on both historical and synchronic axes. The former will trace the processes of change in time which produced in Old French an accentual system quite distinct from that of its Latin forebear, while the latter identifies that system as a coherent structure in particular texts in particular moments in time. The intersection of these axes will appear in a comparison of major texts showing prosodic states of the language in widely separated moments in time.

In a second chapter, the accentual model thus derived will be applied to verse-texts from 1200 to 1950 without reference to their semantic content.[95] Only then will this content be examined in the light of the independently derived accentual scansion. This review of a representative spread of texts over eight hundred years will reveal a sustained tradition of poetic composition in which accentual patterning contributes to the creation of meaning.

Notes to the Introduction

1. William Shakespeare, 'Sonnet XVIII', in *The New Oxford Book of English Verse*, ed. by Helen Gardner (Oxford: Oxford University Press, 1972), p. 145. Accented syllables in bold.
2. Though individual readers may accent any word they choose, we refer to the general structure of the language common to all users ('langue', as Saussure terms it, as opposed to an individual's use of it, 'parole'). To accent 'more' would give prominence to a grammatical word which occurs relatively frequently in the language and twice in the line. In English, 'more' or the suffix

'-er' appears each time a comparison in made. So the reason for not accenting 'more' is that informational weight marked by accent correlates with a word's relative rarity of occurrence, an idea formalised in Zipf's Law. The gist of this statistical law for our purposes is that in any sample of English or French a few words (e.g. *the, le, he, il, this, ce*) are used very often and most are used rarely. The idea of 'informational weight' is illustrated by the 'telegram test'. In a telegram for which one pays by the word, the message 'I shall be arriving on Wednesday by the last train' will take the form 'Arriving Wednesday last train', where only infrequently occurring words critical to the message appear. For an account of Zipf's Law see Colin Cherry, *On Human Communication* (Cambridge, MA: MIT Press, 1966), pp. 103–11.

3. In 'Recherches sur la prosodie et la métrique du français', Paul Verluyten observed that 'la prosodie du français, contrairement à celle de certaines autres langues modernes, est restée presque aussi mystérieuse que celle des langues mortes' (unpublished doctoral thesis, University of Antwerp, 1982, p. 256). Twenty years later, little had changed when in *Mètres et rythmes du vers classique: Corneille et Racine*, Valérie Beaudouin wrote: 'La question de l'accent du vers dans l'alexandrin [...] est le lieu d'âpres débats tout comme celle de l'accent dans la langue' ((Paris: Champion, 2002), p. 38).

4. Benoît de Cornulier shows that the notion of a mid-line pause is just a notion. The cesura in French verse is 'le revers négatif' of the juxtaposition of hemistichs, having no independent existence. See Cornulier, *Théorie du vers: Rimbaud, Verlaine, Mallarmé* (Paris: Seuil, 1982), p. 82.

5. Both quotations from Pierre Corneille, *Le Cid*, II.8, in *Théâtre complet*, ed. by Georges Couton, 3 vols (Paris: Garnier, 1971–74), II, 759. Accented syllable in bold, '#' marks cesura.

6. Arthur Rimbaud, 'Au Cabaret-Vert, cinq heures du soir', in *Œuvres complètes*, ed. by Steve Murphy, 2 vols (Paris: Champion, 1999), II, 290.

7. *La Chanson de Roland*, ed. by Frederick Whitehead (Oxford: Blackwell, 1962), p. 1.

8. Guillaume Apollinaire, 'Les Colchiques', in *Anthology of Modern French Poetry: From Baudelaire to the Present Day*, ed. by C. A. Hackett (Oxford: Blackwell, 1976), p. 111.

9. Jean Froissart, 'Ballade pour se bien porter', in *Anthologie poétique française: moyen age*, ed. by A. Mary, 2 vols (Paris: Garnier-Flammarion, 1967), II, 159–60.

10. Eustache Deschamps, 'Double ballade sur la mort de Guillaume de Machaut', in *Anthologie poétique française*, ed. by Mary, II, 145–46. This cesura is found too in modern poets such as Verlaine and Apollinaire.

11. Since patterned accent in verse is for us an extra-linguistic ordering of linguistic accent itself, a theory of accent in verse will imply insights into the role of accent in other registers of French. See for example Roger Pensom, *Accent and Metre in French: A Theory of the Relation Between Linguistic Accent and Metrical Practice in French, 1100–1900* (Bern: Peter Lang, 2000), pp. 157–72, for sonagram analyses of colloquial speech; and 'Accent et syllabe dans les vers français: une synthèse possible?', *French Language Studies*, 19 (2009), 335–61, for a comparison of accent-distribution in samples of verse and prose.

12. See for example Cornulier, Gouvard, and Fabb and Halle, all quoted and discussed below.

13. The argument of Cornulier's *De la métrique à l'interprétation* (Paris: Garnier, 2009) is a striking expression of this view. See discussion below.

14. Cornulier, *Théorie du vers*.

15. Arthur Rimbaud, 'Le Bateau ivre', in *Œuvres complètes*, ed. by Rolland de Renéville and Jules Mouquet (Paris: Gallimard, 1954), p. 102.

16. Jean-Michel Gouvard, *Critique du vers* (Paris: PUF, 2000).

17. Édouard Dujardin, *Les Premiers Poètes du vers libre* (Paris: Mercure de France, 1922). A view seconded by Hugo Blank: 'Wenn der romanische Vers keinen *festen* Rhythmus aufweist, so bedeutet dies allerdings nicht, dass ihm die vier Grundrhythmen Jambus, Trochäus, Daktylus und Anapäst fremd wären. Ganz im Gegenteil: diese Grundrhythmen sind überall vorhanden' (*Kleine Verskunde* (Heidelberg: Carl Winter, 1990), p. 58). For further discussion and examples, see Christine Lombez, *La Traduction de la poésie allemande en français dans la première moitié du XIXe siècle: réception et interaction poétique* (Paris: Niemeyer, 2009), pp. 1–20.

18. Roger Pensom, *The Literary Technique of the Chanson de Roland* (Geneva: Droz, 1982), and *Accent and Metre in French.*

19. For recurring syllabic count, see, for example, Benoît de Cornulier, *Art poëtique: notions et problèmes de métrique* (Lyon: Presses Universitaires de Lyon, 1995), p. 23.

20. Pensom, *Accent and Metre in French*, and 'Accent et syllabe dans le vers français: une synthèse possible?'.

21. Beaudouin, *Mètres et rythmes classiques.* Unaccented and accented syllables are represented by 0 and 1 respectively.

22. André Van Hasselt, *Le Livre des paraboles* (Namur: Wesmael-Charlier, 1872). Cited by Lombez in *La Traduction de la poésie allemande*, p. 10.

23. François Benoît Hoffmann, 'Je te perds, fugitive espérance! | L'infidelle a rompu tous nos nœuds. | Pour calmer, s'il se peut, ma souffrance,' (*Le Secret, comédie* (Paris: Vente, 1796)).

24. That is, accent on the final pronounced vowel of the word.

25. See n. 17 above.

26. Jean Racine, *Andromaque*, II.1, in *Théâtre complet de Racine*, ed. by Maurice Rat (Paris: Garnier, 1950), p. 131.

27. Mikhail Gasparov, *A History of European Versification*, ed. by G. S. Smith and L. Holford-Strevens, trans. by G. S. Smith and M. Tarlinskaja (Oxford: Clarendon Press, 1996), p. 144.

28. Jean-Michel Gouvard, *La Versification* (Paris: PUF, 1999) p. 86.

29. Alfred de Musset, 'La Nuit d'Octobre', in *Poésies nouvelles*, ed. by Jacques Bony (Paris: Flammarion, 2000), p. 95, in alexandrines divided 6 + 6.

30. Nigel Fabb and Morris Halle, *Meter in Poetry* (Cambridge: Cambridge University Press, 2008).

31. Ibid., p. 5.

32. Ibid., p. 9: 'The metrical grids present one way in which the well-formedness of lines might be determined. We have not shown that this is the way that poets and readers do it, nor have we shown that this is the only logically possible way in which this can be done'. Our summary is perforce an incomplete simplification.

33. Ibid., p. 136. Thus their model for an alexandrine would be 010101 # 010101, which alternates unaccented with accented syllables. The model they refer to for the Sanskrit Vedic 12-syllable line similarly has 'a prevailing iambic pattern' (p. 215).

34. Cornulier, *Art poëtique*, p. 23 (my emphasis). It seems that for Cornulier the term *classique* excludes by definition heterosyllabic verse, as we find it for example in La Fontaine. Cornulier admits that he finds such verse 'terriblement difficile à analyser' (*Art poëtique*, p. 191).

35. Fabb and Halle, *Meter in Poetry*, p. 12.

36. Noam Chomsky, *Syntactic Structures*, Janua Linguarum, series minor, 4 (The Hague: Mouton, 1957). Geoffrey Sampson's observation on Chomsky may also apply to Fabb and Halle: 'The existence of linguistic universals is for Chomsky and his followers, not so much a finding which has emerged from their research despite their expectations, but rather a guiding assumption which determines the nature of the hypotheses they propose in order to account for the data' (*Schools of Linguistics: Competition and Evolution* (London: Hutchinson, 1980), p. 148).

37. For Cornulier, 'L'égalité en nombre syllabique ne peut être métrique que parce qu'elle est *instinctivement* sensible' (*Théorie du vers*, p. 59, my emphasis).

38. See n. 2 above.

39. Cornulier, *Théorie du vers,* p. 279.

40. Gasparov, *A History of European Versification*, p. 144.

41. Gouvard, *La Versification*, p. 86.

42. Claude Lancelot, Antoine Arnauld, and Pierre Nicole, *Nouvelle Méthode pour apprendre facilement et en peu de temps la langue latine, avec une brève instruction sur les règles de la poésie française* (Paris: Vitré, 1650), p. 487. Cited by Gouvard, *Critique du vers*, p. 10.

43. Steve Murphy, 'Effets et motivations: quelques excentricités de la versification baudelairienne', in *Baudelaire: une alchimie de la douleur, études sur les Fleurs du Mal*, ed. by Patrick Labarthe (Paris: Eurédit, 2003), pp. 281–86.

44. Gouvard, *Critique du vers*, p. 85.

45. For Gouvard, the number of syllables in a sub-unit of the line is constrained by Cornulier's 'loi des 8', according to which only sequences of verse-units whose lengths are 8 syllables or less are recognised instinctively by the reader as metrical; sub-units such as 9 + 3 or 10 + 2 are thus illicit.

46. For a detailed review of *Critique du vers*, see *Modern Languages Review*, 97, 4 (2002), 993–94.

47. Though just occasionally Cornulier does succumb to the temptation to ascribe a semantic value to a metrical event: see his identification of 'onomatopée métrique' in *Art poëtique*, p. 81 and p. 87, n. 124.

48. While the usual meaning of the Latin *versus* is 'a turning around', Plautus also uses the word to mean 'a step/figure in a dance' (*Stichus*, V. 7. 2).

49. The word 'strophe' is also derived from the Greek meaning 'to turn'. The measuring unit in classical metre is the foot not the syllable.

50. French song and 'high' lyric poetry had essentially parted company by the fifteenth century. In his *Art de dictier* of 1392, Eustache Deschamps distinguishes between 'musique artificiele' (music proper) and 'musique naturele' (poetry): *L'Art de dictier*, ed. and trans. by Deborah M. Sinnreich-Levi (East Lansing: Colleagues Press, 1994), pp. 60–62.

51. Cited by Gouvard, *Critique du vers*, p. 17.

52. Antonio Scoppa, *Les Vrais Principes de la versification développés par un examen comparatif entre la langue italienne et la française* (Paris: Courcier, 1814), p. 304, cited by Gouvard, *Critique du vers*, p. 17. For an overview of the history of the accentual thesis, see Gouvard, *Critique du vers*, pp. 15–33.

53. Hugo Thieme, *Essai sur l'histoire du vers français* (Paris: Champion, 1916), p. 156.

54. Pierre Lusson and Jacques Roubaud, 'Mètre et rythme de l'alexandrin ordinaire', *Langue française*, 23, (1974), 41–53. A clear and full critique of the Lusson-Roubaud theory is given in Gouvard, *Critique du vers*, pp. 38–49.

55. Georges Lote, *L'Alexandrin d'après la phonétique expérimentale*, 2nd edn, 3 vols (Paris: La Phalange, 1913–14).

56. The identities of the two anonymous professionals among Lote's eighteen informants are divulged by André Spire in his *Plaisir poétique et plaisir musculaire* (Paris: Librairie José Corti, 1949), pp. 463–64.

57. In the following example, the recordings of three readers show syllable-lengths in micro-seconds:

	Ma	pã	sé	ã	tre	né	èr	ã	te	re	vœ	ri (œ)
G	15	39	32	14	41	50	49	15	19	29	10	34
E	17	30	18	19	32	41	49	17	18	19	16	41
R	19	46	40	16	26	18	75	12	19	27	15	33

(I, 97; the line is from Victor Hugo, 'Ma pensée entraînée erre en tes rêveries' (*Hernani*, V. 3)). Whatever the relevance of this to the perception of line-length, it shows a significant correlation between vowel-length and word-accent as we will define it.

58. Lote, *L'Alexandrin d'après la phonétique expérimentale*, II, p. 534.

59. Cornulier, *Art poëtique*, p. 31.

60. Of the 'plusieurs dizaines de personnes' who heard the 'doctored' version of *Les Djinns* recited, '*plusieurs* personnes ont reconnu aisément tous les vers inégaux jusqu'aux vers de 8 syllabes inclus' (Cornulier, *Théorie du vers*, p. 15, my emphasis).

61. Pierre Guiraud thinks that these mutilated alexandrines were perceived as 'regular' since the listener's brain unconsciously rectifies them with reference to the isosyllabic norm (*La Versification* (Paris: PUF, 1970), p. 25). But if so, how many of Cornulier's listeners unconsciously rectified his *vers boiteux* in conformity with the relevant n-syllabic norm of each strophe of *Les Djinns*?

62. E. Koschwitz, *Les Parlers parisiens: anthologie phonétique* (Paris: [n.pub.], 1896), p. 143.

63. Cornulier, *Théorie du vers*, p. 59. He justifies his claim in the experiment on *Les Djinns* discussed above and recorded in pp. 11–69. For a critique of this approach, see Pensom, 'Accent et syllabe dans les vers français: une synthèse possible?', pp. 342–50.

64. Gouvard, *Critique du vers*, p. 44.
65. Whether heard or seen, the process of syllabification involves the informed participation of the reader/listener. He or she is competent in the relevant rules concerning, for example, the deletion of word-final 'ə'.
66. John Hurford, *Language and Number: The Emergence of a Cognitive System* (Oxford: Blackwell, 1987), p. 12.
67. Ibid., p. 110.
68. Cornulier, *Théorie du vers*, pp. 11–69. This, for Cornulier, explains why the octosyllable is the longest common classical French metre not divided into sub-units, as are the decasyllable, 4 + 6, and the alexandrine, 6 + 6. For a possible source of Cornulier's idea, see G. A. Miller, 'The Magical Number Seven Plus or Minus Two', *Psychological Review*, 63 (1956), 81–97.
69. Jean Racine, 'Le Lundi, à Matines', in *Hymnes traduites du Bréviaire Romain: Le Lundi, à Matines*, in *Oxford Book of French Verse*, ed. by St. John Lucas (Oxford: Oxford University Press, 1951), p. 191.
70. Cornulier, *Art poëtique*, p. 191.
71. Jean de La Fontaine, 'Le Corbeau et le renard', in *Fables*, ed. by Alain-Marie Bassy (Paris: Flammarion, 1995), p. 7.
72. Cornulier confesses that 'Les vers "irréguliers" comme en ont écrit Molière et Racine [...] et spécialement La Fontaine, [...] me paraissent térriblement difficiles à analyser' (*Art poëtique*, p. 191).
73. François de Malherbe, 'Stances', in *Poésies*, ed. by Jacques Lavard, 2 vols (Paris : Droz, 1936–37), II, 181.
74. 'C'est l'alternance fixe qui est le premier principe de notre versification. L'isosyllabie, le syllabisme, n'en est que la conséquence' (Paul Verrier, *Le Vers français*, 3 vols (Paris: Didier, 1932), II, 5).
75. 'Le rôle de la rime est [...] nul, ou quasiment nul, dans la détermination de la loi des 8 syllabes' (Cornulier, *Théorie du vers*, p. 23).
76. Beaudouin, *Mètres et rythmes du vers classique*, p. 418.
77. The accentuation of all three examples assumes only oxytonic word-accent.
78. See Jean-Claude Milner, 'Accent de vers et accent de langue dans l'alexandrin classique', *Cahiers de poétique comparée*, 15 (1987), p. 43.
79. 'Le vers des tragédies de Racine emploie plus fréquemment les modèles rythmiques les plus réguliers (001001 et 010101): il n'y a que 25% des seconds hémistiches "irréguliers" ' (Beaudouin, *Mètres et rythmes du vers classique*, p. 414). Oxytonic word-accent within the phrase is assumed for the analysis of her corpus.
80. Édouard Wacken, *Fleurs d'Allemagne et poésies diverses* (Brussels: Labroue, 1850), p. 143.
81. Martin Duffell, *Modern Metrical Theory and the Verso de arte mayor* (London: Department of Spanish Studies, Queen Mary and Westfield College, 1999), p. 45.
82. Jean Racine, *Athalie*, II.2, in *Théâtre complet*, ed. by Rat, p. 666.
83. Not forgetting the octosyllable without fixed cesura, preeminent in medieval verse narrative and found in non-narrative work by poets from Rutebeuf to Hugo.
84. See for example Louis Bonaparte: 'La versification française manque de rythme; les syllabes que nous appelons accentuées sont disposées à caprice sans symétrie, sans aucune raison, de sorte que celles d'un hémistiche ou d'un vers s'opposent quelquefois diamétralement à celles du vers suivant, et ainsi les accents sont variés et sans ordre' (L. Bonaparte, *Mémoires sur la versification française et Essais divers* (1819), cited by Gouvard, *Critique du vers*, pp. 27–28).
85. Voltaire and Corneille both cited by Léon Quicherat, *Traité de versification française* (Paris: Hachette, 1838), p. 150. There are in fact *five* atonic syllables in Corneille's second hemistich.
86. See n. 78 above.
87. Mihai Dinu, 'Structures accentuelles de l'alexandrin chez Racine', *Langue française*, 99 (1993), 63–74 (p. 63).
88. Quicherat, *Traité de versification française*, p. 390. He is quoting a dissertation presented to the Institut by l'Abbé Mablin in 1815.

89. A glance at the first page of Corneille's *Cinna* will qualify him as an exception to Milner's generalisation about atonic runs in classic verse. See n. 78 above.

90. As noted earlier, Saussure distinguishes *parole*, 'la partie individuelle du langage', from *langue*, which is 'sociale dans son essence et indépendante de l'individu'. Ferdinand de Saussure, *Cours de linguistique générale*, ed. by Charles Bally, Albert Sechehaye, and Albert Riedlinger (Paris: Payot, 1971), p. 37.

91. Pierre Corneille, *Horace*, I.1, in *Théâtre complet*, ed. by Couton, I, 836.

92. The imperative form, e.g. *polissez-le!*, is a rare exception.

93. Where the order of pronouns in modern French is concerned, the verdict of K. Sneyders de Vogel is still relevant: 'Il semble qu'il faut chercher la cause de ce phénomène dans l'accent de la phrase' (*Syntaxe historique du français* (Groningen: Wolters, 1919), p. 335).

94. An asterisk marks an unlawful collocation.

95. It is crucial that such scansion should be blind to any consideration of meaning.

CHAPTER 1

The Origin and History of
Word-accent in French,
and its Role in French Verse

Any knowledge of the present supposes some understanding of the past. The early past of modern French and its versification lies in the Late Latin language and culture of the Roman Empire. That modern Italians have to learn Spanish if they want to read *Don Quixote*, tells us how far modern Romance speakers have moved from the spoken Latin of their forebears. The Roman conquest subjected peoples whose various native tongues were mutually incomprehensible to a social and political order whose common language was Latin. The mutual incomprehensibility of, say, modern French and Portuguese speakers has its origins in the impact of the respective native languages on the Latin each people acquired as a second language under Rome.

For what we now know as French, this native language was an early German. In the fifth century, the barriers restraining the incoming Germanic invasion were swept away and Germanic peoples poured into Gaul. Even though the Gaul subdued by Rome had been Celtic-speaking, the ancestor of modern French was the dialect of the Ile-de-France, the domain of the German-speaking Frankish kings. The famous Strasbourg Oaths, sworn in 842, survive in a bilingual text giving the earliest example of what was to become Old French together with its German equivalent.[1] In 813, the Council of Tours had encouraged clergy to give their sermons 'in rusticam romanam linguam aut theotiscam', that is in either the current Romance or German vernaculars.

Rather than the Celtic substrate, it was the influence of German speech-habits on the Latin spoken in Gaul which proved decisive:

> With the dissolution of the Roman Empire and its civilisation perished gradually the unity of the common Latin speech that, despite ever-increasing local differences had up till then linked together the inhabitants of its various parts. The language used in the common intercourse of everyday life, exposed to disintegrating foreign influence, freed from the shackles of tradition, was modified with increasing rapidity and its nascent local characteristics emphasised. Thus the Romance languages in their early stage, Gallo-Roman, Hispano-Roman, Italo-Roman etc., slowly took shape.[2]

The Germanic speech of the Franks influenced both the vocabulary and the sound-system of the spoken Latin of Gaul, and it is this latter which concerns us here. The Frankish system of accentuation was a strong expiratory one and it was in the strengthening of the weak Latin tonic stress that Frankish speech exercised its strongest hold on pronunciation.[3] For example, the accent on the first syllable of classical Latin 'petram' was intensified, producing the 'breaking' or diphthongisation of the vowel to give 'pierre'. The force of this expiratory accent was such that certain Latin polysyllables lost an atonic syllable: *dominus* became *domnu* (Old French *Dons*); *directum* gave *drictu* (Old French *dreit*, modern French *droit*). This expiration brought also the suppression of the vowels of atonic monosyllabic words. In enclisis for example, '*si.st* ampairet', the *e* of *est* has become part of the word that precedes it. In proclisis in '*Qu'elle* Deo raneiet', the [ə] of *Que* is absorbed by the *e* of *elle*. The following are from the eleventh-century *Vie de Saint Alexis*: '*N'at* mais amfant', 'Tut sun aver *qu'od* sei en ad portet', 'Cher filz, cum *t'ai* perdut?', '*Ne.l* reconurent', '*Je.s* (je les) lur dirrai', '*Ki.l* me guardrat', 'fait *l'el* muster venir', 'Ki *si.st* dolente', '*ki.n* report sa dolur'. And in the twelfth-century Oxford manuscript of the *Chanson de Roland*: '*se.m* püez acorder', 'Que *je.l* sivrai', 'Livrez *m'en* ore le guant', '*Si.n* vois vedeir'. Texts in Old French continue to register the suppression of word-final [ə] in frequently occurring articles and atonic pronouns, although as in the cases of *en* and *est*, a full vowel has been absorbed. In both enclisis and proclisis, the attractor-element, for example the *Si* in 'Si.n', has a more marked prosodic identity than the attracted element *en*. Though contextual phonetic factors are complex, certain of these contracted forms have an accentual value and thus a rhythmical role within the verse-unit.[4]

Stress on monosyllables affected the development of personal pronouns. For example, the first person *jo* coexisted with the stressed form *gié*. In Chrétien de Troyes's *Erec et Enide* we find:

> Li rois Artus et la reïne,
> Est ci pres en une gaudine,
> De trez et de tantes *logié*;
> En boene foi le vos lo *gié*
> Que vos veigniez avoeques moi
> Veoir la reïne et le roi.[5]

Here *gié* (the strong form of the first person singular pronoun) is accented on the rhyming vowel *é*. Similarly the indirect object pronoun pairs *me/moi*, *te/toi*, alternate according to their syntactical role, the accented forms occurring both within the phrase and at line-end.

As we have noted, modern French alone amongst her Romance sisters has no semantically distinctive accent but rather a fixed accent on the final full vowel of words with a relatively low frequency of occurrence. Despite the changes that affected accentuation en route from Latin to Romance, the position of the primary accent has not shifted. The position of the accented vowel, for example *cerveau* from the Latin *cerebellum*, may seem to have moved, but its word-final position in modern French is the result of the attrition which weakened and finally deleted the Latin '-um'. This evolution contrasts strongly with that of Italian and Spanish, both of which maintained the Latin final atonic vowel in both masculine and feminine nouns, so that the accented position was 'last but one' or paroxytonic: compare French masculine *labeur* and *latin* with Italian *lavoro* and *latino*.[6]

Not to forget the classical Latin countertonic accent. This secondary accent was weaker than the primary tonic accent: '*o*rnamentum'; '*d*ormitorium'; '*i*nvolare'; '*a*djutare'.[7] The presence of this accent in Latin raises an important question: was there countertonic accent in its successor, Old French? There is phonological evidence that there was. The prosodic oddness of French among its Romance sisters is illustrated by its contrast with for instance Italian and Spanish, in both of which all pretonic vowels remain 'tense' in articulation: in modern French, Latin 'ornamentu' gives 'ornəment'. Here the articulatory contrast between first vowel, which is 'tense' and the second, which is 'lax', results in the alternation '[□] tense / [ə] lax / [ã] tense' being perceived as accentual i.e. [□r.nə.mã]. Both Italian and Spanish give *ornamento*. This phenomenon is already clearly visible in Old French forms: Latin *homicidiu* > Old French *omecire*; *fundamentu* > *fondement*; *sacramentu* > *sairement*; *cantare (ha)beo* > *chanterai*. In these cases, the changes [i]>[e] and [a]>[e] imply a lessening of articulatory effort, that is a move from 'tense' to 'lax' in the articulation of the vowel. The series of changes [i]>[e]>[ə] and [a]>[e]>[ə] were certainly complete by the time of the ninth-century *Séquence de Sainte Eulalie*.[8] The reality of countertonic accent from Old to modern French must therefore be taken into account in our description of the alternation of accent in French verse of all periods. Old French adverbs continue to show this pattern of accentuation acquired under increased expiratory stress: '*fi*erəment', '*pl*einəment'.[9] Overall, Germanic speech habits were responsible for the accentual character of Old French: 'The relatively level accentuation of Early Gallo-Roman was changed into a more up and down system, very like that of modern English except that it was still the syllable that was last or last but one that was strongest'.[10]

Accent and Metre in Old French

Classical Latin had an accentual system, which played only a secondary role in versification. Following classical Greek metre, Latin exploited the alternation of long and short vowel-quantities available in its phonology. The measuring function of Latin metre was based on combinations of metrical feet which joined long with short vowels: the iambus, ˘ – (short + long), the trochee, '– ˘' (long + short), the anapest, ˘ ˘ –, the dactyl '– ˘ ˘' and the tribrach ˘ ˘ ˘. The basic unit of duration, the 'mora', is represented by ˘, '–' being the equivalent of ˘ ˘. This equivalence allowed substitutions of ˘ ˘ for '–' or '–' for ˘ ˘ within the verse-line. Thus an iambus, ˘ –, may be replaced by a tribrach, ˘ ˘ ˘, or a dactyl, '– ˘ ˘', by a spondee, '– –'. Here are some examples of the dactylic hexameter from Virgil's *Aeneid*:

Postquam altos ventum in montis atque invia lustra,	– – – – – – – – – ˘ ˘ – –	13
Ecce ferae saxi deiectae vertice caprae	– ˘ ˘ – – – – – – – ˘ ˘ – –	14
Decurrere iugis alia de parte patentis	– – – ˘ ˘ – ˘ ˘ – – – ˘ ˘ – –	15
Transmittunt cursu campos atque agmina cervi	– – – – ˘ ˘ – – – ˘ ˘ – –	13
Pulverulenta fuga glomerant montisque reliquunt.[11]	– ˘ ˘ – ˘ ˘ – ˘ ˘ – – ˘ ˘ – –	16[12]

Though we may not be equal to savouring the refinements of Roman poetry, we can see that the substitution of spondee for dactyl generates a varied syllabic count: evidently something fundamental happened between the demise of classical Latin metre and the triumph of invariant isosyllabism in Old and modern French verse.

There is clear evidence that in Gaul, by the fifth century, a Latin speaker's sense of the rule-governed combination of long and short vowels in verse was beginning to fade. Though contemporaries were still writing heterosyllabic quantitative verse, the fourth-century Latin hymns of Saint Ambrose were already octosyllabic. He had been guilty too of slips in his Latin scansion, a trend which continued: in the sixth century, the Frankish bishop and historian Gregory of Tours relates that King Chilperic composed hymns in which there were shorts which should have been longs and vice versa. Milo in the ninth century can write 'I hold it no great crime if long or short syllables turn up in the wrong places', which clearly suggests that new ways of writing verse were emerging.[13]

Though in classical Latin verse word-accent was subordinate to the quantitative system, syllabic-accentual verse was always present. Its commonplace nature is shown in the verse-satire with which Julius Caesar's soldiers celebrated his triumph in Suetonius's *Twelve Caesars*:

Caesar Gallias subegit,	8
Nicomedes Caesarem:	7
Ecce Caesar nunc triumphat,	8
Qui subegit Gallias;	7
Nicomedes non triumphat,	8
Qui subegit Caesarem.[14]	7

While sending up Caesar, the former youthful lover of the King of Bithynia, the singers also celebrate the vigour of Latin trochaic verse with its regular accentuation and syllable-count. Unrelated historically to its Latin forerunner, the expiratory accent of Frankish speech was gradually making itself felt in Late Latin verse.

Here are two strophes of the celebrated hymn 'Vexilla regis' by Venantius Fortunatus, Bishop of Poitiers and friend of Gregory of Tours:

Vexi|lla re|gis pro|deunt,	— — | ˘ — | — — | ˘ -
Fulget| crucis| myste|rium,	— — | ˘ — | — — | ˘ ˘
Quo car|ne car|nis con|ditor	— — | ˘ — | — — | ˘ ˘
Suspen|sus est| pati|bulo.	— — | ˘ — | ˘ ˘ | ˘ —
Confix|a cla|vis vis|cera	— — | ˘ — | — — | ˘ ˘
Tendens| manus|, ves|tigia,	— — | ˘ — | — — | ˘ ˘
Redem|ptio|nis gra|tia	˘ — | ˘ — | — — | ˘ -
Hic im|molat'|est hos|tia.[15]	— — | ˘ — | — — | ˘ ˘

The quantitative scansion of these iambic dimeters is shown alongside these strophes; if you read them aloud you may find them falling into accentual 'iambics', 01010101.[16] The poet has arranged things so that in twenty-eight of the thirty-two feet (the feet are marked off with a '|') the accented syllable of the iambus coincides with a Latin word-accent.[17] The lines are thus quantitatively regular while being at the same time regularly isosyllabic and showing a marked 'iambic' rhythm. Fortunatus's own Frankish speech is surely expressing itself in the accentual organisation of his verse.

It is however certain that the Latin hymns of Fortunatus and his predecessors were not accentual in the sense that the English 'iambic' pentameter is. As Michel Burger has demonstrated in his analysis of the Latin hymns of Saint Ambrose, Latin iambic verse shows a variety of accentual types in which the strict alternation of 01010100 is often violated.[18] This leads him, with others, to reject the idea of a meaningful accentual scheme for this verse, but it may be that other factors we have already considered are at work.

To revert to our initial question: how did Fortunatus and his readers/listeners know when a syllabic verse-line had the proper number of syllables? Though varying syllable-count is a standard feature of classical Latin verse, by the time of Fortunatus the classical Latin provision for substituting two short syllables for one long in a metrical foot was being forgotten. Most of Fortunatus's Latin verse was quantitative with irregular syllabic count, but in his Latin hymns, the syllable has replaced the classical 'mora' as the means of measuring the verse-line. From the fourth century onward, Germanic speech-accent was transforming the Late Latin speech of Gaul.[19] We may thus consider the switch in verse from 'mora' to 'syllable' as one of the consequences of the resulting phonological change, and that there is a relationship between the accentual system of Late Latin in Gaul and the organisation of its isosyllabic verse. The apparent disorder of accented positions in Ambrose and Fortunatus may be simply the rule-governed alternation of varied accentual feet.

Clarification comes from Burger's analysis of accentual verse-types in the 428 verses of Ambrose's fourteen octosyllabic Latin hymns.[20] Burger identifies twenty-five types. Here are the four most frequently occurring:

Type 1: Aeterne rerum conditor[21]	01010100	124 occurrences
Type 2: Noctis profundae pervigil	10010100	96 occurrences
Type 3: Hoc omnis erronum chorus	01001010	73 occurrences
Type 4: Soluit polum caligine	10100100	31 occurrences

These frequent types give us the accentual profiles of 76 per cent of the verses in the corpus. Burger's scepticism concerning the overall accentual 'iambic' regularity of this verse is justified, but it is nevertheless clear that its accentual structure is rule-governed. In Type 1, out of a total of 428 (octosyllabic) iambic dimeters 124 are regularly 'iambic' with unaccented and accented syllables alternating. Type 2 alternates accent by combining accentual 'dactyls' with a 'trochee'. Type 3 combines iambs with an 'anapest', while Type 4 shows alternation of 'trochee' and 'anapests'. Thus at least 76 per cent of the verses that Burger studied show *neither* juxtaposed accents *nor* runs of more than two atonic syllables.

But this does not mean that the poet is consciously substituting accentual feet for quantitative ones. His verse is quantitatively regular, hence he must be superadding a rule-governed accentual pattern to the quantitative one. In the examples above, the deployment of a limited repertoire of accentual feet ('iambus', 'trochee', 'dactyl' and 'anapest') avoids both juxtaposed accents and strings of atonic syllables.[22] The resulting rhythm may well facilitate the poet's/listener's perception of the recurring syllabic count via the summation of binary (01, 10) and/or ternary (001, 100) accentual units.

Though the Ambrosian solution of reconciling accentual rhythm with quantity was influential, a radical alternative had emerged. Already in the fifth century, verse was appearing which relied exclusively on rhythm for its form:

a solis ortus cardine	— — ˘ —	— — ˘ —
adusque terrae limitem	˘ — ˘ —	— — ˘ —
Christum canamus principem	— — ˘ —	— — ˘ —
natum Maria virgine	— — ˘ —	— — ˘ —
maior et enim solito	— ˘ ˘ ˘	— ˘ ˘ —
apparuisti omnibus	— — ˘ —	— — ˘ —
ut potestatis ordinem	— ˘ — —	˘ — ˘ —
in lustri mente vinceres.[23]	— — — —	˘ — ˘ —

While the first of these fifth-century quatrains makes perfect sense as classical iambic dimeters with accentual rhythm, the second can *only* make sense accentually, since marking the quantities produces no recognisable pattern.

To recall our experiment in the Introduction with the modern reader's perception of French verse: there it was proposed that our recognition of verse is mediated by its rule-governed alternation of accent. This we found could be explained by Hurford's 'maxima', in our case groups of two and three syllables (twos: 01 and 10, or threes: 001 or 100), which are pre-consciously 'added up' by poet and reader/listener. Since we are now dealing with verse in another language from another time and with the implications of Hurford's findings in mind, we are working with the possibility of a 'human universal' written into the processes of our cognition. We have noted that Verrier's work on French verse from its earliest period convinced him that 'alternation of accent' was the founding principle of all French verse. If our re-appraisal of Burger's work on Saint Ambrose holds water, we can begin to think about the evolution of Old French isosyllabic metres in a framework of alternating accent.

The dominant metres of Old French verse are the octosyllable and the decasyllable. Just as the octosyllable evolved from the iambic dimeter, the decasyllable can be shown to derive from the Late Latin twelve-syllable line which in turn derives from the classical iambic trimeter, made up of three groups of two iambic feet. That is three times four syllables:

Haec nos|tra no|bis con|ferunt| pecca|mina	010101000100	12
Quae pro|uoca|runt iu|dicis| senten|tiam	010101000100	12
Quam nul|la fle|xit dig|na pae|niten|tia	010101010100	12
Parce redemptor.[24]	10010	5

The author of these verses was writing in the seventh century; by that time the substitution of metrical feet, made possible in classical Latin by the counting of one long syllable as two shorts, had fallen victim to phonological change. Such substitution, for example '— —' for '— ˘ ˘', could affect the syllable-count; so now, with its disappearance, a regular count became the norm. The verses above are quantitatively regular, but in addition (except for the *con\|ferunt\|* and ***ju\|dicis\|***) the accented syllable of the iambus coincides in each of the first three lines with the Latin word-accent. As in the 4 + 6 structure of the future decasyllable, in each twelve-syllable line the fourth and tenth syllables are accented. An earlier example of the iambic trimeter cited by Burger, the 'Hymnum apostolorum' from the Bangor Antiphony, shows a freer treatment of the accentual metre:

Precamur patrem regem omnipotentem	01010 # 1001010
Et Iesum Christum sanctum quoque spiritum.	01010 #? 1010100
Ita ueterno iste hoste subacto	10010 # 1010010
Polum nodoso soluit mortis uinculo.	10010 # 1010100
Hoc quam prodiret uera lux mortalia	10010 # 1010100
Contexit alta corda ignorantia.	01010 # 1010100
Sicque erepti nequam iubemur freti	10010 # 1010010
Laudare Deum explosis inimicis.	01010 # 0101010
In fine mundi post tanta mysteria	01010 # 0100100
Adest saluator cum grande clementia.[25]	01010 # 0100100

These quantitative twelve-syllable verses are clearly derived from the iambic trimeter; the Latin word-accent does not always coincide with the iambic long but generates accentual 'trochees' (10) and 'anapests' (001). This practice gives rise to regular alternations of atonic and tonic syllables falling into the pattern we noted in Saint Ambrose's hymns: combinations of the simple repertory of accentual feet 01, 10, 001 and 100.

The emergence of the 4 + 6 structure of the future decasyllable is illustrated more completely by some alphabet poems on the Nativity written down in the ninth century:

1. Audite omnes uersum uerum magnum	01010 # 101010
2. De saluatorem Christum dei filium	01010 # 1010100
3. Cum in Betleem natus fuit de uirgine.	*000*101010100
4. Benigna uox audita est ab angelo,	0101 # 01010100
5. Quam Gabriel adnunciat ad uirginem	01*00* # *01000*100
6. De introitum Christi Dei Filii.	01010 # 1010100
7. Concepti uirgo de sancto espiritu	01010 # 0100100
8. Peperit filium finem et principium,	0101001*000*100
9. Alpha et Ho primum et nouissimum.	1001 # **1***000*100
10. Deus ab austro uenit sicut fulgor	10010 # 101010
11. Ab oriente adorare dominum	01010 # 1010100
12. Et adorabunt Deum in perpetuum.	01010 # 1*000*100
13. Erodes rex iratus erat nimium,	0101 # 01010100
14. Infantes paruulos iussit interficere	0101001010100
15. Propter Iesum, qui natus fuit de uirgine.	1010 # 01010100
16. Festinant magi adorare dominum,	10010 # 1010100
17. Aurum et thus offerebant munera,	1001 # 1010100
18. Myrra electa sepulturae domino.	10010 # 1010100
19. Gaudebunt sancti et gaudebunt angeli	01010 # 0010100
20. Gaudent prophetas, martyres et uirgines	10010 # 0100100
21. Propter Iesum, qui natus fuit de uirgine.[26]	1010 # 01010100

Although the norm is twelve syllables, three lines have eleven syllables (ll. 1, 10 and 17) and two thirteen (ll. 8 and 14). Eighteen verses out of twenty-one (86 per cent) have an accent on the fourth syllable and seventeen (81 per cent) have an accented tenth. Following the standard Latin word-accent, the rhythm is mainly alternating, with six runs of three atonic syllables and two colliding accents. Readers of Ronsard's decasyllabic sonnets will recognise a syntactic family resemblance in eighteen of these twelve-syllable Latin lines.[27] For example:

> 16. Festinant magi # adorare dominum,
> 17. Aurum et thus # offerebant munera,
> 18. Myrra electa # sepulturae domino.

In these lines, the second accent marks a syntactic boundary at its word-boundary: *Festinant magi* is marked off from the dependent infinitival phrase *adorare dominum*; *Aurum et thus* is the grammatical object of *offerebant*; and *sepulturae domino* is an adjectival phrase qualifying *Myrra electa*.

These fixed accents at positions 4 and 10 and the syntactic boundary between the half-lines (hemistichs) are features that will define the French 4 + 6 decasyllable all the way from the anonymous eleventh-century *Vie de Saint Alexis* to Valéry's twentieth-century 'Le Cimetière marin':

> Ce toit tranquille # où marchent les colombes,
> Entre les pins # palpite, entre les tombes;
> Midi le juste # y compose de feux
> La Mer, la Mer, # toujours recommencée!
> Ô récompense # après une pensée
> Qu'un long regard # sur le calme des Dieux![28]

Georges Lote's conviction, that the isosyllabism of French verse was the invention of writers like Saint Ambrose, thus opposes Burger's view: that French syllabic verse arose from classical Latin verse whose gradual decay was driven by the expiratory accent of Germanic speakers.[29]

From Latin to French Verse

Further evidence of typological shift is found in Latin verse composed during the period in which the French language first took written form:

Aeterne orbis conditor	01010101
Christus, parente non minor,	10010101
Originali tempore,	01010101
Dignatus orbi condere,	01010101
Hora sub hac novissima,	10010101
Mundi petivit infima,	10010101
Promissus ante plurimis	01010101
Propheticis oraculis.	01000101
Ut providus Ezechiel,	01000101
Corona plebis Israhel	01010101
Clausam notavit januam	10010101
Summo tonanti perviam.	10010101
Ergo manente viscerum	10010101
Pudore virginalium,	01010101
Divina proles terreae	01010101
Se miscuit substantiae.[30]	01000101

In this hymn derived from the iambic dimeter, though word-accent within the line is Latin, the accented rhyming last syllable of the verse-line is French.[31] As in the hymns of Saint Ambrose, Latin word-accent is arranged to produce varied alternation of accent by our criteria. Here, typically French regular syllable-count, varied accent-distribution and oxytonic rhyme contrast with this contemporary song from the German manuscript which contains the *Carmina Burana*:

Clausus Chronos et serato	10101010	8
carcere ver exit,	101010	6
risu Jovis reserato	10101010	8
Faciem detexit,	101010	6
Purpurato	1010	4
floret prato,	1010	4
ver tene primatum	101010	6
ex algenti	1010	4
renitenti	1010	4
specie renatum.	101010	6
Vernant veris ad amena	10101010	8
— thyma, rosa, lilia,	1010100	7
his alludit filomena,	10101010	8
melos et lascivia.[32]	1010100	7

In contrast with the French-style oxytonic rhyme-syllable of our hymn, the accented rhyme-syllable here follows Latin models, being last but one or two in the last word of the line: *serato, reserato, purpurato, prato*; *exit, detexit*; *lili-a, lascivi-a*. The typical 'trochaic' rhythm of this heterosyllabic song shows, with occasional exceptions, classical Latin word-accent, its fixed rhythm contrasting with the freer alternation of accent in our hymn. As Lote observes: 'La rime est un moyen de marquer d'une manière sensible la fin du vers'.[33] While Latin octosyllables quoted earlier ended with two atonic syllables, in our hymn the alternating rhythm is affirmed by the accent on the last vowel of the rhyme-word, which is the oxytonic accent of French.

This accent commonly affects Latin words when they crop up in Old French texts. In the octosyllabic couplets of the eleventh-century *Sponsus*, we find for example:

> Il li respondent tuit adun
> 'Jhesum querem Nazarenum'.[34]

In the earliest surviving verse written in recognisable French, the *Séquence de Sainte Eulalie,* from a manuscript of the late ninth century, the first assonance-words of the first couplet, *Eulalia* and *anima*, appear to have an accented final vowel which in Latin would have been atonic.[35]

Our model for the scanning of this and all French verse derives from what we have learned so far about the relationship between French and Latin word-accent and from the general definition of accent as an indicator of informational priority. Thus low-frequency monosyllables and paroxytonic disyllables are accented and we mark oxytonic word-accent and countertonic word-accent on all polysyllables of low frequency of occurrence. Frequently occurring words of any length are consequently atonic. Any juxtaposed accents are subject to a deletion/displacement rule with respect to the informational priority of the accents concerned.[36] Note must also be taken of syntactic boundaries within the verse-line which imply an accented position. Such boundaries can result in the accenting of a frequently occurring lexical item.[37] We return to the *Sequence de Sainte Eulalie*:

1. **Buo**na pulcella # fut Eu**la**lia	1001000101	10
2. bel au**ret corps**, # belle**zour** a**ni**ma.	1001001001	10
3. **Vol**drent la **vein**tre # li **deo** i**ni**mi,	1001001001	10
4. **vol**drent la **fai**re # dï**au**le ser**vir**.	1001001001	10
5. **El**le **non** es**kol**tet les mals con**seil**liers	10101001001	11
6. qu'elle **Deo** ra**nei**et, chi **maent sus** en **ciel**	101010010101	12
7. Ne por **or** ned ar**gent** ne para**menz**,	0010010101	10
8. por ma**nat**ce re**giel** ne prei**ement**.	0010010101	10
9. **Nï**ule **co**se # **non** la **pou**ret **om**que **plei**er	0101010101001	13
10. la **pol**le **sem**pre non a**mast** lo **Deo** me**nes**tier.	0101010101001	13
11. E **po**ro **fut** pre**sen**te de Maxi**mi**ien,	001010100101	12
12. chi **rex e**ret a cels dis **sou**re **pa**giens.	**011000**100101	12
13. **Il** li e**nor**tet, # dont lei **non**que **chielt**,	1001001001	10
14. qued **el**le **fui**et # lo **nom** chris**tï**ien	0101001001	10
15. **El**le ent a**du**net # lo **suon** e**lement**,	1001001001	10
16. **melz** sosten**drei**et # les empede**menz**,	1001**000**101	10
17. Qu'elle per**des**se # sa virgini**tét**	1001**000**101	10
18. **po**ro s **fu**ret **mor**te a **grand** ho**nes**tet.	0100101001	10
19. **Enz** enl **fou** la **get**terent, com **ar**de **tost**.	00100100101	11
20. **el**le **col**pes non au**ret**, **po**ro nos **coist**.	10100100101	11
21. A **czo** no s **vol**dret con**crei**dre li **rex pa**giens:	010100100101	12
22. ad **u**ne **spe**de # li **ro**veret to**lir** lo **chief**.	**000**1000100101	13
23. La **dom**ni**zel**le # **cel**le **ko**se **non** con**tredist**,	0101010101001	13
24. **volt** lo **seu**le **laz**sier, si **ruo**vet **Krist**.	1010010101	10
25. In **fi**gure de **colomb vo**lat a **ciel**.	0010**00**010101	11
26. **tuit o**ram, que por nos **deg**net **prei**er,	1010**011**001	10
27. **Qued au**uisset de **nos Chris**tus mer**cit**,	0010**011**001	10
28. post la **mort** et a **lui** nos **laist** ve**nir**	0010010101	10
29. Par **sou**ue cle**men**tia.[38]	0100101	7

That this sequence was probably part of a sung liturgy may explain its irregular syllabism, sixteen only of its twenty-nine lines being decasyllables.[39] Compared with the Latin alphabet poems, this text shows varying syllable-count and absence of regular 'cesura'. In the former, eighteen of twenty-one verses (86 per cent) showed an accented fourth syllable followed by a syntactical boundary: in the *Eulalia,* only fourteen (50 per cent) of the twenty-eight have an accented fourth syllable, thirteen of these being followed by a syntactical limit. Applying to the *Eulalia* the criteria for placing accent used in the Latin examples plus the oxytonic word-accent indicated indirectly by the odd *Eulalia-anima* assonance, we discover that twenty out of the twenty-nine verses (69 per cent) show a regular alternation of accent.[40] These figures suggest that line-length and 'cesura' were secondary to the principle of alternating accent where the *Eulalia*-poet's conception of verse was concerned.

In the earliest manuscript of the assonanced *Vie de Saint Alexis*, composed in the eleventh century, we find the first example of the fully-fledged French decasyllable. Here are the first seven *laisses*:

Bons fut li secles al tens ancienur,[41]	10010* # 010101
Quer fet i ert e justice e amur,	0101 # 001001
Si ert creance, dunt ore n'i at nul prut;	10010* # 010101
Tut est muez, perdut ad sa colur,[42]	1001 # 101001
Ja mais n'iert tel cum fut as anceisurs.	0101 # 010101
Al tens Noe ed al tens Abraham,	0101 # 001001
Ed al David, qui Deus par amat tant,	*0001* # 010101
Bons fut li secles, ja mais n'ert si vailant.	10010* # 010101
Velz est e frailes, tut s'en vat declinant;	10010* # 101001
Si.st ampairet, tut bien vait remenant.	1001 # 010101
Puis icel tens que Deus nus vint salver,	0101 # 010101
Nostra anceisur ourent cristientet.	0101 # *000*101
Si fut un sire de Rome la citet;	01010* # 01*000*1
Rices hom fud, de grant nobilitet:	1001 # 010101
Pur hoc vus di d'un son filz voil parler.	0101 # 001001
Eufemien (si out a num li pedre)	0101 # 0101010
Cons fut de Rome, des melz ki dunc i erent.	10010* # 0101010
Sur tuz ses pers l'amat li emperere.	0101 # 0101010
Dunc prist muiler vailante e hunurede,	0101 # 0101010
Des melz gentils de tuta la cuntretha.[43]	0101 # 01*00*010
Puis converserent ansemble longament;	01010* # 010101
N'ourent amfant, peiset lur en forment.	1001 # 100101
A Deu apelent andui parfitement:	01010* # 010101
'E, reis celeste, par ton comandement	**11**010* # *000*101
Amfant nus done ki seit a tun talent'.	01010* # 01*000*1
Tant li prierent par grant humilitet,	10010* # 010101
Que la muiler dunat fecunditet.	*0001* # 010101
Un filz lur dunet, si l'en sourent bon gret.	01010* # 101001
De saint batesma l'unt fet regenerer;	01010* # 010101
Bel num li metent sur la cristientet.	01010* # *000*101
Fud baptizet, si out num Alexis.	0101 # 001001
Ki lui portat suef le fist nurrir,	1001 # 10101
Puis ad escole li bons pedre le mist;	10010* # 001001
Tant aprist letres que bien en fut guarnit.	10010* # 010101
Puis vait li emfes l'emperethur servir.[44]	0101 # 010101

The 4 + 6 decasyllable became the standard metre for the Old French epic. By our criteria, sixty-one of the seventy verse-units (87 per cent) alternate accent, there being eight runs of three atonic syllables and one juxtaposed accent. Six lines have hemistichs which are rhythmically identical (17 per cent).

Though the syllabic norm seems to be 4 + 6, fourteen lines out of thirty-five show an extra atonic vowel in fifth position, making a total of eleven syllables:

> Puis ad escolə # li bons padre le mist.

Fabb and Halle, following Cornulier, see in this phenomenon the survival of an earlier line-division which allowed the final word of the first hemistich, as in that of the second, a feminine ending:[45]

Fud baptizet #	4 syllables
si out **num** Alexis.	6
Ki lui portat #	4
suef li fist nurrir.	6
Puis ad escolə #	5

Line 2 of *laisse* 4 illustrates both 'licences', the atonic vowel in fifth position and also in line-final position:

> Cons fut de Romə, des melz ki dunc i erənt.

It is clear from the spellings of *tuta* and *cuntretha* that these atonic vowels had syllabic value. The difficulty with the Cornulier-Fabb-Halle hypothesis lies both in the lack of documentary evidence[46] and of any sign of formal organisation where these extra syllables are concerned.[47] In that its fifth atonic syllable matches its thirteenth atonic syllable, l. 2 of *laisse* 4 is a rare occurrence since there is no apparent tendency in this text to arrange such matches in successive lines. In our extract all other examples of an atonic fifth syllable occur randomly in so-called masculine *laisses* which have no line-final atonic syllable.

There is another way of thinking about the 'epic cesura'. We have noted the 86 per cent preponderance of verses alternating accent in the hymns of Saint Ambrose in the fourth century, and the sustained presence of alternation in Carolingian Latin verse in the eighth. Our brief glance at the *Sequence de Sainte Eulalie* revealed its continuity with its Latin antecedents in this respect. It is likely that the *Alexis*-poet sensed the well-formedness of his verse in its 87 per cent alternation of accent, and also in the relationship between the resultant rhythms and syllabic count.

A rapid survey shows that in the first 250 lines of our text there are eighty-two occurrences of a syllabic [ə] in fifth position. However in fifty-nine of these cases (72 per cent), the atonic fifth syllable still permits regular alternation of accent:

> Bons fut li seclə̃s # al tens ancienur.   10010 # 010101

The remaining twenty-three occurrences (28 per cent) give the atonic fifth syllable followed by words with a high frequency of occurrence:

> Dunc **prent** li pedrə # de ses meilurs serganz.   01010 # 000101

These figures suggest a marked tendency to structure the verse-line around accent-distribution. In lines showing a [ə] in fifth position it can 'outbid' syllabic count as the organising principle.

The twelfth century sees the establishment of the alexandrine, which was later to become the 'classic' metre of French narrative and dramatic verse.[48] Here are the opening lines of the anonymous *Siège de Barbastre,* from the last third of the twelfth century:

Plest vos oïr chançon bien faite et conpasee?	100101 # 0101010
Toute est[49] de vielle estoire estraite et porpansee.	010101 # 0101010
Molt fait bien a oïr, pieça ne fu contee;	101001 # 0101010
Tote est de la lingniee que Deus ot tant amee,	0100010 # 0101010
De la geste Aymeri qui prouece a duree.	001001 # 0010010
Ce fu a Pantecoste, cele feste ennoree:	0101010 # 0010010
Li cuens fu a Nerbone, sa grant cité louee.	0100010 # 0101010
Ses fiz ot departiz, chascun tint sa contree;	010101 # 0110010
N'ot a lui que Guillaume a la chiere membree,	001001 # 0010010
Bueves del Conmarchis, Hermenjart la senee.	100101 # 0010010
Dont tint li cuens sa cort en la sale pavee	010101 # 0010010
A trois cenz chevaliers de mesniee privee.	001001 # 0010010
La sale fu molt bien entor encortinee,	010001 # 0101010
De jonc et de mentatre, de rose enluminee.	0100010 # 0101010
Les napes firent metre quant messe fu chantee:	0101010 # 0100010
Aymeris sist au dois, a la chiere membree,	001001 # 0010010
Et Guillaume d'Orange, a cui proëce agree;	001001 # 0101010
Girart servi au dois de la coupe doree,	010101 # 0010010
Et Guielins ses freres tint la verge pelee.	0101010 # 1010010
Des mes qui leanz sont ne vos faz devisee;	010011 # 0010010
De poons ni de cisnes n'i ot onques nonbree;	0010010 # 0010010
Tant en done chascun conme il li agree	001001 # 001010*[50]
Et après mengier ont la quintainne fermee.	010101 # 0010010
Après issirent fors soz Nerbone en la pree,	010101 # 0010010
Et la feste fu haute, si l'orent ennoree.[51]	0010010 # 0101010

Of these fifty verse-units, five show a run of three atonic syllables and two juxtaposed accents. Thus 86 per cent alternate according to our criteria. Five of the twenty-five lines have hemistichs that are rhythmically identical (20 per cent). Overall eighteen hemistichs are 'iambic' and twenty-two 'anapestic'. The tendency, as in the *Alexis,* is to rhythmically differentiate hemistichs in a given line.

What is now needed is an alternative approach to the problem of accent in Old French verse against which to test our conclusions from the historical evidence.

The Evidence from Synchrony

To supplement what we have found in history, i.e. in diachrony, we will now look for evidence in synchrony, that is in the accentual structure of single texts in a single moment in time. These texts will be the *Chanson de Roland,* as it appears in the twelfth-century Oxford manuscript, and Racine's *Phèdre* of 1677.[52] Burger's reading of the hymns of Saint Ambrose relied on a historically-based idea of accent: we will try the distributional method, looking for regularities in the distribution of particular linguistic elements.[53]

Our working hypothesis is that French verse relies on alternating accent and we will be looking for features which might either favour or invalidate our hypothesis. We know that syllabic count is one defining property of French verse and that these syllables appear in words: syllables in their relation to words and to verses will thus be our raw materials. How are syllables arranged into words within the verse-unit? For this we need a mathematician, and Dr. Bob Odone of Exeter University found the answer for us, $W = 2^{n-1}$: W represents the number of possible word-positions on a given string of syllables, and n the number of syllables in the string.[54]

The ten-syllable line normally falls into $4 + 6$: we thus have two strings, one of four syllables and the other of six. So for the first hemistich $W = 2^{4-1} = 2^3$: there are eight possible word-over-syllable positions. For the *Chanson de Roland*, we will concentrate on the major hemistich with its six syllables in which the possible word-positions increase exponentially to thirty-two. *Phèdre* is written in alexandrines, $6 + 6$, and we analyse the first six-syllable hemistich. Here are the word-over-syllable partitions ordered lexicographically. The sample from *Roland* was 716 major hemistichs and that from *Phèdre* 1000 first hemistichs. The figures to the right are the total number of occurrences of each Type in each text:

		La Chanson de Roland	*Phèdre*
1.	(1) (2) (3) (4) (5) (6)	35	52
2.	(1) (2) (3) (4) (5 6)	86	103
3.	(1) (2) (3) (4 5) (6)	13	21
4.	(1) (2) (3) (4 5 6)	59	70
5.	(1) (2) (3 4) (5) (6)	46	52
6.	(1) (2) (3 4) (5 6)	65	87
7.	(1) (2) (3 4 5) (6)	14	15
8.	(1) (2) (3 4 5 6)	7	15
9.	(1) (2 3) (4) (5) (6)	41	63
10.	(1) (2 3) (4) (56)	72	83
11.	(1) (2 3) (4 5) (6)	15	16
12.	(1) (2 3) (4 5 6)	32	32
13.	(1) (2 3 4) (5) (6)	34	31
14.	(1) (2 3 4) (5) (6)	26	32
15.	(1) (2 3 4 5) (6)	7	2
16.	(1) (2 3 4 5 6)	0	0
17.	(1 2) (3) (4) (5) (6)	8	38
18.	(1 2) (3) (4) (56)	30	80
19.	(1 2) (3) (4 5) (6)	10	20
20.	(1 2) (3) (4 5 6)	28	20
21.	(1 2) (3 4) (5) (6)	6	20
22.	(1 2) (3 4) (5 6)	11	20
23.	(1 2) (3 4 5) (6)	2	5
24.	(1 2) (3 4 5 6)	3	6
25.	(1 2 3) (4) (5) (6)	4	31
26.	(1 2 3) (4) (5 6)	12	38
27.	(1 2 3) (4 5) (6)	3	5
28.	(1 2 3) (4 5 6)	3	17
29.	(1 2 3 4) (5) (6)	4	15
30.	(1 2 3 4) (5 6)	2	7

Like Type 16, the polysyllabic Types 31 and 32 have no occurrences.

Zipf's Law, discussed earlier, correlates relative rarity of occurrence with informational weight. Here is the first *laisse* of the *Chanson de Roland*:

> Carles li reis, nostre emperere magnes,
> Set anz tuz pleins ad estét en Espaigne,
> Tresqu'en la mer cunquist la terre altaigne.
> N'i ad castel ki devant lui remaigne,
> Mur ne citét n'i est remés a fraindre,
> Fors Sarraguce, ki est en une muntaigne;
> Li reis Marsilie la tient ki Deu nen aimet,
> Mahumet sert e Apollin recleimet;
> Ne.s poet guarder que mals ne l'i ateignet.

At the 'cesural' accent on the fourth syllable of these nine lines, we find six nouns, one adjective and two verbs, and at the accented tenth two nouns, two adjectives and five verbs. No word with a high frequency of occurrence occupies these accented positions: this confirms the reality of word-accent in Old French and its correlation with informational density, individual members of all the above mentioned classes of parts of speech occurring relatively rarely.[55] Now, in the figures given above, we see that sixteen out of thirty-two Types show a monosyllable in final position. If the last syllable of the major hemistich is a monosyllable, then it too will be accented. Monosyllables are numerous in Old French:

> Enz en vos *bainz* ke *Deus* por *vos* i *fist.*[56]

Those monosyllables (here in italics) capable of standing at the line-end will also be accented when they occur *within* the phrase — an important point for our understanding of the rhythmic structure of later French verse.[57]

Bearing in mind the typological differences which distinguish Old French from the modern French of Racine, an examination of our figures reveals a surprising similarity between the word-over-syllable structures of texts written 500 years apart. In each there is evidence of the same constraint operating on the frequency of certain syllable types. For example, in *Chanson de Roland,* Type 3, e.g. (*li*) (*reis*) (*ki*) (*France*) (*tient*), has thirteen occurrences, while Type 2, e.g. (*li*) (*proz*) (*e*) (*li*) (*gentilz*), has twenty-six occurrences, twice as many. Type 11, e.g. (1) (23) (45) (6), has eight occurrences, while Type 12, e.g. (1) (23) (456), has twenty-two, that is almost three times as many. In *Phèdre*, Type 11, e.g. (*Je*) (*m'abhorre*) (*encor*) (*plus*), has sixteen occurrences, while Type 10, e.g. (*Je*) (*commence*) (*à*) (*rougir*), has eighty-three occurrences, more than five times as many. This despite the fact that the contrasting pairs share the word-over-syllable structure alternating monosyllables and disyllables.[58]

How do we explain the striking disparity in these distributions? If the metric of these verses was, as Cornulier believes, simply a question of recurring syllable-count, then these figures are inexplicable; there could be no constraint operating other than numerical count. Our hypothesis of alternating accent in French verse suggests otherwise: that the disparities in frequency of occurrence of our Types indicate a constraint on precisely those factors which would impede alternation of accent.

The problem is tackled via a two-phased hypothesis: (a) that there is word-accent in French of all periods; and (b) that the above-mentioned constraint discourages juxtaposition of accented syllables in verse. It is, as we have noted, always the case, given the verse-form, that the final syllable of each hemistich carries a linguistic accent marking the close of a syntactic unit:

Madame, au nom des pleurs # que pour vous j'ai versés.[59]

Hence for example Type 19, e.g. (1 2) (3) (4 5) (6), will be rarer than Type 18, e.g. (1 2) (3) (4) (5 6), since the constraint forbids an oxytonic two-syllable word in the (4 5) slot (e.g. (Subir) (un) (malheur) (grave)*). The constraint operates more dramatically in Type 3, e.g. (1) (2) (3) (4 5) (6), whose occurrences, 13 in *Chanson de Roland*, 26 in *Phèdre*, contrast with its frequent sister Type 2, e.g. (1) (2) (3) (4) (5 6), 26 in *Chanson de Roland*, 103 in *Phèdre*.

By accounting for the relatively low frequency of occurrence of these (4 5) (6) Types, this constraint also explains (by its absence) the relative abundance of the related Types in (4) (5 6). In these latter, the poet is free to make the (4) monosyllable either tonic or atonic; either (Et) (dans) (quels) (lieux,) (seigneur), or (de) (quel) (mort) (nus) (murjuns). The results of a fuller analysis of *Phèdre* show that for the Types ending (45) (6), out of 57 occurrences in 1000 hemistichs there are no examples of the type (amant) (doux)*; (parent) (mort)*; (ami) (cher)*; (espoir) (vain)* etc. The systematic avoidance of these classes of lexeme at this point in the line is a powerful negative index of a metrical constraint in operation.[60]

Constraint is also apparent within the hemistich: for example in Type 9, e.g. (1) (2 3) (4) (5) (6), of which there are sixty-three occurrences, there is only one example of a tonic monosyllable in position (4). This rarity must be related to the preponderance of disyllabic oxytones (e.g. *héros, seigneur*) in the (2 3) position, these making up 75 per cent of the words in this position. An oxytone here may not be followed by a tonic monosyllable if alternation of accent is to be maintained. Similarly in Type 10, e.g. (1) (2 3) (4) (5 6), there are only four occurrences (5 per cent) of a tonic monosyllable in position (4), 69 per cent of the words in position (2 3) being oxytones.

Surprising though it was to discover an evidently structured distribution of word-over-syllable Types in the *Roland*, the appearance 500 years later of a similar distribution was even more so. Though our distributional analysis of both texts set aside historical considerations, our synchronic survey has thrown up a clear insight into the *history* of the structures involved. The profile of most and least frequent Types is conserved across what is generally thought to be a linguistic watershed, about 1600, when modern French was emerging.[61]

In the transition from Old French to Middle French (this latter notionally 1350 to the late 1500s) the Germanic expiratory accent progressively levelled out. Its intensity was absorbed by diphthongisation which lowered the force of accent on individual words. This levelling in turn increased the importance of group-final accent and promoted subject/verb/complement (SVC) ordering as the norm.[62] In the ninth-century *Séquence de Sainte Eulalie*, word-order had been flexible, the relative positions of subject, verb and complement being permutable. SVC ordering was then available, so also were the orders SCV (*[que] Krist por nos degnet preier*) and VCS (*Qued auuisset de nos Christus mercit.*) These alternatives gave accentual prominence to differing elements within the sentence. In the earlier period, when tonic stress had been intense, words remained the basic unit of the phrase. Gradually in later Old French and Middle French words closely connected in sense were more and more run together until the phrase became the prosodic unit instead, a progression confirmed by the gradual disappearance of enclisis and the prevalence of *liaison* which blurred word-boundaries.[63]

Despite a gradual levelling of accent within the phrase, poets after five hundred years of linguistic change are clearly still concerned to avoid the juxtaposition of word-accents. This tendency implies that although word-accent in modern French is weaker with respect to intensity than that of Italian or Spanish, it is still present in the structure of the language.

The Evidence from Music

Why do we need such evidence? We have after all a quantity of writing on versification from medieval authorities right down to the eighteenth-century *Encyclopédie*. Though these witnesses generally confirm the isosyllabism of the French verse-line, not one of them tells us how poets and listeners were able to recognise this constant syllabic count. For medieval commentators — and even for later ones writing in Latin — the word *rhythmus* meant simply 'syllabic count', with no acknowledgement of structure within the verse-line other than the 'cesural' pause/accent. Rare indeed is reference to the role in verse of what we know to have been the accentual structure of the spoken language. Exceptionally, in the 1660s, Du Gardin takes note of the importance of word-accent within the hemistich:

> La penultieme de tous motz, dont la derniere est de feminine terminaison, se doit prononcer aucunement longue [i.e. accented]; Exemple: 'Je chante les vertus d'une vaillante vefve.' Les premieres en *chante*, *d'une* et *vefve*' se reciteront aucunement longues. Item: 'Le magnanime coeur ne s'ebransle de peu': *Ni* en *magnanime* est ouy assez longue.[64]

Taking into account the accented positions at the 'cesura' and the rhyme, he will have read these lines as follows:

Je chante les vertus # d'une vaillante vefve.   010001 # 100101
Le magnanime cœur # ne s'esbransle de peu.   000101 # 001001

For this native speaker, even in the case of *une*, the effect of the [ə] is to give prosodic prominence to its preceding vowel.

His remained a minority view even if, now and again, a foreign observer, anticipating the Abbé Scoppa, expressed surprise at the established doctrine which insisted on featureless monotony in the recitation of French verse. In the 1640s, Bannius, a Dutch priest, puzzled by the apparently water-tight seal between what he perceived as the accentual structures of correct spoken French and the atonic syllabism of the recited alexandrine, expressed his bafflement to Mersenne and Descartes. There ensued a dialogue of the deaf: while the Dutchman queried the absence in French poetic declamation of the accentual features of the spoken language, his French correspondents alleged the subjective and affective qualities of French verse, which of course a mere foreigner could never really be expected to grasp.

Bannius's colleague, the internationally known polymath Constantin Huyghens, then took up the cudgels. In correspondence with Corneille, who had dedicated his *Don Sanche* to him, Huyghens enclosed his own accentual scansions of Corneille's verse:

Secrets tyrans de ma pensée	01010101
Respect, amour, de qui les loix...	01010101
Moy-mesme je fay mon supplice	01010101
A force de leur obéir.	01010101
Et forment ma crainte et mes voeux	01010101
Pour ce bel oeil qui les fait naistre.[65]	01010101

Although Huyghens writes fluent and idiomatic French, the 'iambic' rigidity of his scansion reflects the fixed-accent syllabo-tonic metre of his native Dutch. The prosodic relief he gives to possessives, articles and weak pronouns must strike any francophone as 'un-French', making these verses as recited difficult to follow. At all events, he failed to convince Corneille of the inadequacy of 'la maxime qui dicte qu'au vers français il ne vient considérer que le nombre des syllabes', and the status quo prevailed.

So the question is still with us: what has happened in modern French to the alternation of accent that we have detected in Late Latin and Old French verse? The prevalent view is that there is none: how does this square with the confirmed presence of word-accent in the language still today?

From the time of Saint Ambrose down to the trouvères and troubadours, poetry and music were inseparable. The hymns of Ambrose were written to be sung to melodies perhaps composed by the saint himself. At least one, *Aeterne rerum conditor*, survives in manuscript accompanied by its melody. The tune follows the measure of the iambic dimeter, that is one note or group of notes to each of the eight syllables, but alas, the musical notation of this period gives no clue as to the accentuation or duration of individual notes. Our understanding of the Old French and Occitan lyric in the twelfth century is obscured for the same reason, the abundant musical notation accompanying the texts in manuscript giving us no clue as to the rhythmic structure of either music or verse.

The majority of troubadour and trouvère poetry is strophic, that is, it is written in successive strophes which can share a rhyme-scheme. While syllabic count and accent at line-end (and 'cesura' where there is one) are constant from strophe to strophe, the distribution of word-accents within the line/hemistich is not. The manuscripts make it clear however that the same melody, mostly one note to each syllable, is repeated from strophe to strophe. But what is the relationship between the melody and the distribution of word-accent in the text when the text shifts but the tune does not?

Two answers have been proposed in performance: the first ignores the rhythmic structure of the text, giving each syllable and each note within the verse-unit the same duration and intensity.[66] The second imposes on text and melody a regular accentual scheme; following this idea, Jordi Savall and Hesperion XXI (in a recording of songs by women troubadours) perform an Occitan decasyllabic lyric in a sustained 'dactylic' rhythm, 1001 # 001001.[67] This rhythm has clearly been suggested by the opening lines where the 'dactylic' accents coincide with the word-accents:

Vos que.m semblatz del corals amadors   1001 # 001001
Ja non volgra que fossetz tan doptanz.   1001 # 001001

In the late thirteenth century Franco of Cologne developed a notation for the time-values of single notes, groups of notes and rests. The theorists of his time had evolved a system of rhythmic modes loosely derived from the metres of Latin prosody: the first of these is 'trochaic' (– ⌣), that is, in terms of duration, minim + crotchet; the second, 'iambic' (⌣ –), or crotchet + minim; the third 'dactylic' (– ⌣ ⌣) or dotted minim + crotchet + minim, and the fourth 'anapestic' (⌣ ⌣ –), that is crotchet + minim + dotted minim.[68] As set down in Franco's notation, these modes allowed performers to see at a glance what rhythm was required: it is to this mensural notation that Jordi Savall appeals in his realisation of the Occitan lyric cited above. We can know nothing directly of the style of performance of lyrics written down before its advent, but as Gustave Reese observes:

> Old Provençal and Old French had accentuations such as modern French almost completely lacks, and advocates of the modal theory claim that the music must have been stressed in accordance with the stresses in the words, and that the absence of time-value indications in the notation did not greatly matter since a singer would know by observing the distribution of accents in a line of text which rhythmic mode to use.[69]

If the musical notation of the later thirteenth century reflected the performance practice of the pre-mensural tradition, the latter also would have shown the mismatching of musical accent and word-accent that we will find below in Savall's interpretation of the rest of his Occitan song. That such persistent mismatching of musical and linguistic accent belonged to the aesthetic of the trouvère and troubadour tradition is not easy to accept. If word-accent as we have defined it is a property of the French language, would the trouvère, following Christopher Page, have treated the tonic vowel on a par with [ə]? Or, following Savall, would he have indifferently accented either or both?

Gustave Reese gives a third possibility: since the early manuscripts show a single melody for a number of strophes, the non-mensural character of such melody would allow for its reconfiguration from strophe to strophe in accord with the strophe's changing accentual structure. This idea is not popular with our musical colleagues. How could something as grand and serious as the courtly love lyric be 'delivered in the manner of a jazz improvisation?'[70] On reflection they do admit that the organising principle we propose was not entirely foreign to them: they had met it (in short fragments of melody) in the tenor *color* of the isorhythmic motet, in the circulation of motifs in Gamelan, in augmentation and diminution in fugal texture and so forth. But the idea that it could be used as the single basis for the recreation of melodic material goes right against their musical instincts. So the alternatives are either the ironing out of all accent within the hemistich, or the calypso-like distribution of accent brought by the imposition of a fixed rhythmic mode. As far as we know, our third alternative has yet to be explored by specialists in the performance of the trouvère and troubadour repertoire, although a detailed proposal of the scheme has been available for some years.[71]

Meanwhile, we will follow up Savall's insight by looking at a thirteenth-century manuscript collection of songs which uses Franco's mensural notation.[72] The original pre-Franco notation given for these lyrics is non-mensural; we may find evidence supporting Savall's reading of his trobairitz song. First, here are the first two strophes of Savall's song where accentuation follows that of the third ('dactylic') mode:[73]

Vos que.m semblatz del corals amadors[74]	1001 # 001001
ja non volgra que fossetz tan doptanz;	1001 # 001001
e platz me molt quar vos destreing m'amors,	1001 # 001001
qu'atressi sui eu per vos malananz,	10010 #? 01001
ez avetz dan en vostre vulpillatge	1001 # 001001
quar no.us ausatz de preiar enardir,	1001 # 001001
e faitz a vos ez a mi gran dampnatge;	1001 # 001001
que ges dompna non ausa descobrir	1001 # 001001
tot so qu'il vol per paor de faillir.	1001 # 001001
Bona dompna, vostr' onrada valors	1001 # 001001
Mi fai temeros estar, tan es granz,	1001001 #? 001
e no.m o tol negun'autra paors	1001 # 001001
qu'eu non vos prec; que.us volria enanz	1001 # 001001
tan gen servir que non fezes oltratge —	1001 # 001001
qu'aissi.m sai eu de preiar enardir —	1001 # 001001
e volria que.m faich fosson messatge,	1001 # 001001
e pressessetz en loc de precs servir:	1001 # 001001
qu'us onratz faitz deu be valer un dir.	1001 # 001001

Savall's 'dactylic' measure forces 13 mismatches of word- and musical accent in 115 words (11 per cent) while in 18 out of 36 verse-units rhythmic mode and linguistic accent coincide (50 per cent). The 'dactylic' scheme is less rigid than it first appears. After the initial accent, the verse-line runs on in what looks and feels like two 'anapests' (001001). This impression is confirmed by the cesural accent/pause on the fourth syllable which leaves the second hemistich beginning with two unaccented syllables. A song in decasyllables by Gace Brulé, a trouvère, will permit comparison. The 'dactylic' measure is given by the manuscript's mensural notation:

De bone amour et de leaul amie	1001 # 001001
me vient sovent pitiez et remembrance;	1001 # 001001
si que jamais a nul jor de ma vie	1001 # 001001
n'oblierai son vis ne sa semblance.	1001 # 001001
por ce, s'amors ne se puet plus soffrir	1001 # 001001
qu'ele de touz ne face son plaisir	1001 # 001001
et de toutes mais ne puet avenir	1001 # 001001
que de la moie aie bone esperance.	1001 # 001001
Comment porroie avoir bone esperance	1001 # 001001
a bone amor et a leal amie,	1001 # 001001
ne a diaus yeuz n'a la douce semblance.	1001 # 001001
que ne verrai james jor de ma vie.	1001 # 001001
amer m'estuet ne m'en puis plus soffrir	1001 # 001001
celi cui ja ne vanra a plaisir;	1001 # 001001
siens sui, comment qu'il m'en doie avenir	1001 # 001001
et si n'i voi ne confort ne ahie.[75]	1001 # 001001

Here 13 cases of accentual mismatch in 115 words (11 per cent), plus the 'cesural' accent/pause, give a sense of 'anapestic' movement in the second hemistich. 'Dactylic' mode and linguistic accent coincide in thirteen out of thirty-two verse-units (41 per cent).

We cannot know what the original poet-musician intended for the relation between verse-rhythm and musical rhythm. Here are these two strophes scanned in accordance with the model of linguistic accent we have derived from our reading of the historical evidence:

De bone amour et de leaul amie	0101 # *000*101
me vient sovent pitiez et remembrance;	0101 # 010101
si que jamais a nul jor de ma vie	1001 # 001001
n'oblierai son vis ne sa semblance.	0101 # 011001
por ce, s'amors ne se puet plus soffrir	0101 # 001001
qu'ele de touz ne face son plaisir	1001 # 010*0*01
et de toutes mais ne puet avenir	00101 #? 01001
que de la moie aie bone esperance.	1001 # 001001
Comment porroie avoir bone esperance	10101 # 001001
a bone amor et a leal amie,	0101 # *000*101
ne a diaus yeuz n'a la douce semblance	1001 # 001001
que ne verrai james jor de ma vie.	0101 # 001001
amer m'estuet ne m'en puis plus soffrir	0101 # 001001
celi cui ja ne vanra a plaisir;	0101 # 001001
siens sui, comment qu'il m'en doie avenir	0101 #? 001001
et si n'i voi ne confort ne ahie.	0101 # 001001

With the marking of word-accent as we define it, twenty-eight of thirty-two verse-units (87 per cent) alternate accent, one showing juxtaposed accents and three having runs of three atonic syllables. The manuscript's mensural notation agrees with our scansion in eleven of thirty-two verse-units (34 per cent).

So much for the pure decasyllable. But not all trouvère and troubadour verse is so syllabically regular. Three other texts will ring the metrical changes. The first, from the Chansonnier Cangé, fol. 38ᵛ, is a Marian hymn by Thibaut de Champagne, King of Navarre (1201–53). Here, in version A, are the first four strophes from the manuscript. The rhythm is that given by the musical notation:

Version A

De chanter ne me puis tenir	01010101	8
de la tres bele Esperital	01010101	8
cui riens dou mont ne puet servir	01010101	8
cui ja voigne honte ne mal.	01010101	8
que li rois celestiaux	1010101	7
qui en li daigna venir	1010101	7
ne porroit mie soffrir	1010101	7
qui la sert qu'il ne fust saux.	1010101	7
Quant Dex tant la vost obeir	01010101	8
qu'il n'estoit muables ne faux	01010101	8
bien nos i devons donc tenir	01010101	8
dame. roïne naturaux	01010101	8
cil qui vos sert est feaus	1010101	7
vos li savrez bien merir	1010101	7

devant vos porra venir	1010101	7
p*lus* clers qu'*estoile* jornaux	1010101	7
Vostr*e* beauté qui si resplant	01010101	8
fait **tout** le monde resclarcir	01010101	8
par vos vint Dex entr*e* la gent	01010101	8
en terre *por* la mort soffrir	01010101	8
et a l'enemi tolir	1010101	7
nos et g*i*ter *de* torment	1010101	7
p*or* vos **a**vons vengement	1010101	7
et par vos devons garir.	1010101	7
David le sot premieirement	01010101	8
que d*e* lui deviez issir,	01010101	8
quant *il* parla si hautement	01010101	8
par l*a* bouch*e* du saint espir.	01010101	8
v*o*s n'est*e*s mie *a* florir	1010101	7
ainz avez flour si poissant	1010101	7
c*e* est Dex qui onqu(es) ne ment	1010101	7
qui par **tout** fait son plesir.	1010101	7

We count 32 mismatches in 167 words (19 per cent) of which 21 concern atonic monosyllables. Five out of thirty-two lines (16 per cent) show a complete match of modal accent and linguistic accent. The modal accentuation ('iambic' in the octosyllables and 'trochaic' in the heptasyllables) excludes the possibility of 'dactyls', 'anapests', juxtaposed accents and runs of atonic syllables. The alternation of 'iambic' and 'trochaic' quatrains in the strophe is due to the fact that a 'trochaic' pulse would leave the octosyllable without the canonical line-final accent:[76] 10101010? (8); as does the 'iambic' pulse in the heptasyllable: 0101010? (7). Thus this text is simply concerned with reconciling syllabic count and rhythmic mode by arranging for the coincidence of line-final accent and modal accent. This does not tell us what Thibaut himself envisaged for the accentual structure of the rest of the line. Would he deliberately have chosen to sing:

> Plus clers qu'estoile jornaux

in which *estoile* is, by our criteria, doubly misaccented and *clers*, a high-priority adjective, made atonic? Here is the text again (version B), marked with linguistic accent as we have defined it:

Version B

De chanter ne me puis tenir	00100101	8
de la tres bele Esperital[77]	00010101	8
cui riens dou mont ne **puet** servir	01010101	8
cui ja **voigne** honte ne mal.	00101001	8
que li **rois** celestiaux	0010101	7
qui en li **daigna** venir	0010101	7
ne porroit mie soffrir	0101001	7
qui la sert qu'il ne fust saux.	0010101	7
Quant Dex tant la vost obeir	01001001	8

qu'il n'estoit muables ne faux	00101001	8
bien nos i devons donc tenir	10010101	8
dame. roïne naturaux	10010101	8
cil qui vos sert est feaus	1001001	7
vos li savrez bien merir	0010101	7
devant vos porra venir	1010101	7
plus clers qu'estoile jornaux.	1010101	7
*Vostre beau*té qui si resplant	*00*010101	8
fait tout le monde resclarcir	01010101	8
par vos vint Dex *entre la* gent	0101*0001*	8
en ter*re por la* mort soffrir	01*000*101	8
et a l'enemi tolir	0010101	7
nos et giter de torment	1001001	7
por vos avons vengement	0101001	7
et par vos devons garir.	0010101	7
David le sot premieirement	01010101	8
que de lui deviez issir,	00100101	8
*quant il par*la si hautement	*000*010101	8
par la bouche du saint espir.	00100101	8
vos n'este*s* mie a florir	0101001	7
ainz avez flour si poissant	1001001	7
ce est Dex qui onqu(es) ne ment	1010101	7
qui par tout fait son plesir.	0011001	7

This scansion gives one juxtaposed accent and five runs of atonic syllables in thirty-two verse-units of which twenty-six show alternating accent by our criteria (81 per cent). In version A, the straitjacket of the 'iambic' and 'trochaic' rhythmic modes ensures 100 per cent alternation of accent while forcing random correlation with word-accent; version B has 81 per cent alternation of accent, restores the accent of optative subjunctive *voigne*, irons out the aberrant accents of *muables*, *estoile* and by definition restores the atonic character of the eighteen high-frequency clitics accented in version A.

The structure of word-accent in French does not necessarily imply a high incidence of alternating accent such as we find it in version B. In the Introduction an experiment showed that modern French, in colloquial registers and in prose, routinely accommodates both juxtaposed accents and runs of atonic syllables.[78] Because linguistic change since 1250 has not materially affected these features, the predominance of alternation in this verse cannot be due to linguistic factors: it must be the result of the poet's intention. All things considered, the question of the aesthetic of accentuation in the original performance of this verse must remain open. While the poet has contrived a high incidence of varied alternation of linguistic accent in his verse, his choice has been overridden by the invariant structure of the rhythmic modes in the notation used by his successors.

The following song, transcribed again from the Chansonnier Cangé (fol. 13^v–14^r), shows in contrast a conscious exploitation of the rhythmic possibilities offered by varied line-length. Here are its first three stanzas:[79]

Au tans d'aoust que fuille de boschet	1001 # 001001	10
chiet et matist a petit de ventet,	1001 # 001001	10
flours n'a duree,	10010	4
verdure est passee,	010010	5
remaint chant d'oisel;	01001	5
blanche ialee	10010	4
a *la* matinee	010010	5
s'apert ou prael.	01001	5
*A*donc montai sor mon cheval morel,	1001 # 001001	10
si m'en entrai tout le fonz d'un vaucel.	1001 # 001001	10
grant assemblee	10010	4
d'anfanz ai trovee	010010	5
de joste un ormel.	01001	5
la reposee	10010	4
ont enqui juree,	010010	5
delez le prael.	01001	5
N'**i** a celui n'ait fleüste ou frestel	1001 # 001001	10
tuit en iront as voilles saint marcel.	1001 # 001001	10
R*o*bins puree	10010	4
sa teste a juree	010010	5
qu'il **a** de novel	01001	5
pype achetee	10010	4
si sera sonee	010010	5
s'il puet a revel.	01001	5

The accents marked are again those given by the longs in the musical notation. Though we have become used to thinking of French verse-accent as predominantly either 'iambic' or 'anapestic', the rhythmic mode is again 'dactylic'. For Lote all such verse is simply un-French: 'un mécanisme brutal qui soumet le texte et le brise inexorablement selon un schema donné'. Reminding us that accent at 'cesura' and line-end are canonical, he concludes that: 'Au contraire, à l'intérieur, parfois des vers courts, et toujours dans les hémistiches des grands vers, les autres syllabes sont traitées sans aucun souci des toniques'.[80] Lote's case rests on his finding that the rhythmic structure given by the musical notation of this lyric repertoire randomly violates the principle of oxytonic/paroxytonic word-accent. But are the accents random? Of the ninety-five words in this text eight are misaccented (8 per cent): for example *fuille* has an accented 'ə' and *cheval* has its accent on an atonic syllable. But out of forty-four polysyllables in these verses, just six fall accentual victims to the dactylic straitjacket. In the other thirty-eight the text has matched word-accent with the modal rhythm of the melody. In only two instances is an atonic monosyllable accented (*Au tans d'aoust*; *la matinee*).

If Lote's contention were true, it would make no difference which syllables within the verse-unit were accented. Suppose we take him at his word when he reminds us that: 'le mouvement de la langue française, et celui du latin mediéval, qui lui a été assimilé de très bonne heure, est iambique et anapestique: il n'est ni trochaique ni dactylique'.[81] Here is our text accented 'iambically':

Au **tans** d'aoust que fuille de boschet	0101 # 010101	10
chiet et matist a petit de ventet,	0101 # 010101	10[82]

verdure est p*a*sse*e*,	010101	5
remain*t chant* d'*o*isel;	01010	5
blanche i*a*le*e*	10101	4
a l*a* matine*e*	010101	5
s'*a*pert *ou* prael.	10101	5
Adonc montai sor m*o*n cheval morel,	0101 # 010101	10
si m'*en* entrai tout l*e fonz* d'*un* vaucel.	0101 # 010101	10
grant assemblee	01010	4
d'*a*nfanz *ai* trovee	101010	5
D*e* joste *un* or*m*el.	10101	5
La reposee	01010	4
*o*nt enqui juree,	101010	5
D*e*lez l*e* prael.	10101	5
N'*i a* celu*i* n'ait fleüste *ou* frestel	0101 # 010101	10
tuit en iront as voilles saint marcel	0101 # 010101	10
Robins puree	01010	4
sa teste a juree	101010	5
qu'*i*l a d*e* novel	10101	5
pype achetee	01010	4
si sera donee	101010	5
s'*il* puet *a* revel.	10101	5

The 'iambic' matrix harmonises with word-accent in polysyllables in all but nine out of the forty-four cases, but it forces into accentual prominence twenty-two atonic monosyllables, as against two in the original version, i.e. *eleven* times as many. In this (fake) 'iambic' version, thirty-one out of the total of ninety-six words are misaccented (32 per cent) compared to the eight out of ninety-six (8 per cent) in the 'dactylic' version. More significantly, six high-priority monosyllables, *chiet* [falls], *chant* [song], *fonz* [bottom], *tuit* [everybody], *test(e)* [head], *pyp(e)* [pipe, whistle] are made atonic. Even more significantly, in ll. 3, 5 and 6, atonic line-final [ə] is accented. Only seven out of the thirty verse-units in the 'iambic' version (23 per cent) show complete matching of 'iambic' modal rhythm with linguistic accent.

In contrast, our anonymous poet-composer has, in his own 'dactylic' version, marked the fixed accent-positions (at cesura and line-end) while minimising conflict with linguistic accent.[83] Thus twenty-one of thirty verse-units agree with a scansion of the text according to our model (70 per cent).

A further interesting feature of this little lyric is that, while minimising accentual mismatch, the distribution of note-value over syllable allows rhythmic variation which produces a pleasing alternation of accent. Each of the opening decasyllables of each strophe opens and closes with an accented syllable, and the final [ə] of the feminine rhymes, *passee, matinee, trovee, juree*, in carrying the 'dactylic' pulse over the line-end creates in the following line what looks and feels like an equivocation of 'anapest' and 'iamb':

Flour n'a dure*ə*,	1001[0	4
verdure est passe*ə*,	01]001[0	5
Remain*t* chant d'oisel.	01]001]	5

Our poet-composer is organising the tension between syllabic count and rhythmic matrix in order to produce an alternation of accent in keeping with the accentual structure of his French. The marked correlation of musical and linguistic accent in this song suggests the competent work of a single hand. While our thirteenth-century *chansonnier* is for the most part editing the work of notable poets who had lived half a century before, poets who had left their own melodies in non-mensural form, 'Au tens d'aoust' evokes instead a poet-composer working with new notational forms.

It has not escaped us that this lyric shows the very feature that Benoît de Cornulier finds so troublesome in the verse of La Fontaine: a mixture of ten-, four- and five-syllable lines will not fit with the isosyllabist idea of verse which stands or falls on a fixed syllabic count. Though Cornulier denies any metrical role to accent within the hemistich, in this text it is discovered to be essential to our perception of the verse-form.

In the following two strophes of a lyric by Richard de Fournival (d. 1220), the rhythm again follows the 'trochaic' mensural notation of the Chansonnier Cangé. The poet is considering the merits of a younger as against an older mistress:

Chascuns qui de bien amer	1010101	7
cuide avoir non	0101	4
ne set *ou* moins a d'amer	1010101	7
ne ou moins non.	0101	4
l*i* uns dit et vuet prover	1010101	7
et par raison	0101	4
qu'assez fait mieuz a loer	1010101	7
dame *a* baron	0101	4
qu*e* pucele pour amer,	1010101	7
mais je di que non[84]	00101	5 [*sic*]
chascuns a droite achoison	1010101	7
s'il jug*e* le jeu a bon	1010101	7
qu'ai esprouvé;	0101	4
queque nus i ait trové	1010101	7
j'ai mis mon cuer en jone damoisele	1001 # 0101010	10
dont ja ne partirai mon gré.	01010101	8
Celui puet on escuser	1010101	7
de mesprison,	0101	4
qui egaument vuet donner	1010101	7
selonc son bon.	0101	4
Por ce vuil par droit mostrer,	1010101	7
et sanz tençon,	0101	4
qu*e* jon*e* dame *a* loer	1010101	7
a plus haut don.	0101	4
qu'*a* la pucele panser	1010101	7
ni a fors le non.	0101	4
Mais dam*e* rent guierredon	1010101	7
et pucele est tost chanjanz	1010101	7
et sanz bonté.	0101	4
J'*en* ai mon voloir osté.	1010101	7
s'ai mis mon cuer en jone dame et bele	0101 # 0101010	10
dont ja ne partirai mon gré.[85]	01010101	8

This text shows 17 accentual mismatches in 149 words (11 per cent) and 19 of the 34 verse-units (56 per cent) show matching of 'dactylic'/'iambic' rhythm and linguistic accent. Just as in 'Au tans d'aoust' cited above, the apparent metrical alternation between lines of seven and four syllables is enforced by the overflow of the 'trochaic' pulse from the longer line to the shorter one, in contrast to the last two lines of each strophe which are both syllabically and accentually out of step. The penultimate line of the first strophe is a decasyllable. Were the 'trochaic' rhythm to be maintained throughout this line, the 'cesural' syllable, syllable 4, would lack the 'cesural' accent:

> J'**ai** mis mon cuer? #

At this point, the manuscript's musical notation clearly indicates a shift to the 'dactylic' mode which restores the cesural accent:

> J'**ai** mis mon **cuer**. #

The corresponding decasyllable of strophe 2 begins with an atonic syllable, thus generating an integrally iambic line which satisfies the requirement for fixed accents at both cesura and line-end. The atonic final vowel of the penultimate line of both strophes is immediately followed by an atonic syllable at the head of the last line. This link maintains the 'iambic' rhythm across the line-end via a 'dactylic' 'bridge':

> S'ai] [mis mon] [**cuer** # en] j[one] d[ame e]t b[ele
> Dont] ja ne partirai mon gré.

Dont is the 'tail' of the 'dactyl' [*ele dont*] and at the same time the head of the 'iambic' foot [*dont ja*]. Though these lines are heterosyllabic, the recurrent rhythmic pulse confirms that they are metrically well-formed. Both this text and the preceding one profit from the flexibility available within what looks like a rhythmic straitjacket. Here is the text again, this time scanned in accordance with our model:

Chascuns qui de bien amer	0100101	7
cuide avoir **non**	1001	4
ne set ou **moins** a d'amer	0101001	7
ne ou **moins non.**	00**11**	4
li uns dit et **vuet** prover	0010101	7
et par raison	0101	4
qu'assez fait **mieuz** a loer	0101001	7
dame a baron	1001	4
que pucele pour amer.	0010*00*1	7
mais je **di** que non.	00101	5 [*sic*]
chascuns a droite achoison	0101001	7
s'il **juge** le **jeu** a bon	0100101	7
qu'**ai** esprouvé;	1001	4
queque nus i **ait** trové,	0010101	7
j'ai mis mon **cuer** en jone damoisele	0101 # 0101010	10
dont ja ne partirai mon **gré.**	01010101	8
Celui puet on escuser	0101001	7
de mespris**on,**	0101	4
qui egaument **vuet** donner	0010101	7
selonc son **bon.**	0101	4

Por ce vuil par droit mostrer,	0110101	7
et sanz tençon,	0101	4
que jone dame a loer	0101001	7
a plus haut don.	0101	4
qu'a la pucele panser	*0001*001	7
ni a fors le non.	0101	4
Mais dame rent guierredon	0101001	7
et pucele est tost chanjanz	0010101	7
et sanz bonté.	0101	4
J'en ai mon voloir osté	0100101	7
s'ai mis mon cuer en jone dame et bele	0101 # 0101010	10
dont ja ne partirai mon gré.	01010101	8

Here 87 per cent of thirty-two verse-units alternate accent, two showing juxtaposed accents and two having runs of three atonic syllables. According to the manuscript's mensural notation, nineteen of thirty-four verse-units alternate accent as predicted by our model (56 per cent).

Between these thirteenth-century lyrics and the verse of modern French lies the period of Middle French during which word-accent was levelled with consequences for the relations between word, syllable and syntactical ordering. Meanwhile, the measuring role of accent in verse might have quietly disappeared, leaving only syllabic count to guarantee the verse form. However, of this matter the texts will speak for themselves. The early fourteenth century brought remarkable innovations in musical notation. The modal system of the Chansonnier Cangé was gradually replaced by one which made possible the notation of more varied rhythmical combinations. The Franconian system was refined in the *Ars Nova* of Philippe de Vitry (1291–1361), Bishop of Meaux and correspondent of Petrarch. In the songs of Guillaume de Machaut (1300–77), canon of Reims, these innovations are deployed in his settings of his own verse. Along with his polyphonic setting of the Mass, we find a more intimate repertoire in which strophes on the same rhymes are sung by a single voice to a repeated melody. Here is a *chanson roial* from the *Remède de Fortune*, a mainly octosyllabic essay in erotic autobiography, interlarded with musical settings of his own verse. Machaut's melody is in the triple rhythm common in the earlier Franconian notation of trouvère lyrics, and the rhythm given here is that of its musical notation:

Version A

Joie, Plaisence et douce norriture,	1001 # 1011011	10 + ə
Vie d'onour prennent maint en amer;	1101 # 101101	10
Et pluseurs sont qui n'i ont fors pointure,	1001 # 1011011	10 + ə
Ardour, dolour, plour, tristece et amer.	1101 # 101101	10
Si dient; mais acorder	1000101	7
Ne me puis qu'en la souffrence	10010101	7 + ə
D'amours ait nulle grevance,	10100101	7 + ə
Car tout ce qui vient de li	1010101	7
Plaist a cuer d'ami.	10101	5
Amours, je say sans doubtance	10100101	7 + ə
Qu'a cent doubles as meri	1010101	7
Ceaus qui t'ont servi.	10101	5

Car vraie Amour en cuer d'amant figure	1001 # 1011011	10 + ə
Tres dous Espoir et graci-eux Penser:	1101 # 101101	10
Espoirs attrait Joie et bone Aventure;	1001 # 1011011	10 + ə
Dous Penser fait Plaisence en cuer entrer;	1101 # 101101	10
Si ne doit plus demander	1000101	7
Cils qui a bonne Esperence,	10010101	7 + ə
Dous Penser, Joie et Plaisence,	10100101	7 + ə
Car qui plus requiert, je di	1010101	7
Qu'Amours l'a guerpi.	10101	5
Amours, je say sans doubtance	01010011	7 + ə
Qu'a cent doubles as meri	1010101	7
Ceaus qui t'ont servi.[86]	10101	5

We are struck here by the violent disagreement of word-accent and musical accent. Of the forty-eight polysyllables in our text, twenty (42 per cent) are, by our criteria, misaccented, and many of these are in no way random. Line-final [ə] in the rhyme-series *norriture/pointure/figure/Aventure* persistently coincides with a primary accent at the head of the bar. Elsewhere the note-values are imposed on the text in ways that generate juxtaposed accents (*maint en*; *amant*; *graci-eux*) which make hay of normal word-accent. Also some high-priority words (e.g. *pluseurs*, *dient*, *cuer*, *say*) are atonic. The *Ars Nova* had indeed advanced the notation for the combining of rhythmic cells, but here the resulting impact on the relation between text and melody violently subjugates the former to the latter.[87] Though our review of texts from the trouvère repertoire certainly found a measure of disagreement between word-accent and musical accent, we encounter in Machaut extreme dissonances absent from the earlier repertoire. Of the thirty-two verse-units here, only five show alternating rhythm in harmony with word-accent (16 per cent).

Clearly Machaut was abandoning ordered linguistic word-accent as the basis for settings of his own verse. If so what was it that made this song perceptible as verse? Alas, not even 'recurrent syllabic count' can come to our rescue if these verses of Machaut are typical, which indeed they are. Their alternation of ten-, seven- and five-syllable lines puts them in that class of lyrical composition which for Cornulier does not count as verse at all.

A second example from Machaut is in the newer style of quadruple rhythm (4/4). The four-line refrain is repeated between the stanzas:

REFRAIN		
Douce dame joli-e,	0101011	6 + ə
Pour Dieu ne penses mi-e,	0101011	6 + ə
Que nulle ait signorie	0101010	6 + ə
Seur moy fors vous seulement.	1010101	7
I		
Qu'ades sans tricherie	0101010	6 + ə
Cherie	010	2 + ə
Vous ay et humblement	010101	6
Tous les jors de ma vie	0101010	6 + ə
Servie	010	2 + ə
Sans vilain pensement.	010101	6

Helas! et je mendi-*e*	0101011	6 + ə
D'esperance *et* d'ai-*e*;	0101011	6 + ə
Dont m*a* joie *e*st fenie	0101010	6 + ə
S*e* pité ne **vous** en prent.	1010101	7
II		
Mais v*o* douc*e* maistrie	0101010	6 + ə
Maistrie	010	2 + ə
Mon **cuer** si **durement**	010101	6
Qu'ell*e* le contralie	0101010	6 + ə
Et lie	010	2 + ə
En *a*mour tellement	010101	6
Qu'il n'**a** de riens envi-*e*	0101011	6 + ə
Fors d'**être** en v*o* bailli-*e*;	0101011	6 + ə
Et si ne li ottrie	0101010	6 + ə
V*o* cuer nul aligement.	1010101	7
III		
Et **quant** ma maladie	0101010	6 + ə
Garie	010	2 + ə
Ne s*e*ra nullement	010101	6
Sans **vous**, douce anemie	0101010	6 + ə
Qui lie	010	2 + ə
Est*e*s de m*on* tourment	010101	6
A jointes mains depri-*e*	0101011	6 + ə
Vo **cuer** puis qu'*i*l m'oubli-*e*	0101011	6 + ə
Que **temprement** m'ocie	0101010	6 + ə
C*a*r trop l*a*ngui longuement.[88]	1010101	7

The strophe starts with alternate six- and two-syllable lines and ends with an orphan seven-syllable line. There is slightly less disagreement between word-accent and musical accent; the dominance of 'iambic' rhythm recalls the fixed modal notation of our examples from the Chansonnier Cangé. Of the forty-two polysyllables thirteen are misaccented (31 per cent); the accenting of line-final schwa continues unabated as does the juxtaposition of word-internal accents and the accenting of clitic monosyllables. Again, some high-priority words are without accent. Of thrity-four verse-units, fourteen show alternating accent by our criteria (41 per cent).

The real puzzle is the relationship between Machaut the poet and Machaut the composer. Suppose we take Machaut the poet independently of the musician. Here is 'Joie, plaisence et douce nourriture' scanned in accordance with linguistic accent as we define it, i.e. as if it had not been set:

Version B

Joie. **Plaisence** # et **douce** norriture,	1001 # 0101010	10 + ə
Vie d'onour # prennent **maint** en amer;	1001 # 101001	10
Et pluseurs **sont** # qui n'i ont fors pointure,	0101 # 0010010	10 + ə
Ardour, dolour, # **plour**, tristece et amer.	0101 # 101001	10
Si **dient**; mais acorder	0100101	7
Ne me puis *qu'en la sou*ffrence[89]	00**10**0010	7 + ə
D'amours ait nulle grevance,	01010010	7 + ə
Car tout ce qui **vient** de li	0100101	7
Plaist a **cuer** d'ami.	10101	5

Amours, je **say** sans doubt**a**nce	01010010	7 + ə
Qu'a cent **doubl**e**s** *as* m**e**ri	001**0001**	7
Ceaus qui t'**ont** servi.[90]	10101	5
Car vraie A**mour** en **cuer** d'amant figure	0101 # 0101010	10 + ə
Tres **dous** Es**poir** et graci**eux** Pen**ser:**	0101 # 010101	10
Es**poirs** at**trait** Joie et **bon**ne Aven**ture:**	0101 # 1010010	10 + ə
Dous Penser fait Plaisence en **cuer** entrer:	101 #? 0010101	10
Si ne doit plus demander	1001001	7
Cils qui a **bon**ne Esperence,	10010010	7 + ə
Dous Penser, **Joie** et Plaisence,	10110010	7 + ə
Car qui plus requiert, je di,	0010101	7
Qu'Am**ours** l'a guerpi.	01001	5
Am**ours**, je **say** sans doubt**a**nce	01010010	7 + ə
Qu'a cent **doubl**e**s** *as* m**e**ri	001**0001**	7
Ceaus qui t'**ont** servi.	10101	5

When we sang this song from the notated values of Machaut's melody, we encountered frequent displacement of oxytonic word-accent: *Ardour*; *amours*; *Espoirs*; *Pleisence*. Even more striking, this displacement was repeatedly coupled with an accented [ə] in line-final position: *Aventure*; *souffrance*; *grevance*; *Esperence*. In addition, the accented positions in the melody created strong juxtapositions of accent involving atonic clitics: *maint en*; *en cuer*; to say nothing of the independent accenting of clitics such as *je, a, en*; and the accenting of adjacent syllables in the same word: *amant*, *graci-eux*.

Recited (as in version B above) rather than sung, the incongruity evaporates. Once we assume the text's conformity with linguistic word-accent as we have found it in the historical record, we find that Machaut the poet shows a flexible handling of the relationship between word-accent and varied syllabic count. Once word-accent has been marked, a varied landscape of alternating accent appears. In version B, out of thirty-two verse-units twenty-eight show alternation of accent (88 per cent), while four have a run of three atonic syllables. One has juxtaposed accents:

> Dous Pen[ser, Joie] et Pleisance

though these are separated by a minor syntactic juncture.

In this repertoire we face again the problem of the relation of strophe to melody. Since, as in our examples from the Chansonnier Cangé, the same melody is repeated from strophe to strophe, the musical accentuation will remain constant while the word-over-syllable distribution will shift. Thus, even if the composer were in the first strophe to ensure the conformity of musical accent with linguistic accent, this relationship would from strophe to strophe become random. For example in l. 4 of 'Joie, plaisence et douce nourriture' version B, the syllabification is thus:

> Ar|dour|, do|lour|, plour|, tri|stece| et| a|mer|.   **1** 2 3 **4** 5 6 7 8 9 **10**

In the corresponding line of strophe 2, we find:

> Dous| Pen|ser| fait| Plei|san|ce en| cuer| en|trer| **1** 2 3 **4** 5 6 7 8 9 **10**

which accented as in strophe 1 would give:

> Dous| Pen|ser| fait| Plei|san|ce en| cuer| en|trer|.

To maintain the musical accents of strophe 1 in succeeding strophes would result in complete absence of agreement between musical and linguistic accent.

In version B of 'Joie, plaisence et douce nourriture' the word-over-syllable layout shows a strong correlation with linguistic accent. If this was intended by Machaut the poet, its overlaying with an incompatible musical rhythm by Machaut the composer must also have been. This treatment of word-accent, familiar to modern anglophones conversant with West Indian calypso, will characterise the relationship between music and text from Machaut right down to the French *air de cour* in the sixteenth century. D. P. Walker draws our attention to the observations of Edward Filmer, a contemporary English connoisseur, on the vagaries of these French court composers in their setting of verse-texts:

> The French when they compose to a ditty in their own Language being led rather by their free Fant'sie [*sic*] of Aire (wherein many of them do naturally excel) than by any strict and artificiall scanning of the line, by which they build, doe often, by disproportion'd Musicall Quantities, invert the natural Stroke of a Verse, applying to the place of an *Iambicke* foot, such modulation as Iumps rather with a Trochay.[91]

Filmer's remarks raise a question of principle. From Machaut to Guédron in the 1580s, does the persistent indifference of composers to the defining oxytonic accent of French imply that, in Middle French and early modern French, such accent had ceased to exist? We have already noted that the weakening of the tonic accent of Old French was decisive in the development of the phonology and syntax of later French. While the 'word' in Old French was, as in modern English, free-standing with clear boundaries, the 'word' in the French of Machaut was losing its segmental identity. The emergence of *liaison* and *enchaînement* were part of a process in which the phrase instead became the basic unit.[92]

This seductively simple account fails however to explain reference to word-accent by francophone commentators like Palsgrave, for whom 'l'accent est une élévation de la voix sur quelques mots ou syllabes dans une phrase';[93] and Du Gardin who, as we noted earlier, found word-accent within the hemistich:

Je chante la vertu # d'une vaillante dame.

Discount the evidence of such valid witnesses, the hard evidence is still there: the constraints we discovered in our analyses of the *Chanson de Roland* and *Phèdre* are operating here on the distribution of word-accent within the hemistich. No-one can deny the presence of word-accent in the twelfth-century *Chanson de Roland*, and the same constraints were still working, we found, in the alexandrine of Racine, 500 years later. Were there no word-accent, there would be no such constraints.

In the posthumous fourth volume of his magisterial *Histoire du vers français*, Georges Lote summarises his view of the relation between syllabic count and rhythm in French verse. He finds that the high verse of the French Middle Ages 'avait été articulé uniquement sur deux accents, celui de la césure et celui de la rime'. Only more popular verse-forms took up the possibilities offered by the alternation of tonic and atonic syllables, he adds, while still observing strict syllabic count. For him, the even delivery of syllables in the declamation of high verse had 'une allure lourde et pesante qui déplaisait à beaucoup et, à mesure que les années passaient, devait déplaire encore davantage'.[94] For him, this unaccented syllabism remained the cultural norm for the recitation of verse, segregating high verbal art from the rhythms of everyday speech and prose. Certainly this account explains a great deal. As Lote tells us, sixteenth-century setters of French syllabic verse appear to have had little idea where the accent ought to fall, other than at the rhyme and now and then at the cesura. And not just composers: in the 1552 edition with music of his *Amours*, Ronsard gives a long list of the sonnets which could be sung to the same setting by Janequin, thus implying that these sonnets were either rhythmically indistinguishable or that their rhythm was irrelevant. We might suspect the poet of having one eye on the commercial advantage offered by this flexibility, were it not that the union of poetry and music was a central tenet of the humanist programme. In his *Art poétique* Ronsard says that 'la poësie, sans les instrumens ou sans la grace d'une ou plusieurs voix, n'est nullement agréable'.[95]

Respect for classical models was affirmed by another member of the Pléiade, Antoine de Baïf, who in 1570 founded the Académie de poësie et de musique. Baïf aimed to restore the harmony of word and note by remodelling the metric of French in imitation of the Greek. French theatre would regain the intimate union of metre, song and dance proper to the Athenian stage:

Car leurs vers avoyent la mesure,	001000010
Qui d'une plaisante batture	100010010
Frapoit l'oreille des oïans.	0101001
Et des Chores la belle dance	001001010
En chantant gardoit la cadance	001010010
Au son des hauboys s'egayans.	01001001

(*Euvres en rime de Jan Antoine de Baïf, secrétaire de la chambre du Roy*, ed. by Charles Marty-Laveaux, 5 vols (Paris: Lemerre, 1881–90), III, 2.) In imitating classical metre, the basic assumption was that, in their *vers mesurés*, Greek feet were to be represented by alternations of longs and shorts: a dactyl (– ˘ ˘) would therefore consist of a long (–), plus two shorts (˘ ˘), a minim plus two crotchets. Lote points out that members of Baïf's Académie placed a long at the 'cesura' and at the rhyme, but also felt that contrast between long and short was necessary within the hemistich. Lote cites examples to show however that in most cases there is little or no correlation between these alternations and the structure of French word-accent. Here are some lines by Ronsard with the rhythm indicated by Costeley's melody:

Je veux aymer ard**ante**ment:	10011111
Aussi veux-je qu'**é**galement	10011111
On m'ayme d'**une** amour ard**ante**.[96]	100100011[97]

But this apparent chaos is not universal. As in the concord of scansion and linguistic accent which we saw in certain songs of the Chansonnier Cangé, a much closer correspondence can arise. Take these verses by Nicolas Rapin, a follower of Ronsard:

Chevaliers généreux, qui avez le courage François,	001001001001001
Accourez, accourez secourir l'héritier de vos Rois.	
Secourez vostre Roy naturel, si vaillant, si guerrier!	
A la peine, à la charge, à l'assaut, le premier, le dernier:	

Un Roy ne s'est jamais veu   0101001
De tant de grace pourveu.

A cheval, à cheval, cazaniers, tout l'affaire laissé:
Le loyal coutelas à la main et le casque baissé,
Debatez courageux votre honneur, vostre vie et vos biens.
Ne souffrez ce tyran, qui s'accroist de la perte des siens,
Ravir le sceptre et ses lois
Du grand royaume François.[98]

Here the sustained 'anapests' of ll. 1–4 contrast with the 0101001 of the final couplet, in an interesting parallel to 'Au tans d'aoust' of the Chansonnier anticipating the eighteenth- and nineteenth-century experiments of Hoffman and Van Hasselt. These four poets have in common, across a span of six hundred years, keen awareness of word-accent and its potential in the organisation of French verse.

The Seventeenth Century

The operatic composer Jean-Baptiste Lully, a contemporary of Racine, enjoyed a reputation as a sensitive setter of French verse. He frequently attended the Comédie française where he would have heard the celebrated actress La Champmeslé declaiming the alexandrines of Racine. She had been for a time Racine's mistress, and it is likely that the playwright, renowned among his intimates as a reciter of verse, had polished her style. Working closely with his librettist Quinault, Lully gave to his recitative, that is the sung narrative parts of the operatic score, rhythms which were new to audiences used to a more syllabic style.[99] His score for *Alceste* may well give us objective evidence for the role of accent in the French which Lully, Quinault and Racine all spoke.[100]

Our method here, as in the thirteenth-century examples, is to gauge whether the accents indicated by the musical notation match the points in the verse-line which our theory predicts will receive a linguistic word-accent. In a musical bar with four crotchet beats, the first has the main accent, the third has a secondary one. Here are a pair of alexandrines from the Lully-Quinault *Alceste*:

Tu me //vois arrê//té sur le /point de par//tir,
Par les //tristes cla/meurs qu'on en//tend reten//tir.[101]

Following Lully's musical notation, the syllable following a double slash is marked by a primary or secondary bar-accent (first or third beat of the bar) and the single slash is followed by an accent produced otherwise. Lully has several ways of marking such an accent: he can do it by increasing a note's duration relative to that of a preceding note:

this happens with *point* which is under a quaver, and *clameurs* where the tonic vowel is matched with a crotchet. Or he can throw it into relief by a sudden change in pitch — either up or down. In the present specimen, accents on *vois, arrêté, partir, tristes* and *retentir* are marked by both bar-accent and lengthening. *Point* achieves prominence through pitch-contrast and lengthening, while *clameurs* is marked by lengthening alone.

Lully takes for granted not only that cesural and line-final accents are fixed (*arrêté, partir, clameurs, retentir*), but also that certain words within the hemistich must carry an accent (*vois, point, tristes, entend*). Each of these accented words belongs to the class of lexical items that have a relatively low frequency of occurrence and are thus critical to the message — as compared to *tu, me, sur, le, par, les, on*, all of which are atonic.[102]

Here is a longer sample from Act IV, scene 2, of *Alceste* in which Alcide seeks passage from Charon the infernal boatman:

ALCESTE:	Sortez Ombres, faites-moi place,	8
	Vous passerez une autre fois.	8
CHARON:	Ah! Ma barque ne peut souffrir un si grand poids!	12
ALCESTE:	Allons,il faut que l'on me passe.	8
CHARON:	Retire-toi d'ici, Mortel, qui que tu sois,	12
	Les Enfers irrités puniront ton audace	12
ALCESTE:	Passe-moi sans tant de façons!	8
CHARON:	L'eau nous gagne, ma barque crève!	8
ALCESTE:	Allons, rame! Dépêche, achève!	8
CHARON:	Nous enfonçons!	4
ALCESTE:	Passons, passons!	4
CHARON:	Nous enfonçons!	4
ALCESTE:	Passons, passons!	4

The composer writes *faites-moi place* with a length-accent on *faites*, while the accent on *place* coincides with a primary bar-accent. In Charon's indignant response, the accent on *si* is produced by the lengthening of its note, a quaver in contrast to the preceding and following semiquavers. In reply to the hero's peremptory demand, the boatman's emphatic riposte accents the countertonic syllable of the verb, *Retire-toi d'ici!* by placing a full quaver on it in contrast to the rapid series of four semiquavers which follows, the 'cesural' accent on *ici* falling on the primary accent of the following bar. In the next line all the accents result from the interposing of full quavers in a series of semiquavers, the final accent on *audace* coinciding with the primary accent of the next bar. All these are reinforced by pitch-contrasts, adding vehemence. The urgency of the hero's injunction is also heightened by the juxtaposed accents which Lully arranges by joining a full crochet on the second syllable of *Allons* to the bar-accent on *rame*, the two being separated by a crotchet rest.

The interest of this passage lies largely in its alternation of alexandrines with shorter lines. The composer has at his disposal a flexible system of notation that enables him not only to mark fixed verse-accents but also to follow the profile of alternating accent within the hemistich. Evidently the judgement of Lully's peers, that his was a 'natural' style reflecting the reality of French speech, counters the claim that accent within the verse-phrase has no metrical function and is, as Gouvard affirms, a simple question of chance.[103] Everywhere in *Alceste* we find accent alternating systematically in the musical realisation. All the accents we have noted in the foregoing examples are predicted by our theory: if the metre here were defined only by a recurring syllable-count, Lully would have been quite free to place musical accents at points within the verse-line not predicted by our theory.[104]

The negative evidence is even more compelling, namely what Lully *does not* do. Much of his setting of recitative shows patterns of shorter notes with their own tendency to alternate accent. For example in the exchange between Alcide and Charon, we read the former's words to the gathered Shades: *Vous passerez une autre fois.* The syllables in *Vous passer [...]* and *une autre* are written in short notes, semiquavers, all at the same pitch and of the same length. How do we justify marking *passerez* with a countertonic accent when there is in the music no pitch- or length-contrast? The answer lies in Lully's treatment of groups of semiquavers. We have seen that in a bar of four crotchets the first and third carry respectively the primary and secondary bar-accents and that these match the word-accents of Quinault's text. Suppose that these groups of four semiquavers alternate accent on the first and third as do the four crotchets which make up a bar of 4/4. It may follow that alternation of accent in the verse-text will match alternation of accent in the notation of groups of four semiquavers, albeit with lower values of intensity. All perception of accent is contextual. No prosodic features have an independent existence; they can only be defined by their relations with the neighbouring units. Here are two examples from Act II, scene 5:[105]

|7 ♪ ♪♪| ♪   ♪|♪♪ ♪ ♪|♪
|7 n'y ré pond pas   a re tar dé mes pas.

And some further examples from Scene 6:

♪| ♪ ♪ ♪ ♪| ♪ |♪ ♪ ♪ ♪|♪
Se roit en cor plus doux   son heu reux é poux.
| ♪ ♪♪ ♪|♪   ♪| ♪ ♪♪ ♪|♪♪
Rien à re dou ter.   Votre âme im pa ti en te.
♪| ♪ ♪ ♪ ♪|♪
Les noeuds d'une a mi tié

Here all the syllables accented by Lully are as predicted by our theory. In each case, the tonic syllable is matched with either a primary (first) or secondary (third) musical accent within the bar. Counter-examples might have forms such as:

|♪ ♪ ♪ ♪|♪* | ♪ ♪ ♪ ♪|♪*[106]
|le maî tre de moi   l'Heu reux en fant naît

Here the accented first syllable of *maître* is mismatched with the unaccented second beat of the bar, as are the oxytonic accents of both *heureux* and *enfant*. I have not found any such counter-examples in this act of *Alceste*.

As the exchange between Alcide and Charon suggests, the librettist writes a mixture of long and short lines whose rhythmic contrasts prompt a varied dramatic setting from the composer. The agreement between verse- and musical rhythm required the careful avoidance on Lully's part of any mismatching. Just as popular Roman audiences were,

Cicero reports, offended by false quantities in the recitation of Latin verse, so Lully's reputation as a sensitive setter of French verse is witness to a refined awareness of the prosodic features of the language on the part of both composer and audience.

In order to test and consolidate our conclusions so far, here are two longer passages of recitative from the Lully-Quinault *Thésée* with Lully's accentuation.[107] Firstly, in Act V, scene 2, Médée, enchantress and unrequited lover of Thésée, pours out her heart in a tête-à-tête with Dorine, her *confidente*:[108]

DORINE:	Que Thésée est content de son bien heureux sort.[109]	001001 # 010101	12
MÉDÉE:	Dorine, c'en est fait, tout est prêt pour sa mort.	010101 # 001001	12
DORINE:	Quoi! Ce grand appareil est sa mort qu'on prépare?	101001 # 0010010	12
	Le Roy le doit choisir icy pour successeur.	010101 # 010101	12
	Votre soin pour luy se déclare.	001010010	8
MÉDÉE:	J'ay caché mon dépit sous ma feinte douceur;	001001 # 001001	12
	La vengeance ordinaire est trop peu pour mon coeur;	001001 # 001001	12
	Je la veux horrible et barbare.	001010010	8
	Je m'éloignais tantôt exprès pour tout savoir.	010101 # 010101	12
	Du secret de Thésée il faut me prévaloir,	001001 # 010101	12
	Le Roy l'ignore encor, *et pour me* satisfaire	010101 # 0101010	12
	Contre un fils inconnu, j'arme *son* propre père:	101001 # 1010010	12
	J'immolay mes enfants j'osay les égorger,	001001 # 010101	12
	Je ne serais pas seul inhumaine et perfide	010101 # 0010010	12
	Je ne puis me venger à moins d'un parricide.	001001 # 0101010	12

Here in Quinault's twenty-eight verse-units we find twenty-seven (96 per cent) which conform to our model for alternation. In Lully's setting, there is 100 per cent alternation. In one instance Lully disagrees with our scansion by accenting a clitic: 'j'arme *son* propre père'. He thus ratifies a scansion according to our model in twenty-six of twenty-eight verse-units (93 per cent). The composer obtains full alternation by accenting high-frequency monosyllables: *so, pour, son*. Exit Dorine and enter the King. In the following scene, Médée is in conversation with the King, Theseus' rival in love:

MÉDÉE:	Ce vase *par mes* soins vient d'être empoisonné;	010101 # 010101	12
	Vous n'aurez qu'à l'offrir...vous semblez étonné?	001001 # 001001	12
LE ROY:	Ce héros m'a servi; malgré moi je l'estime,	001001 # 1010010	12
	Puis-je lui préparer un injuste trépas?	100101 # 001001	12
MÉDÉE:	L'espoir *de votre a*mour, la paix *de vos é*tats,	010101 # 010101	12
	Tout dépend d'immoler cette grande victime.	001001 # 0010010	12
	Contre un rival heureux faut-il qu'*on vous a*nime?	100101 # 0101010	12
	La vengeance a bien des appas;	00101001	8
	Est-ce trop la payer s'il vous en coute un crime?	001001 # 0101010	12
LE ROY:	Je n'ay rien fait jusqu'à ce jour	01010001	8
	Qui puisse ternir ma mémoire;	010010010	8
	Si près *de mon tom*beau faut-il trahir ma gloire?	010101 # 0101010	12
	Ne vaudrait- il pas mieux étouffer mon amour?	010101 # 001001	12
MÉDÉE:	Vous avez un fils à Trézène,	001010010	8
	Il faudra toujours l'éloigner.	00101001	8
	Votre peuple pour luy n'aura *que de la* haine;	001001 # 0101010	12
	Il adore Thésée, il veut le voir régner.	001001 # 010101	12
	Laisserez-vous un fils sans nom et sans empire?	00101 # 0101010	12

Tandis qu'un étranger jouira de son sort,	010101#001001	12
Et peut-être osera s'assurer par sa mort...	001001#001001	12
LE ROY: Je cède aux sentiments *que la na*ture inspire,	010101#0101010	12
Je me rends, l'Amour seul n'était pas assez fort.	001001#001001	12

In this passage thirty out of thirty-nine (77 per cent) of Quinault's verse-units conform to our model. Lully's disagreements with us concern the eight runs of atonic syllables we would find. Apart from one run of three atonic syllables, the composer again manages almost full alternation (97 per cent) by accenting atonic syllables: *par, votre, vos, vous, mon, de, Tandis, la*. Overall, 83 per cent of Quinault's verse-units in these two passages conform to our model, all of which save one (*son propre père*) are ratified by the composer, who manages 98 per cent alternation in his setting of the total sixty-seven verse-units.

Our examination of the dialogue between Alcide and Charon confirmed our assumption that in Lully's setting of verse, word-accent would be matched with alternating accentual positions within the bar. Just as in 4/4 rhythm a bar of four crotchets would alternate marked/unmarked/marked/unmarked, so an equivalent bar of eight quavers would alternate marked and unmarked positions, just as would a bar of sixteen semiquavers.[110] In short, the composer uses this matrix to distinguish those syllables which carry a linguistic accent from those which do not. The musical accent like the prosodic accent marks those elements of the message which are informationally critical.[111]

Here accent on monosyllables with a low frequency of occurrence (e.g. *sort, prêt, peu* etc.) and oxytonic word-accent (*choisir, caché, encor, rival* etc.) are consistently given musical accent within the bar. There is no case of such a word-accent being matched with an unmarked position within the bar and only one — 'Je me rends, l'*Amour* seul' — where a word-accent is deleted to avoid juxtaposed accents. Lully shows full recognition of countertonic accent in polysyllables: *successeur, éloignais, prévaloir, satisfaire, égorger, parricide, empoisonné, préparer, étranger, sentiments*. Similarly marked in the setting is the consistent deletion of countertonic accent where juxtaposed to an immediately preceding word-accent:[112] *grand appareil, la vengeance ordinaire, seul inhumaine, dépend d'immoler, toujours l'éloigner, étranger jouira, osera s'assurer*. The consistency of Lully's response is striking: each time, the 1001 textual rhythm is matched with a [**quaver** + two semiquavers + **quaver**] group in which accent is expressed by *both* position *and* duration.

We mark in italics ten atonic monosyllables which are accented by Lully. In seven an accented atonic monosyllable breaks a run of three atonic syllables. While our scansion finds ten such runs, Lully allows only one, finding for it the following notational solution:

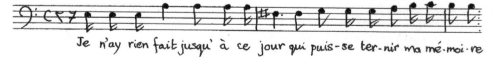

LE ROY: Je n'ay rien fait *jusqu'à ce* jour.

The first syllable of *jusqu'à* (*jus*) is placed under a quaver directly following a crotchet on *fait*. It thus loses prominence, being shorter than the crotchet. It is immediately followed by a pair of semiquavers on *à ce* which make up the final atonic quaver of the bar. Fine-tuning indeed, enough to show that Lully's notation is capable of recording up to three atonic syllables.[113]

Otherwise Lully's notation shows alternating accent. In doing so, as we have seen, it gives accentual prominence to words which are for us atonic: *Tandis, pour, par* etc. If these exceptions prompt an objection to our earlier conclusions concerning the way alternation of musical accent is maintained during the progressive diminution of note-values, remember that in these two passages, word-accent as we define it correlates with Lully's musical accentuation in 95 per cent of all instances.[114] While this is irrelevant to the form of the verse, it is strong confirmation of the composer's intention to match linguistic accent with musical accent.

The Eighteenth Century

A comparator for Lully and his views on textual rhythm is found in Jean-Philippe Rameau, whose final version of *Hippolyte et Aricie* was published in 1757.[115] Though he saw himself as an 'imitator of Lully', the originality of Rameau's music and his musical theory stirred up critical controversy. The libretto by Simon-Joseph Pellegrin is in a variety of metres; Rameau sets the recitatives with one note per syllable. While the recitative is built on irregular alternation of alexandrines and eight-syllable lines, arias and choruses show an even more varied alternation of metres. Take for example a Huntress's aria in Act IV, scene 3:

Amans, quelle est votre foiblesse?	010101010	8
Voyez l'Amour sans vous alarmer;	100100101	9
Ces mêmes traits dont il vous blesse	010101010	8
Contre nos coeurs n'osent plus s'armer.	100100101	9
Malgré ses charmes	01010	4
Les plus doux,	101	3
Bravez ses armes,	01010	4
Faites comme nous;	0100	5
Osez sans alarmes,	010010	5
Attendre ses coups;	01001	5
Si vous combattez la victoire est à vous.	01001001001	11
Vous vous plaignez qu'il a des rigueurs,	010101001	9
Et vous aimez tous les traits qu'il vous lance!	01010010010	10
C'est vous qui les rendez vainqueurs;	01010101	8
Pourquoi sans défense	010010	5
Livrer vos coeurs?	0101	4

Such freedom in syllabic count makes it impossible to see this as verse in Cornulier's sense of the term. When no one of the last six lines here has the same number of syllables, the notion of 'recurring syllabic count' is inoperative. If the rhyme-scheme suggests that the Abbé Pellegrin is convinced that he *is* writing verse, then the 'versiness' here can only be attributable to its rhythm. The musical rhythm is close to that of the thirteenth-century song we looked at earlier. Just as the rhythm of 'Au tans d'aoust' was dictated by a dactylic matrix, 1001001001, here Rameau sets the verse to strict 6/8 rhythm, that is two groups of three quavers to a bar. This gives two accented

positions per bar on the first and fourth quavers. The thirteenth-century setter was
obliged to begin his verses on an accented position; Rameau is able to vary this by
beginning his verse-line on the unaccented third quaver of the bar, thus avoiding an
initial descending foot, e.g *Amans, quelle est, Malgré ses charmes* etc.

This follows the natural tendency of oxytonic French to move in 'iambs' and 'anapests'.
The twenty-seven bars of this *air* present fifty-four accented positions. Eight are
occupied by atonic syllables or words: the rest coincide with linguistic word-accent.
This 85 per cent coincidence of word-accent with musical accent confirms that
perception of 'versiness' will arise from this correlation.[116]

To illustrate Rameau's treatment of more regular verse, here, with Rameau's
accentuation, are two extracts from *Hippolyte et Aricie*, typical of his setting of the
dramatic recitative which carries the plot forward.[117] The storyline is roughly that of
Racine's *Phèdre*, ending though with the happy reunion of the lovers. Here, in Act I,
scene 2, Hippolyte and Aricie, sundered by the hostility of their respective families,
confess their love:

	HIP.:	Princesse, quels apprêts me frapp*ent dans ce* temple.	010101 # 01*0001*	12
	AR.:	Diane préside en ces lieux;	01001001	8
		Lui consacrer mes jours, c'est suivre votre exemple.	010101 # 01*0001*	12
	HIP.:	Non, vous les immolez ces jours si précieux.	100101 # 01*0001*	12
5	AR.:	J'exécute du roi la volonté suprême;	001001 # *000101*	12
		A Thésée, à son fils, ces jours sont odieux.	001001 # 011001	12
	HIP.:	Moi, vous haïr! Quelle injustice extrême!	1001 # 100101	10
	AR.:	Je ne suis point l'objet de votre inimitié?	010101 # *000101*	12
	HIP.:	Je sens pour vous une pitié	0101*0001*	8
10		Aussi tendre que l'amour même	00100101	8
	AR.:	Quoi? Le fier Hippolyte...	101001	6
	HIP.:	Hélas! Je n'en ai que trop dit;	01001001	8
		Je ne m'en repens pas,	001001	6
		Si vous avez daigné m'entendre;	*000*10101	8
15		Mon trouble, *mes soupi*rs,[118] vos malheurs, vos appas,	010101 # 001001	12
		Tout vous annonce un coeur trop sensible et trop tendre.	100101 # 001001	12
	AR.:	Ah! que venez-vous de m'apprendre?	10101001	8
		C'en est fait; *pou*r[119] jamais mon repos est perdu.	001 # 101001001	12
		Peut-être *votre in*différence [Air in 3/4]	01010101	8
20		Tôt ou tard me l'aurait rendu;	00100101	8
		*Mais votre a*mour m'en ôte l'espérance.	0101 # 010101	10
		C'en est fait; *pou*r jamais mon repos est perdu.	001 # 001001001	12
	HIP.:	Qu'entens-je? Quel transport de mon âme s'empare?	010 # 001001001	12
	AR.:	Oubliez-vous qu'on nous sépare!	0101*0001*	8
25		Quel temple redoutable et quel affreux lien!	010101 # 100101	12

Act II, scene 2, takes place in the Underworld where the offending Theseus is judged
by Pluto:

TH.:	Inexorable roi de l'empire infernal,	010101 # 001001	12
	Digne frère et digne rival	10101001	8
	Du Dieu qui lance le tonnerre.	01010001	8
	Est-ce donc pour venger tant de monstres divers	001001 # 001001	12
5	Dont ce bras a purgé la terre,	00100101	8
	Que l'on me livre en proie aux monstres des enfers?	100101 # 010101	12
PL.:	Si tes exploits sont grands, vois quelle en est la gloire;	100101 # 100101	12
	Ton nom sur le trépas remporte la victoire;	010001 # 010001	12
	Comme nous, il est immortel;	00101001	8
10	Mais, d'une égale main puisqu'il faut qu'on dispense	100101 # 001001	12
	Et la peine et la recompense,	00100101	8
	N'attends plus de Pluton qu'un tourment éternel.	001001 # 001001	12
	D'un trop coupable ami trop fidèle complice,	100101 # 001001	12
	Tu dois partager son supplice.	01001001	8
15 TH.:	Je consens à le partager.	00100101	8
	L'amitié qui nous joint m'en fait une joie suprême;	001001 # 010101	12
	Non, de Pirithoüs tu ne peux te venger	100101 # 001001	12
	Sans me punir moi-même.	100101	6

Fifty of Pellegrin's sixty-seven verse-units (75 per cent) in these two passages show alternating accent; we find fifteen runs of three atonic syllables and two accented clitics. Rameau's reading gives eleven runs of three atonic syllables, one juxtaposed accent,[120] and two accented clitics; for him, 80 per cent of these verse-units alternate accent. In two verse-units which alternate for us, Rameau introduces an extra accent: in the first passage, l. 6, 'ces jours sont odieux', and in l. 18, 'pour jamais mon repos'. There is thus a 72 per cent coincidence between verse-units which alternate for Rameau and the 75 per cent which alternate for us.

Unlike Lully, Rameau allows runs of three atonic syllables, setting them in a characteristic way. In 'me frappent dans ce temple',[121] the atonic run is marked as it were downhill in decreasing note-values from the full crotchet on frapp:

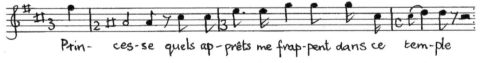

This is followed by a quaver on ent and then semiquavers on dans ce with a full crotchet on temple. An exactly parallel procedure is followed in 'suivre votre example', in 'jours si précieux', 'roi la volonté suprême', 'objet de votre inimitié', 'Je sens pour vous une pitié', 'Du Dieu qui lance le tonnerre', 'ton nom sur le trépas'. These atonic sequences are notated via contrasts of note-length: the quaver is half the initial crotchet while the following semiquaver is not only half the quaver but also perceived as the onset of the unaccented second quaver of a two-quaver group. Evidently for Rameau the run of three atonic syllables is a legitimate component of the verse-unit as opposed to being unwanted 'noise' in a context of sustained alternation.

As in Lully, alternation is managed through the matching of accent in the music with accent in the verse. In a bar of 4/4, the first and third crotchet beats will be prominent, while in a 4/4 bar of eight quavers, the head quaver of each group of two is more marked than the second. Further subdivision creates an analogous scheme in which the head of each group of two semiquavers is more marked than the second. Also as in Lully, the text here shows no violations of the accord of word-accent with marked rhythmic positions. There are three places where a normally atonic monosyllable falls in a marked position. In l. 19, in which the 4/4 recitative gives way to an Air in 3/4, there is a potentially accented 'ə': 'Peut-être *votre in*différence' places the [ə] of 'votre' under the head quaver of a two-quaver group. In ll. 5 and 8 *la* and *de* are similarly placed. Since these three anomalies occur in bars where the 4/4 rhythm has moved to 3/4, there is room for doubt over their interpretation. What happens normally is illustrated in l. 2: the sequence *Diane préside en ces lieux* is matched in 4/4 metre by *Di* under a quaver which is the second (i.e. unmarked) in the two-quaver group making up the first crotchet; *an* is under the head quaver (i.e. marked) of the second crotchet while *ə pré* fall under the two semiquavers which make up the secondary (unmarked) quaver of that crotchet. Continuing, in *...side en ces lieux*, *...side* falls on the head (marked) quaver of the final crotchet of the bar, while the atonic *en ces* are under the two semiquavers which make up the remaining secondary (unmarked) quaver. The line-final accent on *lieux* is on a crotchet at the head of the following bar in 3/4.

So far, word-accent has been mainly oxytonic. In contrast, the succeeding alexandrine shows in *Lui consacrer mes jours* a trisyllabic oxytone which we predict will bear a countertonic accent *consacrer*.[122] The note-values over this hemistich are as follows:

Di - a - ne pré-side en ces lieux hui con -sa- crer mes jours

Non, vous les im - mo - lez

Lui has an unmarked semiquaver,[123] while the syllables *consa...* are under a pair of semiquavers with *con...* under the first, giving it relative accentual prominence. The final syllable *...crer* falls under the head of a pair of quavers, the weak partner of which accompanies atonic *mes*. *Jours*, at the 'cesura', falls under a dotted quaver at the head of the following bar. This gives the 'iambic' hemistich:

> Lui consacrer mes jours.

The reality of the countertonic accent for Rameau is clear in l. 4: *Non, vous les immolez*. *Non* falls on a high-pitched, long, dotted crotchet (worth three quavers), followed by atonic *vous les* on two semiquavers making up the second (unmarked) quaver of the third crotchet of the bar. The countertonic of *immolez* is under a long dotted quaver (worth three semiquavers) while the following atonic syllable is paired with the weak remaining semiquaver. The 'cesural' accent, like all such 'cesural' and line-final accents, is matched with the following primary bar-accent.

There are further examples of polysyllabic oxytones where Rameau accents the countertonic: in l. 8, *de votre inimitié*, the countertonic *i* falls on the first of a two-quaver group; in l. 19, the accented syllables of *indifférence* are similarly matched; as are the italicised vowels in l. 21: 'Mais votre amour m'en ôte l'*espérance*'. In l. 25, the countertonic of *redoutable* falls under the first of a bar-final pair of semiquavers, and the following 'cesural' accent is at the head of the next bar.[124]

It might be objected that these matches are the mechanical outcome of the rhythmic properties of the bar, but this account does not explain the overall coincidence of musical and word-accent in Rameau. Given those same rhythmic properties, the composer might have simply ignored linguistic word-accent, setting for example l. 3 as *Lui consacrer mes jours, # c'est suivre votre exemple** (compare l. 5, 001001 #); l. 16 as *Tout vous annonce un coeur # trop sensible et trop tendre** (compare ll. 11, 101001, and 21, 010101); l. 4 as *Est-ce donc pour venger # tant de monstres divers** (compare l. 16, 100101 #); or l. 12 as *N'attends plus de Pluton # qu'un tourment éternel**, all of which are possible in terms of Rameau's rhythmic alternation without violation of accent at 'cesura' or line-end.

'Enfin Gluck vint'

In 1752, the arrival in Paris of an Italian opera company precipitated a musical and cultural crisis. Grumbling opposition to the by now old-fashioned state-subsidised French opera exploded in 'la guerre des bouffons' in which acclaim for the melodic and dramatic freshness of Italian comic opera was vigorously countered by conservative followers of Lully and Rameau. Jean-Jacques Rousseau supported the Italians, going so far as to publish an article in which he argued that the French language was inherently unsuitable for singing! After much heated debate, the italophiles prevailed and the national opera of Lully and Rameau lost its standing. Nothing appeared to take its place until a Bohemian, Christoph Willibald Gluck, brought peace to the capital by announcing that a good opera could indeed be written to French words, and soliciting Rousseau's help in creating 'a noble, sensitive and natural melody [...] suited to all nations'. His operas, beginning with *Iphigénie en Aulide* (1774) on a libretto adapted from Racine, took Paris by storm; this first success was followed by revised versions of *Orfeo* and *Alceste*, both of course with French libretti.[125]

Here are two extracts from his *Alceste* of 1776 with Gluck's accentuation.[126] In Act II, scene 3, Admète learns that his wife, Alceste, is to die on his behalf:

Admète:	Tu m'aimes, je t'adore, *et tu rem*plis mon **coeur**	010*0*01 #010101	12
	d*e*s plus vives alarmes.	1010010	6
Alceste:	Ah! cher épou**x**, pardonne *à ma dou*leur;	1001 # 010101	10
	Je n'ai **pu** te cacher mes larmes.	001001010	8
Admète:	Et qui les **fait** couler?	010101	6
Alceste:	On t'a **dit** à quel prix les **Dieux** ont con**senti**	001001 # 010101	12
	De calmer leur colère et t'**ont** rendu des **jours**	001001 # 010101	12
	Si **tendrement** chéris.	010101	6
Admète:	Connais-**tu** cet ami, victime volontaire?	001001 # 0101010	12
Alceste:	Il n'**aurait** pu survivre *à ton tré*pas.	0101 # 010101	10
Admète:	Nomme-**moi** ce héros!	001001	6
Alceste:	Ne m'**interroge** pas!	010101	6
Admète:	*Réponds-moi!*[127]		
Alceste:	Je ne puis!		
Admète:	T*u* ne peux?		
Alceste:	Quel martyre!	010*0*01 # 1010010	12

Admète:	Explique-toi!		
Alceste:	Tout mon **coeur** se déchire.	0101 # 0010010	10
Admète:	Alceste!		
Alceste:	Je frémis!	010101	6
Admète:	Alceste, au **nom** des Dieux, au **nom** *de cet a*mour	010101 # 010101	12
	Si **tendre** si fidèle, qui fait **tout** mon bonheur;	010101 # 001001	12
	qui **comble** tous mes voeux.	010101	6
	Romps ce silence odieux,	100101	6
	dissipe *ma fray*eur mortelle!	010101010	8
Alceste:	Mon cher Admète, hélas!	010101	6
Admète:	Tu me glaces d'effroi;	001001	6
	Parle! Quel est celui *dont la pi*tié cruelle	100101 # 1001010	12
	L'entraîne à s'immoler pour moi?	01010101	8
Alceste:	**Peut-tu** le demander?	010101	6
Admète:	O silence funeste!	0010010	6
	Parle enfin, je l'exige!	1011010	6
Alceste:	Eh! Quelle **autre** qu'Alceste	1010010	6
	devait mourir pour toi?	010101	6

This charged and intimate exchange between husband and wife is written in mixed metres which convey its broken and ejaculatory nature. Though intermittent rhyme and the absence of recurrent syllabic count make it impossible to see this as verse in Cornulier's sense, the writing moves in units which rely on the relation between syntax and rhythm for the recognition of recurrence. We find here thirty-four such units of six syllables of which ten include monosyllables for us atonic but accented by Gluck.[128] While twenty-eight of Du Rollet's forty verse-units (70 per cent) show alternating accent, Gluck's setting alternates regularly in 92 per cent.

Gluck avoids the six atonic runs here by accenting clitics; however, oxytonic and countertonic accent are consistently matched with alternating musical accent, with the single exception of *Réponds-moi*. Accent internal to the phrase is musically marked: *vives alarmes*; *tendrement chéris*; *victime volontaire*; *silence odieux*; *frayeur mortelle*; *silence funeste*. The marking is consistently managed by alternating note-values.

Et t'ont ren-du des jours si ten-dre-ment ché-ris

Romps ce si-lence o-di-eux

'[*tendrement*] [*chéris*]' = [**dotted quaver** + semiquaver + **head quaver**] + [weak quaver + **crotchet**] and '[*silence odieux*]' = [semiquaver + **quaver**] + [semiquaver + semiquaver + **crotchet**].[129]

Bearing in mind Gluck's reputation with his Parisian audiences as a proponent of French as an operatic language, it may be that his accenting of clitics is more than just a move to ensure alternation. Although the accented personal pronoun in *et tu remplis mon coeur* may be for the sake of alternation, that in *Parle enfin, je l'exige!* is not. Together with the other accented personal pronouns and possessives, we may have here a hint of the way Gluck and his audiences spoke their French. More thorough exploration of these operatic scores might in future cast welcome light on the accentual prosody of modern French.

Meanwhile in Act III, scene 3, the heroine, in search of Admète in the Underworld, encounters the infernal powers:

Grands Dieux! Soutenez mon courage![130]	010010010	8
Avançons! Je frémis! Consommons notre ouvrage,	001001 # 0010010	12
Ah! Quel séjour affreux!	100101	6
Tous mes sens sont saisis d'*une te*rreur soudaine:	001001 # 1001010	12
Tout de la Mort *dans ces ho*rribles lieux	1001 # 010101	10
Reconnaît la loi souveraine.	001010010	8
Ces arbres desséchés, ces rochers menaçants,	010101 # 001001	12
La terre dépouillée aride et sans verdure,	010101 # 0101010	12
Le bruit lugubre et sourd de l'onde *qui mu*rmure,	010101 # 01010	12
Des oiseaux de la nuit les funèbres accents:	101001 # 001001	12
Cet antre, *cet au*tel, ces spectres effrayants,	01*0*001 # 010101	12
Cette pâle clarté *dont la lu*mière obscure	001001 # 1001010	12
Répand sur ces objets *une nou*velle horreur,	01*0*001 # 100101	12
Tout de mon coeur glacé redouble *la te*rreur,	100101 # 010101	12
Dieux! Que mon entreprise est affreuse et cruelle!	100101 # 0010010	12
La terre se refuse à mes pas chancelants,	01*0*001 # 001001	12
*Et mes ge*noux tremblants s'affaissent sous le poids	100101 # 01*0*001	12
*De ma fra*yeur mortel,	010101	6
Ah! l'amour me redonne une force nouvelle!	101001 # 0010010	12
A l'autel de la Mort lui-même *me con*duit,	001001 # 010101	12
Et des antres profonds de l'éternelle nuit	001001 # 010101	12
J'entends sa voix qui m'appelle.	01010010	7

This passage shows the following adjective + noun phrases: *Grands Dieux!*; *séjour affreux*; *terreur soudaine*; *horribles lieux*; *loi souveraine*; *arbres dessèchés*; *rochers menaçants*; *bruit lugubre*; *funèbres accents*; *spectres effrayants*; *pâle clarté*; *lumière obscure*; *nouvelle horreur*; *coeur glacé*; *pas chancelants*; *genoux tremblants*; *frayeur mortel*; *force nouvelle*; *antres profonds*; *éternelle nuit.*[131]

Gluck follows then without exception our model for word-and-phrase accent. To take a few examples: *Grands Dieux!* has a single accent since *grand* has a relatively high frequency of occurrence and low informational value: the composer places it under the unaccented final crotchet of a 4/4 bar. *Loi souveraine* consists of two low-frequency words with high informational value, both of which are thus accented. The countertonic of *souveraine* is in juxtaposition to the informationally prior accent on *loi* and is deleted. Gluck gives *loi* accentual prominence by placing it on a quaver among unmarked semiquavers. The most telling touch here is *éternelle nuit* with its emphatically preposed adjective. The adjective's countertonic accent is doubly determined, standing under a dotted quaver at the head of the bar. Gluck confirms countertonic accent in polysyllables: *dessechés*; *dépouillée*; *effrayants*; *entreprise*; *éternelle*; and also further instances of the deletion of countertonic accent when preceded by an oxytonic word-accent: *Je frémis! Consommons* [...]; *pas chancelants.*[132]

Du Rollet's text contains thirty-nine verse-units of which twelve show a run of three atonic syllables and twenty-seven (69 per cent) have alternating accent. In his setting, Gluck follows Lully's example in that all but three of these atonic runs are reduced to regular alternation by the accenting of a clitic. This raises an interesting question: do these interventions of Lully and Gluck reflect the way verse was read by contemporaries? Was a presumption of alternating accent built into reading aloud? While our reading of Du Rollet's text finds 69 per cent of his verse-units alternating regularly, in Gluck's reading, this figure rises to 92 per cent.

High-frequency elements are accented by the composer nine times: *d'une*; *ces*; *qui*; *dont*; *une*; *la*; *et*; *ma*; *me*. With the exception of *me*, Gluck has gone out of his way to throw most of these into relief. *D'une*, *ces*, *qui*, *la* and *ma* are all given prominence by the lengthening of the note-value, while *dont* is placed at the head of its bar. These accented clitics do ensure alternation, but the fact that they owe their prominence to lengthening as well as to accented position strongly suggests that these are *accents d'insistance* which reflect the spoken French of the composer. The juxtaposition of accents is subject to linguistic constraint, but the affective emphasis of these clitics takes us into the domain of *parole*, that is of living speech.

For the surviving runs of three atonic syllables, Gluck finds notation that avoids accent. Take these three examples:

La terr[*e se re*]fuse à mes pas chancelants

[*Et mes ge*]noux tremblants s'affaiss[*ent sous le*] poids.

The first syllable in each of these bracketed atonic runs is sung to the unaccented second of a pair of quavers while the remaining atonic syllables fall under a pair of weak semiquavers which follow a quaver rest, twice at the bar-end. This solution parallels Rameau's rendering of atonic runs by the progressive diminution of note-values.[133] Throughout this passage correlation between the patterning of word/phrase accent and the alternation of musical accent-positions is sustained by the progressive subdivision of crotchets into quavers and quavers into semiquavers; this gives strong confirmation from an eighteenth-century French-speaking composer of the accuracy of our accentual scansion and of the predictive power of our model.

Overall, of the seventy-nine verse-units in these two passages, fifty-five alternate in accordance with our model (70 per cent). This scansion is matched by that of the composer with the single exception of *Réponds-moi* in the first passage.

The Nineteenth Century

Gluck's fusion of the Italian and French styles inspired the vocal music of the outstanding French composer of the following generation.[134] Hector Berlioz's epic recreation of Virgil's *Aeneid* in *Les Troyens à Carthage* has been described as 'the Romantic consummation of the French opera tradition in the line of descent from Rameau and Gluck'.[135] Here are two excerpts from *Les Troyens,* libretto and music both by Berlioz.[136] In the first, from Act I, scene 4, a festival is in progress and Didon, queen of Carthage, is in recitative with Anna, her sister. Berlioz's accentuation:

Didon:	Les chants joyeux, l'aspect *de cette* noble fête[137]	0101 # 010101010	12
	Ont fait rentrer la paix en mon coeur agité.	010101 # 001001	12
	Je respire, ma soeur, oui, ma joie est parfaite,	001001 # 1010010	12
	Je retrouve le calme *et la sérénité.*	001001 # 010101	12
Anna:	Reine d'un jeune empire	1001010	6
	Qui chaque jour s'élève florissant	010101 # 010101	12
	Reine adorée *et que le* monde admire,	1001 # 0101010	10
	Quelle crainte avait pu vous troubler un instant?	101001 # 001001	12
Didon:	Une étrange tristesse,	0010010	6
	Sans cause, tu le sais, vient parfois m'accabler.	010001 # 101001	12
	Mes efforts restent vains contre *cette fa*iblesse,	001001 # 1010010	12
	Je sens transir mon sein qu'un ennui vague oppresse,[138]	010101 # 0101010	12
	*Et mon vi*sage en feu sous mes larmes brûler...	100101 # 001001	12
Anna:	Vous aimerez, ma soeur...	010101	6
Didon:	Non, toute ardeur nouvelle	1001010	6
	Est interdit à mon coeur sans retour.	0101 # 001001	10
Anna:	Vous aimerez, ma soeur...	010101	6
Didon:	Non, la veuve fidèle	1011010	6
	Doit éteindre son âme et détester l'amour.	101001 # 010101	12
Anna:	Didon, vous êtes reine, et trop jeune et trop belle	010101 # 0010010	12
	Pour ne plus obéir *à cette* douce loi;	010101 # 010101	12
	Carthage veut un roi...	010101	6
Didon:	Puissent mon peuple et les dieux me maudire	1001 # 0010010	10
	*Si je qui*ttais jamais cette anneau consacré!	100101 # 001001	12
Anna:	Un tel serment fait naître le sourire	0101 # 0101010	10
	De la belle Vénus;	001001	6
	*Sur le li*vre sacré, les dieux refus*ent de l'*inscrire.	101001 # 01010010	12

The following passage from Act IV, scene 1, gives us Didon, abandoned by Enée, still with Berlioz's accentuation:

Didon:	Va, ma soeur, l'implorer.[139]	101101	6
	De mon âme abbatue,	0010010	6
	L'orgueil a fui. Va! ce départ me tue	0101 # 1001010	10
	Et je le vois s*e* préparer.	10010101	8
Anna:	Hélas! Moi seule fus coupable	010101010	8
	En vous encourageant à former d'autres noeuds.	010101 # 010101	12
	Peut-on lutter contre les dieux?	01011001	8
	Son départ est inévitable	001001010	8
	*E*t pourtant il vous aime.	1010010	6
Didon:	Il m'aime! Non! Non! son coeur est glacé.	0101 # 101001	10
	Ah! je connais l'amour, et si Jupiter même	100101 # 0100110	12
	M'êut défendu d'aimer, mon amour insensé	010101 # 001001	12
	De Jupiter braverait l'anathème!	0101 # 0010010	10
	Mais, va ma soeur, allez, Narbal, *le* supplier	0101 # 01011001	12
	Pour qu'il m'accorde encore	0101010	6
	Quelques jours seulement.	101001	6
	Humblement je l'implore;	10010010	6
	Ce que j'ai fait pour lui pourra-t-il oublier?	010101 # 101001	12
	Et repoussera-t-il cette instance suprême?	001001 # 0010010	12
	De vous, sage Narbal, de toi, ma soeur, qu'il aime?	011001 # 0101010	12

These passages give us the rare opportunity of seeing a composer setting his own words. In the first, Berlioz avoids all but one of the eleven runs of three atonic syllables predicted by our model by accenting high-frequency clitics/monosyllables.[140] To take two extreme examples:

> Les chants joyeux, l'aspect *de cette* noble fête;
> *Et mon vi*sage en feu sous mes larmes brûler.

To avoid atonic (*de cette*) and (*Et mon vi*), 'cette' and '*E*t' are emphatically placed at the head of the bar, at a primary accent-position. In:

> Je retrouve le calme et la sérénité,

the article is again at the primary bar-accent and this time substantially lengthened, its note-value being five quavers. This vehemence is in sharp contrast to his predecessors' handling of what our theory describes as atonic runs. Lully's response to Quinault's text is, with one exception, to interrupt such runs with an accented clitic. But this accent is never primary, arising rather through dotting or simple alternation among quavers or semiquavers within the bar. For his part, Rameau finds a notation which maintains the atonic character of these runs, again well within the bar.

Query: is Berlioz the composer a different animal from Berlioz the poet? When he put together the libretto for his opera, did he perceive as such what we describe as 'runs of three atonic syllables'? Or does the prominence of accented clitics in his melody reflect an accentuation already there in Berlioz's libretto as he recited it? The accentuation we hear in the music may arise from the semantic values of his verse. If so, this expressive exaggeration would take us from the domain of *langue* to that of *parole*.

In the remaining seven examples, the musical accenting of clitics is less extreme, being expressed through secondary bar-accent, a dotted quaver, or the head-element of a three-quaver triplet. The only run of three atonic syllables to survive this treatment is:

Sans caus[*e, tu le*] sais [...].

This fragment is under notation compressed in a way not found elsewhere: [caus] is marked by a crotchet at the head of the bar and the following [ə] by a brief semiquaver, the atonic [*tu le*] lying under the second and third of a group of triplet quavers, the first of which quavers is replaced by a quaver rest. The effect is for the voice to slide over the atonic syllables with their shortened unaccented quavers. This intimate aside from Didon to her sister has the expressive urgency of colloquial speech.

As compared with those of Lully and Rameau, Gluck's accented clitics achieved, as we have seen, extra relief through lengthening of note-values, and in one case by coincidence with a primary bar-accent. Berlioz's more emphatic treatment of atonic runs can be seen as a continuation and development of that of Gluck. As in Gluck, adjective + noun phrases here show without exception accent within the phrase: *chants joyeux*; *noble fête*; *coeur agité*; *jeune empire*; *Reine adorée*; *étrange tristesse*; *ennui vague*; *ardeur nouvelle*; *veuve fidèle*; *douce loi*; *anneau consacré*; *livre sacré*; and in the second passage: *âme abbatue*; *amour insensé*; *instance suprême*; *sage Narbal*, which show a 100 per cent correlation of word- and musical accent.

As before, the countertonic of polysyllables always attracts musical accent: *sérénité*; *florissant*; *aimerez*; *détester*; *implorer*; *encourageant*; *inévitable*; *défendu*; *Jupiter*; *seulement*; *Humblement*. Note also the deletion of the countertonic in juxtaposition to an oxytonic accent in the preceding syllable: *coeur agité*; *Reine adorée*; *parfois m'accabler*; *anneau consacré*; *âme abbatue*; *amour insensé*; and, two for the price of one, *De Jupiter braverait l'anathème*.

Of the forty-six verse-units of the first passage, thirty-four (74 per cent) satisfy our criteria for alternation; in the thirty verse-units of the second passage, the figure is twenty-five (83 per cent). Thus, overall, fifty-nine of seventy-two verse-units conform (78 per cent). Our scansions are ratified by the composer with the exception of *Non, la veuve fidèle* in the first passage. Of the seventy-two verse-units here sixty-eight alternate regularly on the composer's evidence.

Music and Lyric in the Nineteenth Century

Our hypothetico-deductive method will again enable us to make predictions to be tested on the expert witness, the francophone composer. As before, our pre-emptive scansion of a verse-text will be compared to the scansion implicit in the musical setting. Fauré's setting of Leconte de Lisle's ode 'La Rose' is in triple rhythm (3/4) with a melody moving mostly in short notes.[141] Here are two versions of the the text, the first marked in accord with our theory (with respect to group-final accent, paroxytonic/oxytonic and countertonic word-accent) and the second with Fauré's note-values, showing accent through relative duration and marked accent-position within the bar:

A	B
Je dirai la Rose aux plis gracieux.	Je dirai la Rose aux plis gracieux.
La Rose est le souffle embaumé des Dieux,	La Rose est le souffle embaumé des Dieux,
Le plus cher souci des Muses divines,	Le plus cher souci des Muses divines,
Je dirai ta gloire, ô charmes des yeux,	Je dirai ta gloire ô charmes des yeux,
Ô fleur de kypris, reine *des col*lines!	Ô fleur de kypris, reine des collines!
Tu t'épanouis *entre les beaux* doigts	Tu t'épanouis entre les beaux doigts
de l'Aube écartant les ombres moroses;	de l'Aube écartant les ombres moroses;
L'air bleu devient rose et roses les bois;	L'air bleu devient rose et roses les bois;
La bouche et les seins des vierges sont roses!	La bouche et les seins des vierges sont roses!
Heureuse la vierge aux bras arrondis	Heureuse la vierge aux bras arrondis
Qui *dans les hal*liers humides te cueille![142]	Qui dans les halliers humides te cueille!
Heureux le front jeune où tu resplendis!	Heureux le front jeune où tu resplendis!
Heureuse la coupe où nage ta feuille!	Heureuse la coupe où nage ta feuille!
Ruisselante encor du flot paternel,	Ruisselante encor du flot paternel,
Quand de la mer bleue Aphrodite éclose	Quand *de la mer* bleue Aphrodite éclose
Etincela nue aux clartés du ciel,	Etincela nue aux clartés du ciel,
La terre jalouse enfanta la rose;	La terre jalouse enfanta la rose;
Et Olympe entier, d'amour transporté,	Et Olympe entier, d'amour transporté,
Salua la fleur avec la Beauté!	Salua la fleur av*ec la* Beauté!

These decasyllables, unlike those of the twelfth-century *Saint Alexis*, do not have the 4 + 6 division; here the mid-line ('cesural') accent falls on the fifth syllable. In his five-syllable hemistich, the poet has three options for alternating accent: 01001, 00101 and 10101. In version A, twenty-two hemistichs follow the pattern 01001 and eleven follow 00101 with five hemistichs not alternating consistently. Of these, three have runs of three atonic syllables and two have juxtaposed accents.

In the first four lines, both versions A and B show an identical regular alternation of accent, their rhythm being as follows:

Je dir**ai** la Ro # se aux plis graci**eux**.	00101 # 01001
La **Rose** est le **sou** # ffle embaum**é** des D**ieux**,	01001 # 00101
Le plus cher souc**i** # des **Muses** div**ines**,	00101 # 01001
Je dir**ai** ta glo**i** # re, ô charmes des y**eux**.	00101 # 01001

The alternation is achieved through that of long and short notes, the long carrying the accent, either dotted quavers or quavers, the short being semiquavers.

In the next four lines Fauré accents the countertonic of *épanouis* and evidently maintains alternation by accenting the clitic *les*. The other two are in both versions accentually regular and identical:

De l'**Au**be écart**ant** # les **om**bres mor**oses** [...]	01001 # 01001
La **bou**che et les s**eins** # des v**ie**rges sont r**oses**	01001 # 01001

For accents within the line the composer uses both position and duration. The cesural accents on *écartant* and *seins* are matched with dotted quavers ending groups of simple quavers; each dotted quaver is also at the lowest pitch in its group.

In the following quatrain, the music overrides our scansion, in the interest of alternation. Our scansion leaves a string of three atonic syllables in:

> Qu**i** *dans les ha*lliers [...].

Fauré 'repairs' this is by accenting *dans*, giving regular alternation:

Qu**i** dans les hall**ie**rs hum**ides** te cue**ille**!	01001 # 01001

What looks like an *accent d'insistance* on *tu resplendis*, falls on the first of triplet quavers at the head of the bar. The first and last lines of this quatrain alternate regularly in both versions:

Heur**euse** la v**ie**rge aux bras arr**ondis**	01001 # 01001
Heur**euse** la c**ou**pe où n**age** ta fe**uille**!	01001 # 01001

The final quatrain begins with an alternating line:

Ruissel**ante** enc**or** du fl**ot** pat**ernel**.	00101 # 01001

Our accent on the following *Quand* implies this punctuation:

> Qu**and**, de la mer bl**eue**, Aphrod**ite** écl**ose**.

Quand takes a group-accent since it adjoins a syntactical boundary. In Fauré's version *Aphrodite* has a countertonic accent marked by a full quaver at the head of the bar, and that of *étincela* is marked within the bar by a dotted quaver. The next two lines alternate accent throughout:

La terre jalouse enfanta la rose;	01001 # 00101
Et Olympe entier, d'amour transporté.	00101 # 01001

This throws into sharp relief an irregularly accented final line in Fauré's version:

Salua la fleur avec la Beauté!	10101 # 01101

By our criteria the only non-linguistic accent would be the *accent d'insistance* on *la*.

Overall, Fauré offers confirmation, firstly, of accent on high-priority lexical items *within* the phrase: *plis gracieux, souffle, embaumé, cher souci, charmes des yeux, fleur de kypris, reine des collines, ombres moroses, roses les bois, bras arrondis, nage ta feuille, flot paternel, terre jalouse, enfanta la rose, Olympe entier* and *d'amour transporté*; and secondly, of countertonic accent on polysyllables: *t'épanouis, Aphrodite' étincela* and *Salua*. As for the negative evidence: the musical text respects word-accent as we have defined it. There are *no* examples of musical accent contradicting word-accent, as in *embaumé*, épanouis*, Ecartant*, Heureux*, Etincela** and *enfanta**. There are three cases in which normally atonic clitics are subject to what looks like an *accent d'insistance*: *les beaux doigts*; *tu resplendis*; *avec la Beauté*. Only this last clitic has been accented through lengthening. These emphases confirm the composer's attention to the alternation of accent, which he observes in sixteen out of the nineteen lines. With only one run of three atonic syllables, Fauré's setting alternates accent in 97 per cent of the verse-units.

Of the ode's thirty-eight verse-units thirty-two (84 per cent) alternate accent according to our model. The composer's musical accents are matched by our predictive scansion in all thirty-two of these hemistichs, and his musical alternation overall rises to 97 per cent, with a single run of atonic syllables. Twice where our scansion has runs of atonic syllables, Fauré 'normalises' by restoring alternation:

A.	Tu t'épanouis *entre les beaux*[143] doigts
B.	Tu t'épanouis entre les beaux doigts

and:

A.	Qui *dans les hal*liers humides te cueille!
B.	Qui dans les halliers humides te cueille!

Fauré never places a musical accent on the atonic syllable of a polysyllable, for example:

La Rose est le souffle *embaumé* des Dieux*	01001 # 01001

or:

Quand de la mer bleue *Aphrodite* éclose.*	10001 # 01001

If syllabic count were the only criterion for verse structure, as most critics claim, composers would have been free to distribute musical accents to any vowel of a polysyllable.[144]

Leconte de Lisle's choice of the 5 + 5 division of the decasyllable makes it impossible to obtain strict alternation of accent within the hemistich by repeating a given rhythmic unit. The arithmetic is straightforward: the requirement for a 'cesural' accent at position 5 means that neither repeated feet of two (01) nor of three syllables (001, 100) will go exactly into a five-syllable unit as they would into the normal six-syllable one. In the

5 + 5 of our ode above, 00101 and 01001 dominate.[145] The only possible arrangement repeating a single foot is the 'trochaic' hemistich, 10101, whose initial accent and non-oxytonic character run against the prosodic norm;[146] this solution is avoided by the poet. As we have seen, the canonical status of the 6 + 6 verse-line may be largely due to its divisibility by both three and two, making the combinations 010101 and 001001 readily available.

It is certain that in the modern French period, the odd-syllable verse-unit is a minority sport. In my old copy of the *Oxford Book of French Verse*, out of 156 texts from the seventeenth century to the nineteenth, only seven are written in odd-syllable verse-units. An exception to this tendency is Paul Verlaine, who experimented extensively with lines of five, seven and nine syllables. One of the nine-syllable lines in his 'Art poétique' describes the *vers impair* as 'plus soluble dans l'air', reflecting perhaps the varied movement of such metres as compared with those which allow the repetition of a single rhythmic unit (01 or 001).[147]

Here is another song by Fauré, a setting of Verlaine's 'En sourdine' which is written in seven-syllable lines. Version A shows our scansion of the text and version B the layout of the composer's musical accents:

A	B
Calmes *dans le* demi-jour	Calmes dans le demi-jour
Que les branches hautes font,	Que les branches hautes font,
Pénétrons bien notre amour	*Pénétrons* bien notre amour
4 *De ce si*lence profond.	*De ce si*lence profond.
Mêlons nos âmes, nos coeurs	Mêlons nos âmes, nos coeurs
Et nos sens extasiés,	Et nos sens extasiés,
Parmi les vagues langueurs	Parmi les vagues langueurs
8 Des pins et des arbousiers.	Des pins et des arbousiers.
Ferme tes yeux à demi,	Ferme tes yeux à demi,
Croise tes bras sur ton sein,	Croise tes bras sur ton sein,
Et de ton coeur endormi	Et de ton coeur endormi
12 Chasse à jamais tout dessein.	Chasse à jamais tout dessein.
Laissons-nous persuader	Laissons-nous persuader
Au souffle berceur et doux	Au souffle berceur et doux
Qui vient, à tes pieds, rider	Qui vient, à tes pieds, rider
16 Les ondes du gazon roux.	Les ondes du gazon roux.
Et quand, solennel, le soir,	Et quand, solennel, le soir,
Des chênes noirs tombera,	Des chênes noirs tombera,
Voix *de notre* désespoir,	Voix de notre désespoir,
20 Le rossignol chantera.	Le rossignol chantera.

How does the seven-syllable verse-unit differ from the five-syllable one? Unlike the six-syllable unit, neither can be composed of a repeated rhythmic unit, so that the former will share the latter's mixed rhythmic character, its 'irregularity'. Here are the possible alternating combinations for the seven-syllable line (called the heptasyllable): 0101001, 0100101, 0010101, 1010101 and 1001001. Options increase with the syllabic count, so the straitjacket which cramped the five-syllable hemistich is loosened here. The composite rhythmic structure of both these metres distinguishes them from the six-syllable unit with its possibility of a repeated oxytonic foot (01, 001).

Version A shows regular alternation in fifteen of twenty verse-units (75 per cent), of which fifteen Fauré ratifies thirteen (65 per cent). In Fauré's setting overall seventeen verse-units alternate (85 per cent). In l. 1B he accents *dans*; in 3B, *Pénétrons* has an unaccented countertonic; 7B accents *parmi*; in 11B, the initial *Et* falls on the primary bar-accent and in 12B *tout* has an *accent d'insistance* given it by a dotted crotchet on the secondary bar-accent. Line 20B shows a juxtaposed accent on the countertonic of *chantera*, emphatically sung with a jump of a perfect fourth to a primary bar-accent whose minim, tied to a dotted crotchet, is sustained for seven of the eight quavers of the bar. In version B, these stylistic gestures stand out so firmly because of the background regularity.

Our scansion finds five runs of three atonic syllables, in l. A1 Ca**lm**es *dans le* demi-jour', A4 *De ce si*lence, A7 *Parmi les* vagues lang**ueu**rs, A11 *Et de ton* **coeur** and A19 **Voi**x *de notre* désespoir; while the composer's scansion puts in l. B3 *Pénétrons* and B4 *De ce si*lence, restoring alternation to our ll. A11 and A19 by accenting an atonic monosyllable. Fauré is quite at home with line-initial accent; it takes prominence in ll. 1, 9, 10, 12, 13 and 19, placed five times out of six on the primary bar-accent. This setting confirms our prediction on the accenting of high-priority lexical items within the phrase. These particularly affect noun phrases carrying affective weight: *branches hautes*; *silence profond*; *sens extasiés*; *vagues langueurs*; *coeur endormi*; *souffle berceur*; *chênes noirs*. Again we see confirmed countertonic accent on polysyllables: *arbousiers*, *persuader* and *chantera*.

Why is the *vers impair* so infrequent in modern French? The current generally accepted view is that recurring syllabic count alone defines French verse, the upper limit being set at eight syllables by Cornulier's 'loi des 8'. If this were so, there is no reason why verses of five and seven syllables should not occur just as frequently and naturally as those of six and eight. Yet they remain in a stubborn minority. Cornulier puts the same question 'Existe-t-il un poème tout en 7–5?' — but does not answer it.[148] In a later book, he finds a way of avoiding the problem of the scarcity of odd-syllable lines and hemistichs.[149]

The evidence before us in this music example is utterly clear. The arithmetic of the odd-syllable verse-unit renders impossible rhythmic solutions found everywhere in even-syllable ones, thus reducing the poet's combinatory options. If we compare Leconte de Lisle's ode with the following randomly selected passage of alexandrines the same picture emerges just as clearly:

Alors ne pense pas que j'épouse un visage:	010101 # 001001
Je règle mes désirs suivant mon intérêt.	010001 # 010101
Si Doris me voulait, toute laide qu'elle est,	001001 # 001001
Je l'estimerais plus qu'Aminte et qu'Hippolyte;	001001 # 010101
Son revenu chez moi tiendrait lieu de mérite:	010101 # 001001
C'est comme il faut aimer. L'abondance des biens	000101 # 001001
Pour l'amour conjugal a de puissants liens:	001001 # 000101
La beauté, les attraits, l'esprit, la bonne mine,	001001 # 010101
Echauffent bien le coeur, mais non pas la cuisine;	010101 # 001001
Et l'hymen qui succède à ces folles amours,	001001 # 001001
Après quelques douceurs, a bien des mauvais jours.	001001 # 010101

Une amitié si longue est fort mal assurée	010101 # 001001
Dessus des fondements de si peu de durée.	010101 # 001001
L'argent dans le ménage a certaine splendeur	01*0001* # 001001
Qui donne un teint d'éclat à la même laideur.	010101 # 001001
Et tu ne peux trouver de si douces caresses	*000*101 # 001001
Dont le go**û**t **du**re autant que celui des richesses.	00**11**01 # 001001

In these seventeen alexandrines from Corneille's *Mélite* (I, 1), each of the thirty-four hemistichs has one syllable more than the hemistich in Leconte de Lisle's ode. Five have runs of three atonic syllables and one juxtaposed accent. Eighty-two per cent of this random sample of classical alexandrines show regular alternating accent. In the six-syllable unit, alternation of accent can take four possible forms, 001001, 010101, 100101 and 101001; in these hemistichs, of those with alternation ten have 010101 and eighteen 001001 while none show either 100101 or 101001. The absence of these demonstrates this dramatic poet's tendency to write accent-alternating hemistichs which repeat the same rhythmic unit (01 or 001).[150]

Why should the five-syllable hemistich have played such a minor role in the history of the French decasyllable? The answer cannot lie in syllabic count, since the official doctrine states that any number below nine will do. It can only be found by considering the rhythmic character of the French verse-line. Firstly, odd syllable-count obliges the poet to vary the rhythmic units which make up his or her hemistich, i.e. the said hemistich cannot be composed by repeating a given rhythmic unit (01 or 001). Secondly, if we accept that the rhythm of the verse-unit is constitutive of its metre — that is that it has a measuring function which enables us to recognise the verse as verse — then the poet is further challenged by the fewer combinatory possibilities in the five-syllable unit, 01001, 00101 or 10101. For Cornulier rhythm is irrelevant to the metrical structure, so the constraints imposed by the *vers impair* are invisible to him.

Here is another setting of a Verlaine text by Fauré, the famous song 'Green'. It is written in alexandrines and 3/4 rhythm, which gives a rapidly moving vocal line. Indeed the score displays bars filled with semiquavers for the voice over repeated quaver chords in the accompaniment. On the basis of our operatic studies so far, we might expect to find a strong correlation between word-accent and musical accent. Here is the text, first with the scansion according to our model:

A

	Voi**ci** des fruits, des f**leu**rs, des **feu**illes et des **bran**ches	010101 # 01*00*010
	Et **puis** voi**ci** mon **coeu**r qui ne bat que pour **vous**.	010101 # 001001
	Ne le dé**chi**rez pas avec vos **deux** mains **blan**ches	100101 # 0101010
4	Et qu'à vos **yeu**x si **beau**x l'**hum**ble pré**sent** soit **doux**.	*000*101 # 100101
	J'a**rrive** **tout** couvert encore de ro**sée**	010*1*01 # 01*00*010
	Que le **vent** du matin **vient** glacer à mon **front**.	001001 # 101001
	Souffrez que ma fatigue un ins**tant** repo**sée**	01*0001* # 0010010
8	**Rê**ve des **chers** ins**tants** qui la dé**lasse**ront.	100101 # *000*101
	Sur votre **jeu**ne **sein** laissez rouler ma **tête**	000101 # 0101010
	Toute sonore encor de vos derniers **bai**sers,	100101 # *000*101
	Laisse-**la** s'apaiser de la **bonne** tem**pête**	101001 # 0010010
12	Et que je **dorme** un **peu** puisque **vous** repo**sez**.[151]	010101 # 001001

And here it is with Fauré's accentuation:

B

	Voici des fruits, des fleurs, des feuilles *et des* branches[152]	010101 # 0101010
	Et puis voici mon coeur qui ne bat que pour vous.	010101 # 001001
	Ne le déchirez pas avec vos deux mains blanches[153]	010101 # 0101010
4	*Et qu'à vos* yeux si beaux l'humble présent soit doux.	010101 # 100101
	J'arrive *tout* couvert encore *de ro*sée	010001 # 0101010
	Que le vent du matin vient glacer à mon front,	101001 # 101001
	Souffrez *que ma fa*tigue un instant reposée	010101 # 0010010
8	Rêve des chers instants *qui la dé*lasseront.	100101 # 010101
	Sur votre jeune sein laissez rouler ma tête	010101 # 0110010
	Toute sonore encor *de vos de*rniers baisers,	100101 # 010101
	Laissez-la s'apaiser de la bonne tempête	101001 # 0010010
12	Et que je dorme un peu puisque vous reposez.	010101 # 001001

Fauré's setting takes us back to the question raised by our discussion of Lully's setting of Quinault: is accentual alternation maintained during the progressive diminution of note-values? We discovered in our review of *Alceste* decisive negative proof that syllables or words that our model defines as accentuable never fell on the second or fourth semiquavers of a group composing a crotchet. The same principle proves to be crucial for this setting of 'Green': the 3/4 pulse is realised in the piano part through a persistent pattern of six quavers to a bar throughout, while the voice part is written in semiquavers for much of the time. The result is a marking for accent of the first semiquaver of each pair of semiquavers which coincide with the quaver pulse, although each case must be decided on its contextual merits.[154] On the basis of Lully's text, we expect that accentuable syllables of Verlaine's text will fall either on the first quaver of a group of two or on the first semiquaver of a group of two.[155]

The accents of the first line fall, uncontroversially, on nouns, where syntactic and high-priority lexical accent coincide. Whereas accents on *fruits* and *fleurs* are carried by dotted quavers, those on *feuilles* and *et* derive from rhythmic alternation in a group of four semiquavers, the accent on *feuilles* being overdetermined by a crescendo hairpin. In the second line *puis*, at a minor syntactical boundary, coincides with the primary bar-accent (the semiquaver concerned is marked *forte* by Fauré) while the breathgroup-final *coeur* and the intraphrasal *bat* have prominent quavers in initial position on the second and third crotchets of the bar. This bar confirms our general idea about the matching of linguistic and metrical accent in that it shows alternation in a group of four semiquavers and also in two groups of quaver + two semiquavers. In a group of four semiquavers, the metrical accent falls on 1 and 3, whereas the quaver + two semiquavers unit is perceived as two quavers, i.e., 100. Had his only criterion been the placing of group-final accent, nothing would have prevented Fauré writing a rhythm which gave us:

(a)   [...] qui ne bat que pour vous*   010101

instead of:

(b)   [...] qui ne bat que pour vous.   001001

In this hemistich there is no group-final accent until *vous*, to which of course Fauré gives the primary bar-accent. Like Lully, he is working on assumptions that correspond closely to our model for the role of accent in French verse. If he were not, then accent-distributions which our model defines as unlawful would proliferate in settings such as example (a)* given above.

Line 4 provides a valuable clue to the composer's perception of juxtaposed accent.

Our model defines both *beaux* and *l'humble* as accented and clearly the composer agrees. While *beaux*, at the 'cesura', is on a syntactic boundary, *l'humble* is intraphrasal. Fauré accents *beaux* with a full crotchet after a semiquaver, while *l'humble* takes a quaver followed by two semiquavers. In this 3/4 bar, all three accented syllables in [...] *yeux si beaux l'humble pré* [...] coincide with the onset of one of the three whole crotchets. Once again, Fauré overdetermines the accent on *l'humble* by placing it at the beginning of a diminuendo.

In the second strophe, *J'arrive tout couvert* with its atonic run emerges from a progressive diminution of note-values. The accent on *arrive* is of both position and duration, and is marked by a whole crotchet on the second beat of the 3/4 bar. The atonic value of the [ə] is due to the shorter quaver note-value which marks it in the context of the longer (accented) preceding crotchet.[156] Similarly the semiquaver of the following *tout* is perceived as atonic following the quaver on the [ə]. By contrast, the *de* in the following *cou[vert encore de] rosée* is marked as tonic taking the third in a group of four semiquavers with their alternating rhythm. In *Que le vent du matin, Que* is at the onset of the last whole crotchet of the bar *and* under a dotted quaver which follows a quaver rest: it is thus perceived as accented by both position and relative length. In *Souffrez que ma fatigue un instant reposée*, the first two accents derive from rhythmic alternation among semiquavers while those on the 'cesural' *fatigue* and on *instant* are marked rather by relative length, under quavers in a bar otherwise consisting entirely of semiquavers. In *Rêve des chers instants qui la délasseront,* the first and strongest accent is a crotchet at the head of the bar. While each of the following four syllables is under a quaver, the first, *ve*, though on a quaver at the head of the second crotchet, is perceived as atonic by contrast with the preceding crotchet; the quaver on *des* is also atonic as the second of a group of two quavers. *Chers* is accented by position as the first of the final group of two quavers. The accent on 'cesural' *instants* is marked by a dotted crotchet at the bar-head, while the *la* in *qui la dé* is under the head of the last two-quaver group of the bar. The countertonic of *délasseront* is under a dotted quaver at the bar-head, a strong index of the countertonic's accentual status. The last vowel is under a long minim tied over into the otherwise empty following bar.

In the third strophe, *Sur* votre *jeune sein* begins on a weak off-beat quaver followed by dotted quavers on the full vowels of *votre* and *jeune* and *sein*, the last at a bar-head. We might then expect continued 'iambic' rhythm in *laissez rouler ma tête* but Fauré has other ideas: the accent on *laissez* is given a full crotchet while the three syllables of *rouler ma* fall under an expressive triplet of quavers with group-accent on the first, giving the juxtaposed accent *laissez rouler.*

Then in *toute sonore* the accented vowels take quavers while between them the atonic [ə] and *o* are under shorter semiquavers. The accent on *vos* is marked by alternation *and* relative pitch, rising to F, a diminished seventh above the A flat on *de*. In contrast to previous *laissez rouler*, the following 'La*issez-la*' shows the normal leftward displacement of accent in such syntax. The dominant 'dactylic' rhythm in *Laissez [la s'apai][ser # de la] [bonne tem]pête* is realised by the composer in a bar made up of three groups of quaver triplets, each group having an accented first quaver. The cross-rhythm created by the three-against-two between voice and accompaniment cannot fail to impress the listener as a musical metaphor for *s'apaiser*.

The *que* of the last line is under a quaver at the head of the bar, very likely an *accent d'insistance* expressing a fervent wish.

Of the thirty-six polysyllables here, only one, ***rouler***, shows an aberrant accent, the tonic syllables of all the others being given by Fauré's notation. His emphatic bar-head accent on the countertonic of *délasseront* marks an expressive reversion to *parole*. Also of the fifteen high-priority monosyllables here, fourteen are clearly marked for accent. Accent within the phrase is confirmed by Fauré's notation on *humble present, instant repose, chers instants, jeune sein, derniers baisers* and *bonne tempête*. Though our model finds eight runs of three atonic syllables here, the only one to be observed by Fauré is *J'arrive tout couvert*, 010001. This is set as it were downhill, in decreasing note-values — crotchet, quaver, semiquaver: after the accented crotchet on *riv*, each note, being shorter than its predecessor, is perceived as atonic. Though this procedure, which we have noted in the recitative of both Rameau and Gluck, is clearly known to Fauré, he nevertheless opts to break other atonic runs with *et, à, de, ma, la, votre* and *vos*. None of these is marked for accent by length, correlating only with the alternating pulse in strings of either quavers or semiquavers. We clearly have a hierarchy of accents: accent in alternating pulse can be stepped up by the introduction of the downhill gradations. Maybe atonic runs in verse serve to give further prominence to the tonic syllables which frame them.

With our predicted alternation in sixteen of twenty-four verse-units (67 per cent), Fauré agrees in fifteen (63 per cent), while twenty-two out of twenty-four of his verse-units alternate regularly (92 per cent).

To round off this survey, here is 'Les Ingénus', another poem by Verlaine, also in alexandrines but this time set by Claude Debussy.[157] Our scansion first:

A

Les hauts talons luttaient # avec les longues jupes,	010101 # 0101010
En sorte que, selon le terrain et le vent,	0101 # 01001001
Parfois luisaient les bas de jambes, trop souvent	0101 # 01010101
4 Interceptés! — *et nous ai*mions ce jeu de dupes.	0101 # *000*101010

Parfois aussi le dard d'un insecte jaloux	010101 # 001001
Inquiétait le col des bell*es sous les* branches,	010101 # 01*00*010
Et c'étaient des éclairs soudains de nuques blanches	001001 # 0101010
8 *Et ce ré*gal comblait nos jeunes yeux de fous.	*000*101 # 010101

Le soir tombait, un soir équivoque d'automne:	0101 # 010010010
Les bell*es, se pen*dant rêveuses à nos bras,	010*001* # 010*001*
Dirent alors des mots si spécieux, tout bas,	100101 # 010101
12 Que notre âme depuis ce temps tremble et s'étonne.	00100101 # 10010

B

Les hauts talons luttaient # avec les longues jupes,	010101 # 010101
En sorte que, selon le t*err*ain *e*t le vent,	0101 # 01010101
Parfois luisaient les bas de jambes, trop souvent	0101 # 01010101
4 Interceptés! — *et nous ai*mions ce jeu de dupes.	0101 # *000*10101

Parfois aussi le dard d'un insecte jaloux	010101 # 001001
Inquiétait le col des belles s*ou*s les branches,	010101 # 010101
Et c'étaient des éclairs soudains de nuques blanches	001001 # 010101
8 *Et ce ré*gal comblait nos jeunes yeux de fous.	*000*101 # 010101

*Le soir tom*bait, un soir équivoque d'automne:	1001 # 01001001
Les belles, se pendant rêveuses à nos bras,	010*001* # 010*001*
Dirent alors des mots si spécieux, tout bas,	100101 # 010101
12 Que notre âme depuis ce temps tremble et s'étonne.	00101001 # 1001

This song is of especial interest to us since its accompaniment moves in a sustained alternation of accented and unaccented positions. It is in triple time, three quavers to the bar 'doucement soutenu' according to the composer's instruction. The tempo, 'modéré', allows prominence to the quaver beats, each of which is subdivided into semiquavers, giving a trochaic feel to the accompaniment.[158] Each group of two semiquavers in the piano part presents most often a falling interval, giving further accentual prominence to the first note in each of the three pairs of semiquavers. This extra weight allows the composer to use the unaccented second semiquaver to begin a phrase from the text on an unaccented note.

The entry of the voice on *Les hauts talons* follows the alternating pattern with *Les* falling on the unaccented second semiquaver of the second quaver-group in the bar, thus allowing *hauts* to coincide with the accented head semiquaver of the final quaver-group. The accented syllable of *talons* then falls on the primary bar-accent at the head of the first quaver group. Closely following this scheme, the accented syllable of *luttaient* coincides with the head semiquaver of the second quaver group and *avec* with that of the third. The accented syllable of *longues* falls at the head of the next bar and the tonic syllable of *jupes* is given relief by its matching whole quaver, whose enhanced duration marks the canonical verse-accent at the line-end. In *En sorte que*, the two syllables of *sortǝ* are matched with the first semiquaver group of the bar, producing an alternation of tonic/atonic. Debussy observes the syntactic accent on *que*, by placing it under the following whole quaver. After matching the tonic syllable of *selon* with a bar-initial semiquaver, he overrides the linguistic word-accent in *terrain* by maintaining the existing 'iambic' rhythm, giving *terrain*, which irons out the poet's alternation of 01 and 001.

The pulse being set by the semiquaver-pairs in the accompaniment is 'trochaic', but the composer creates 'iambic' counter-alternation by consistently matching atonic syllables with unaccented semiquaver positions, and word-accent with accented semiquavers. For example, in:

Les **hau**ts talons lu**tt**aient avec les longues jupes,

atonic *Les* coincides with an unaccented position, i.e. the first semiquaver of the series [semiquaver rest + semiquaver + two-semiquaver group], while *hauts* is matched with the accented first element of the two-semiquaver group. The rest of the line continues the alternation of atonic and tonic syllables with matching unaccented and accented rhythmic positions. Elsewhere alternation is weakened in ' — *et nous aimions*', where the run of atonic syllables is translated by three full quavers, which iron out any rhythmic contrast. This notation is repeated later in *Et ce régal* and *Le soir tombait*.[159]

Debussy uses a range of notational possibilities to follow the accentual patterning of Verlaine's verse. The *Parfois aussi* which begins the second strophe sets up the alternation 0101. But in the following bar, the poet evokes the threatening insect by a sudden switch to 'anapestic rhythm': *le dard d'un insecte jaloux*. Debussy achieves this 01001001 thus:

with 'semiquaver + "full quaver" + semiquaver + semiquaver + triplet-semiquavers + full quaver': the accent on *dard* is reinforced by contrasted duration, a full quaver preceded by an atonic semiquaver and followed by two semiquavers. The tonic syllable of *insecte* coincides with the accented first of the semiquaver triplets at the bar-head, while that of *jaloux* is marked by the contrast between a full quaver and the immediately preceding semiquaver triplets. The text's reversion to 'iambic' rhythm is followed in the melody. In l. 7, the melody manages the 'anapestic' 001001 of *Et c'étaient des éclairs* firstly by a contrast of duration, sandwiching the full quaver on *c'étaient* between pairs of semiquavers, while the tonic syllable of *éclairs* coincides with a primary bar-accent. In the rest of the line, the 'iambic' rhythm of the text is mirrored by the alternation of accented and unaccented semiquavers, with the line-end accent on *blanches* resting on a dotted crotchet at the head of a bar. In l. 8, the three atonic syllables of *Et ce régal* are accompanied by undifferentiated full quavers, as in *et nous aimions*. The following bar illustrates the range of rhythmic possibilities open to the composer's notation. While the musical accent on the tonic syllable of *régal* is confirmed by its position at the head of the bar, that on *comblait* results from the contrast between the full quaver which marks it and the pair of semiquavers which precedes it. In *nos jeunes yeux de fous*, the 'iambic' measure culminates in a strong melodic accent on the final *fous*, the result of a jump of a fifth.

Debussy begins the third strophe by setting the first three syllables of *Le soir tombait* to a bar of three full quavers, a device which we saw in *et nous aimions* (l. 4) and *et ce régal* (l. 8). The effect is to flatten any sense of alternation until we get to the bar-accent on *tombait*. Then everything changes, with more rapidly moving short notes over *un soir équivoque d'automne*. Once again the composer finds the notational means to follow the 'anapestic' movement of the line. He marks the anomalous cesural pause at the fourth syllable with a rest on the third semiquaver beat, the accent on the second *soir* falling at the head of a triplet of semiquavers. This leads to a second triplet, at the head of which falls the accent on *équivoque*, coinciding with the bar-accent. The accent on *automne* is enhanced by the contrast of its quaver with the rapidly moving semiquaver triplets which precede it. The two runs of atonic syllables in l. 10 are boldly overridden in the melody by a recurring 'iambic' pulse which accents *se* and *à*. In l. 11, the initial accent on *Dirent* coincides with the head of a semiquaver triplet group, whose two unaccented members (100) create the melodic counterpart of the 'dactylic' unit which interrupts the otherwise 'iambic' flow of l. 11 where verse and melody agree. Though the culminating l. 12, marked 'Lent' by the composer, begins with an 'anapest' (*Que notre âme*), he carefully marks *depuis* with an accent-sign. This cuts across the normal downhill notation which would have given two 'anapests' (*Que notre âme depuis**). This 'dactylic' intrusion makes *depuis ce temps* feel like an intercalated phrase delaying the completion of the syntax. This completion comes with *tremble* on the second quaver of the next bar, also marked with an accent-sign by Debussy. This levelling of the rhythm in slow whole quavers at the same pitch on *temps tremble* is the composer's response to the juxtaposed accents in the verse-text, the accentually neutral quavers bringing a sense of suspended movement after the freer articulation of the 'anapest'.

The first quatrain shows one incompatibility between versions A and B where Debussy imposes an 'iambic' rhythm on *selon le terrain et le vent* (l. 2). In the second quatrain, Debussy again maintains the 'iambic' pulse in l. 6 by placing *sous* on the first element of a semiquaver group. This is the only anomaly in the quatrain. In the third quatrain, l. 9, Debussy suppresses the word-accent on *soir*, and in l. 10 maintains the 'iambic' pulse by placing *se* and *à* in accented positions. In version A, there are four runs of three atonic syllables while version B shows two. Both versions show a single instance of juxtaposed accents (*temps # tremble*) where they are on either side of a likely 8 + 4 'cesura'.

To conclude, Debussy's reading of the accentual structure of this text affirms, as did Fauré: firstly, the linguistic status of the countertonic accent on oxytonic trisyllables (*Interceptés!, Inquiétait, spécieux*); and secondly, the accenting of high-priority lexical terms *within* the phrase in noun phrases (*hauts talons, longues jupes, insecte jaloux, éclairs soudains, nuques blanches, jeunes yeux*), verb phrases (*Parfois luisaient, régal comblait*) and others such as *les bas de jambes*, *jeu de dupes*, *le col des belles* and *des mots si spécieux*. In a single instance the composer displaces word-accent in defiance of the oxytonic norm, (*terrain*), and elsewhere places a clitic (*se*) and two prepositions (*à* and *sous*) in musically-accented positions. Overall, our scansion finds that nineteen of twenty-four verse-units alternate (80 per cent). The composer's scansion ratifies our alternating verse-units in seventeen instances (71 per cent).

An Overview

Our defence and illustration of alternating accent in French verse has located its origins in Late Latin verse and has presented evidence for its continued operation from Old French in the *Séquence de Sainte Eulalie* and the *Chanson de Roland* down to modern French in Racine's *Phèdre* and the lyrics of Verlaine. While word-accent in French seems to be a linguistic fact, alternation of accent in verse is evidently not; this is clearly shown by comparison of word-accent distribution in verse with that in prose and recorded speech. We must conclude that this alternation is a cultural practice, a tradition, 'the disciplined imitation by each writer of his predecessors' linguistic usage in the formulation of verse'.[160] Our laborious discovery of this practice is then a discovery of something completely obvious, at least to the poets we have so far cited. Critics to whom it is not obvious and for whom accent in French verse is *aléatoire*, may need to look more closely at a verse-tradition which for them is devoid of living rhythm.

Historical data on the evolution of French word-accent from Late Latin squared with our finding of a 69 per cent predominance of alternating accent in the verse-units of the *Séquence de Sainte Eulalie*, and 91 per cent for the eleventh-century *Alexis*. In a synchronic perspective, analyses of word-over-syllable distribution in the *Chanson de Roland* and in Racine's *Phèdre* revealed persistent constraints on the ordering of words within the hemistich. These constraints as a recurrent property of French verse decisively confirmed the presence of accent within the phrase as well as within the word.

The evidence from music, initially problematic, eventually proved critical. Although the unmeasured musical notation of the earliest manuscripts of the trouvère repertoire give no indication of the relation between musical and linguistic accent, advances in notational technique in the later thirteenth century enabled composers (or copyists) to indicate musical rhythm by the alternation of long and short notes in fixed modal patterns, 01010101, 1010101 and so forth. This notation revealed the correlation, or not, of musical accent with word-accent as we have defined it. However, the musical rhythmisations of these songs may be the contribution of the copyist. In Thibaut de Champagne's 'De chanter ne me puis tenir', we saw that the copyist's version of the notation showed alternation of accent in 16 per cent of thirty-two verse-units, there being frequent mismatches of word-accent and musical accent. The 'iambic' or 'trochaic' straitjacket imposed on the melody excluded the possibility of 'dactyls', 'anapests' or runs of three atonic syllables. The poetic text scanned according to our criteria gave an 81 per cent predominance of alternating accent.

As the flexibility of musical notation increased in the fourteenth century, we find growing disagreement between word-accent and musical accent. The lack of coincidence shown in 'De chanter ne me puis' is compounded by Machaut's blithe disregard for the word-accent which structures his own verse. The striking contradiction between the undeniable reality of word-accent and the indifference to it shown by certain composers, is in part resolved by another fact: French verse written from the trouvères to Ronsard shows alternation of accent whatever the interpretation placed upon it by the composers, from Machaut in the fourteenth century to the *vers mesurés* of Mauduit in the sixteenth. Our scansion of one of Machaut's poems showed an 88 per cent predominance of alternating accent.

Ronsard arranged for a large number of his sonnets to be sung to the same melody, but we know that each of these sonnets, just like the strophes of the trouvères, was rhythmically unique. Here are the first quatrains of two of his sonnets with our scansions:

Bien que l'esprit humain s'enfle par la doctrine	100101 # 100001
De Platon, qui le chante influxion des cieux,	001001 # 010101
Si est-ce sans le corps qui sera ocieux,	010101 # 001001
Et auroit beau vanter sa celeste origine.	010101 # 001001
Bienheureux fut le jour, où mon âme sujette	001001 # 001001
Rendit obeyssance à ta douce rigueur,	010101 # 001001
Quand d'un trait de ton oeil tu me perças le coeur,	001001 # 000101
Qui ne veut endurer qu'un autre luy en jette.[161]	001001 # 010101

Assuming that the first of these was set to a melody faithful to its accentual structure, to sing the second to the same musical rhythm would again make hay of word-accent:

Bienheureux **fut** le **jour, où** mon âme sujette	100101 # 100001
Rendit **obeyssance** à **ta** douce **rigueur,**	001001 # 010101
Quand **d'un** trait de ton **oeil** tu me perças le **coeur,**	010101 # 001001
Qui **ne** veut **endurer** qu'un autre luy en jette.	010101 # 001001

In this version the thematic *âme* is unaccented, as is the low-frequency verb *rendit*; *obeyssance* has an accented atonic syllable, and [ə] (*douce*, *autre*) and clitics (*ta, un, de*) gain accents. Even if we assume that rhythm in this verse has no informational or aesthetic function, it is difficult to imagine that Ronsard the poet would have been happy with this state of affairs.

Whatever the difficulties troubling the relation between verse and music before 1650, our comparison of word-over-syllable structure in the twelfth-century *Chanson de Roland* and the *Phèdre* of Racine had proved decisive. Clearly the constraints on word-accent distribution operating in the former were still present in the latter. This necessarily implied the continuing presence of word-accent in a modern French text (and of a tradition exploiting it), since if there were no such word-accent in Racine's French there could be no constraints on it. *Either* word-accent was continuously present in French from 1100 to 1700, *or* it vanished sometime in Middle French only to re-appear in modern French.

Who could argue for this latter option? Rather the monotonous declamation which so exasperated Lote must be cultural rather than language-based in origin. Whatever treatment it received at the the hands of composers or *comédiens*, the verse that we have so far scanned shows a predominance of alternating accentual structure. Racine was writing French verse with alternating accent while learned opinion was repeatedly claiming that it was made of nothing but syllabic count and rhyme.[162]

In our review of music in modern French, we found composers confirming the reality of alternating accent. For Machaut in the fourteenth century and Costeley in the sixteenth, the words were expected to fit the melody; for Lully and his successors the art of operatic recitative became that of wedding musical accent to the accentual patterning of verse.[163] In Lully's music we found a refined system of alternating accented positions which was unaffected by the progressive diminution of note-values from crotchet to semiquaver. Together with alternation of contrasting note-values, this technique made possible the notation of patterned alternating accent and of runs of three atonic syllables. The composer confirms our alternating scansions of Quinault's libretto in all but one instance.

The Abbé Pellegrin's libretto for Rameau's *Hippolyte et Aricie* exploits an even freer mixture of metres than that found in Quinault. Our scansions of extracts from Pellegrin's recitative are closely matched by Rameau, in whose setting 80 per cent of his verse-units have regularly alternating accent. Certain lyric interludes show no recognisable syllabic norm, freely combining lines of eleven, ten, nine, eight, five and four syllables. Though these, by Cornulier's criteria, cannot be called 'verse', the example we looked at showed an 85 per cent correlation of musical and linguistic accent. If there is here perception of 'versiness', such a correlation must be essential to it.

The historical importance of Gluck was that he restored French confidence in the singability of the language. He follows Lully in that word- and musical accent consistently agree: oxytonic and countertonic accent are always placed under alternating musical accent while accent internal to the phrase is always marked: *vives alarmes*, *silence funeste*, *tendrement chéris*. This latter is managed by alternating note-values: [**tendrement**] [chéris] = [**dotted quaver** + semiquaver + **head quaver**] + [weak quaver + **crotchet**]. There are signs too of increased insistence on the expressive accenting of atonic monosyllables: Gluck emphasises them either by placing them under bar-accent or by lengthening the note-value. His flexible notation follows that of Rameau in avoiding accent in runs of atonic syllables by downhill diminution of note-values.[164] While overall 70 per cent of Du Rollet's verse-units conform to our accentual predictions, Gluck's reading makes 92 per cent of them alternate regularly.

Berlioz wrote and set his own verse in *Les Troyens*. Our extracts show a predominance of alexandrines and six-syllable verse-units, which permit the repetition of both 01 and 001 within the unit. Where our model identifies twelve runs of three atonic syllables in seventy-six verse-units, Berlioz restores alternation in all but one by the accenting of a clitic. This procedure contrasts with Gluck's acknowledgement of four such runs in his notation, and even more visibly with Rameau's whose notation in recitative permits twelve runs of atonic syllables. We see here a preference for more sustained alternation in dramatic verse. Berlioz also has a (romantic?) penchant for juxtaposed accent of which we find seven in seventy-six verse-units as compared with only one in Gluck and none in Rameau. Berlioz's setting amply vindicates our finding of alternation in his libretto.

In contrast to the medieval lyric with its single melody repeated from strophe to strophe, settings of the nineteenth-century lyric are all through-composed. The composer thus acknowledges the accentual uniqueness of the individual strophe and finds a notational language to do it justice. In Fauré's setting of Leconte de Lisle's decasyllabic ode 'La Rose', all the verse-units we identify as alternating are confirmed by the composer. In Verlaine's seven-syllable 'En sourdine', our scansion predicts regular alternation in fifteen out of twenty verse-units, thirteen of which are ratified by Fauré. He is quite at home with the poet's line-initial accent; there are six examples, five placed under a primary bar-accent. In his setting of the twenty-four verse-units of 'Green', Fauré confirms our scansion of fourteen of the fifteen verse-units we identify as alternating and disagrees with us in nine. This disparity is due to Fauré's restoring the alternation to seven of eight runs of atonic syllables, by accenting a clitic. His scansion thus finds that twenty-two out of the twenty-four verse-units alternate regularly (92 per cent). Since our disagreement concerns Fauré's treatment of atonic runs, the witness of Berlioz may be relevant. We remember that in our extracts from *Les Troyens* only one of eleven atonic runs survives in Berlioz's notation: in the others alternation is restored insistently. We have no way of knowing what Verlaine thought about this: we do know that the notational means was available to Fauré for recording these runs, had he wanted to. If Berlioz the composer was of one mind with Berlioz the poet, it may be that alternation via an accented clitic was not unusual in the declamation of his contemporaries.

With Debussy, we have a song written in the the twentieth century. His handling of Verlaine's alexandrines in 'Les Ingénus' (1904) differs however from Fauré's in his treatment of atonic runs. Our scansion shows five such runs, of which the composer 'normalises' three. He does this by accenting *sous*, *se* and *à*, while for the other two he finds novel notational forms.

Here is a digest of the numbers illustrating the constitutive role of alternating accent in the history of French verse: for the early period, the first column shows the percentage of verse-units of a given text which alternate by our criteria, and the second shows the degree of correlation between linguistic accent and musical accent in the text:

Séquence de Sainte Eulalie	69%	–
Vie de Saint Alexis	87%	–
Siège de Barbastre	88%	–
Gace Brulé	87%	41%
Thibaut de Champagne	81%	16%
'Au tens d'aoust'	70%	70%
Fournival	87%	56%
Guillaume de Machaut	88%	16%

And here are the numbers for modern French: the first column shows the number of verse-units in a given text which show alternation of accent; the second column shows the number of verse-units in which our scansion and that of the composer coincide; column three gives the total of alternating verse-units according to the composer:

Quinault-Lully	83%	81%	98%
Pellegrin-Rameau	75%	72%	80%
Rollet-Gluck	70%	69%	92%
Berlioz	78%	76%	95%
Leconte-Fauré	84%	84%	97%
Verlaine-Fauré 1	75%	65%	85%
Verlaine-Fauré 2	67%	63%	92%
Verlaine-Debussy	80%	71%	80%

These figures confirm what this chapter has argued: that from the eleventh to the nineteenth centuries, French verse was defined by a structured relation between syllable count and word-accent. We have progressively illustrated what it is about French verse that distinguishes it from its Romance congeners and which still gives rise to disagreement among commentators.

Language-structure obviously decides what resources are available to the poet. Where word-accent is concerned, French is either oxytonic (*ami*) or, until recently, paroxytonic (*amiə*). Italian and Spanish are dominantly paroxytonic (e.g. Italian *amore*, Spanish *alegre*), but also proparoxytonic (e.g. Italian *horribile*, Spanish *fàbrica*) and oxytonic (e.g. Italian *felicità*, *canto*, Spanish *corazón*, *murió*). This variety evidently creates opportunities and imposes constraints. Whereas syllabification for French or Italian verse is straightforward, in Spanish, 'poetic licences' affecting syllabification combine with word-accentual variety to decide accent-distribution within verse-units.

For the French relation between syllable and accent, the approximate isosyllabism and irregular accentuation of the ninth-century *Séquence de Sainte Eulalie* gave way by the eleventh century to the accentually ordered decasyllable of the *Vie de Saint Alexis*; syllabically regular also, save for its 'epic cesura'. The twelfth-century Spanish *Cantar de mio Cid* was still undecided on both counts:

Mio Cid Rruy Díaz # por Burgos entrava,	5 + 6	2 + 2 accents
en su conpaña # sessaenta pendones.	5 + 8	1 + 2
Exienlo ver # mugieres e varones,	4 + 7	2 + 2
burgeses e burgesas # por las finiestras son,	7 + 6	2 + 2
plorando de los ojos, # tant avién el dolor;	7 + 6	2 + 2
de la sus bocas # todos dizían una rrazón:	5 + 9	1 + 3
'Dios, qué buen vassallo # si oviesse buen señor'.[165]	6 + 6	4 + 3

The metre of this verse puzzles scholars uncertain whether it is syllabic or accentual.[166] Its origin lies in the collision between Late Latin metres and the accented Germanic speech of fifth-century Visigothic invaders; but, unlike French, it did not evolve into a syllabically and accentually stable form. The decasyllable of the *arte mayor* in the 1400s still showed a variable syllabic count. In the sixteenth century, literary Spanish adopted the Italian eleven-syllable line, the *endecasíllabo*; this became the main metre for narrative verse and the literary lyric. Spanish contemporaries of Verlaine and Baudelaire still show some syllabic irregularity together with marked irregularity of accent-distribution within the line. Here are three stanzas of a poem by Gustavo Bécquer (1836–70) in *endecasíllabos*:

Olas gigantes que os rompéis bramando[167]	12	4 accents
en las playas desiertas y remotas,	11	3

envuel*to entre la* sábana *de es*pumas,	11	3
¡llevad*me con vo*sotras!	7	2
Ráf*agas de huracá*án, que *arreba*táis	11	3
de **al**to bos*que las mar*chitas hojas,[168]	11	4
arrastrado en el cielo torbellino,	11	3
¡llevad*me con vo*sotras!	7	2
Nub*es de tempes*tad que **ro**mpe el rayo	11	4
y en fuego ornáis *las despren*didas orlas,	12	4
arrebata*do entre la* niebla obscura,	11	3
¡llevad*me con vo*sotras![169]	7	2

As in Italian, paroxytonic word-accent in Spanish results in atonic hemistich-final and line-final syllables, the Spanish alexandrine counting fourteen syllables. There is no alternation of accent. Though accent is clearly prominent in Bécquer's poem, the abundance of atonic runs makes it difficult to envisage it being subject to the kind of formal ordering we have found in French verse.

Italian verse, which 'incorporated the heritage of Latin verse in the most direct and straightforward way', settled like French into isosyllabic forms, with the pre-eminent 4 + 7 *endecasillabo*[170] corresponding to the French 4 + 6 decasyllable.[171] Whereas in the sixteenth century, the second hemistich of the *endecasillabo* becomes 'firmly iambic',[172] both hemistichs of the French decasyllable and alexandrine vary accentually in the ordered way that we have already noted in texts from the *Vie de Saint Alexis* down to Leconte de Lisle.[173] French verse then shows neither the Italian fixed syllabo-tonic 'iambics' nor the unstable syllabification and free accentuation of the Spanish verse-line. Unlike its siblings, its precociously settled isosyllabism maintained the alternation of accent emergent in Late Latin.

So far inferences from our hypothesis have proved productive and we can proceed to its second phase: if alternation of accent is a formal reality in French verse, then it will be available to the poet as potential stylistic raw material. Until now, our French verse-texts have served only as punchbags for metrical analysis with no consideration of their meaning. In our second chapter sanity returns with an exploration of the *poetry* of verse. A review of representative texts from the twelfth to the twentieth centuries may further help our understanding of the mysterious charm of poetry in French. Readers of Baudelaire know at least two things about his verse: one is that it is syllabically regular, and the other is that it is magical. It may be that we will learn more about the craft of this verse. We can hope also to discover the origin of its magic.

Notes to Chapter 1

1. The oldest surviving manuscript calls the language '*romana* lingua' (my emphasis). Paris, Bibliothèque nationale de France, MS fonds latin 9768, fol. 12[v].
2. Mildred Pope, *From Latin to Modern French* (Manchester: Manchester University Press, 1966), p. 11.
3. Ibid., p. 15.
4. Ibid., p. 217, for further comment and illustration.
5. Chrétien de Troyes, *Erec et Enide*, ed. by Mario Roques (Paris: Champion, 1978), p. 121.
6. Again, unlike French, Italian word-accent can occupy different positions: *távola, compito, semplice*. This accent can be phonemic, distinguishing such pairs as *mando* [I send] and *mandò*

[he sent]. The French word-final 'ə', as in 'machine' which corresponded to the final vowel in 'macchina', though having till recently syllabic value in verse, has disappeared almost entirely from standard spoken French.

7. Tonic accents in bold, countertonics in italic. Evidence for the reality of countertonic word-accent in modern French is given in Pensom, 'Accent et syllabe dans les vers français', pp. 340–42.

8. See Pope, *From Latin to Modern French*, p. 112.

9. As do modern French trisyllabic verb-forms, *lèverai* [l□vəʀe], *mènerait* [m□nəʀe], in contrast to disyllabic forms: infinitive [lɔve], imperfect [fɔze] etc. The spontaneous tendency to maintain alternation appears also for example in *garde-fou* [gaʀdəfu].

10. Pope, *From Latin to Modern French*, p. 102.

11. Virgil, *Aeneid*, 4, 151–56, in *Aeneidos, liber quartus*, ed. by H. M. Stephenson (Oxford: Clarendon Press, 1924); Latin accentuation in bold. For help in the scansion of classical Latin verse see G. B Nussbaum, *Vergil's Metre: A Practical Guide for Reading Latin Hexameter Poetry* (London: Bristol Classical Press, 2001). Since the semantic content of this and other texts cited in this chapter is not relevant to our discussion, translation is unnecessary. Because in our following chapter the argument turns to the relation between accent-patterning and meaning, translations will be provided for texts before 1600.

12. Thus, though the syllable-count varies from line to line, the number of 'morae' is fixed at 24, since the dactylic hexameter is made up six times '– ˇ ˇ': that is, six times four 'morae'.

13. Gregory of Tours, *History of the Franks*, VI, 46. For Milo, author of the *Vita Amandi*, in 20,000 dactylic hexameters, see Anna Lisa Taylor, *Epic Lives and Monasticism in the Middle Ages: 800–1050* (Cambridge: Cambridge University Press, 2013).

14. Suetonius, *The Twelve Caesars*, trans. by Robert Graves (Harmondsworth: Penguin, 1960), p. 31. Note here the coincidence between the metrical accent and the Latin word-accent on the penultimate vowel of polysyllables.

15. Venantius Fortunatus, 'Vexilla regis', cited by Ernst Robert Curtius, *European Literature and the Latin Middle Ages*, trans. by Willard Trask (Princeton, NJ: Princeton University Press, 2013), p. 389. Accented syllables bold, misplaced accents in bold italics.

16. Henceforth, the quotation marks in 'iambic', 'anapestic' etc. distinguish the accentual terms from the quantitative ones, which are without quotation marks.

17. The exceptions are *Fulget crucis* and *Tendens manus*. Classical Latin tonic word-accent fell on the penultimate or antepenultimate syllable of polysyllables, disyllabic words being accented on the first. A secondary accent emphasised the initial syllable of words which contained one or more pre-tonic syllables: '*o*r-na-men-tum' (see D. S. Raven, *Latin Metre* (London: Bristol Classical Press), p. 32).

18. Michel Burger, *Recherches sur la structure et l'origine des vers romans* (Geneva: Droz, 1957), pp. 82–89.

19. See W. von Wartburg, *Evolution et structure de la langue française* (Bern: Francke, 1946), p. 43.

20. Burger, *Recherches sur la structure et l'origine des vers romans*, pp. 82–85.

21. Accented syllables in bold.

22. Of Burger's Types 5–25, which cover 104 verses, he finds that six Types (covering forty-nine verses) show runs of atonic syllables and eight show juxtaposed accents (that is in twelve verses only). This leaves seven Types (covering forty-four verses) in which accent alternates in the way I propose. This means that by Burger's own accentual criteria, 86 per cent of Ambrose's octosyllables meet our criteria for rule-governed alternating accent. Since Burger does not acknowledge countertonic Latin word-accent, it is further possible that the head-count for strings of atonic syllables should be reduced.

23. The first of these quatrains is by Coelius Sedulius (d. *c.* 450 CE), the second is anonymous from the fifth century; both are cited without attribution by Raven, *Latin Metre*, p. 38. Accented syllables in bold.

24. Cited in Burger, *Recherches sur la structure et l'origine de vers romans*, p. 91; boundaries between feet added.

25. Cited in Burger, *Recherches sur la structure et l'origine des vers romans*, pp. 109–10. Note alternation of accent by our criteria.

26. Text given in 'Poetae Latini Aevi Carolini', in *Monumenta Germaniae Historia*, cited by Burger, *Recherches sur la structure et l'origine des vers romans*, pp. 110–11. This is an extract from a conflation of two incomplete manuscript texts.

27. 'Qui voudra voir # un Dieu qui me surmonte | Comme il m'assault, # comme il se rend vainqueur, | Comme il r'enflamme # et r'englace mon cuœur, | Comme il reçoit # un honneur de ma honte' (Pierre de Ronsard, *Poèmes*, ed. by André Barbier (Oxford: Blackwell, 1946), p. 58).

28. Paul Valéry, 'Le Cimetière marin', in *The Penguin Book of French Verse 4: The Twentieth Century*, ed. by Anthony Hartley (Harmondsworth: Penguin, 1959), p. 64.

29. Georges Lote, *Histoire du vers français*, 4 vols (Paris: Boivin et Cie; Aix-en-Provence: Université de Provence, 1949–88), I, 50.

30. Quoted without provenance in Lote, *Histoire du vers français*, I, 98. Question: how do we know that these line-final syllables are accented? Answer: the Latin rhyme-syllable is tonic but never word-final or line-final. In our hymn, it *remains* tonic but is both word- and line-final. Elsewhere, musical notation in manuscripts from French scriptoria show that in fully syllabic pronunciation, Latin words were accented oxytonically, e.g. Aeterne rerum conditor. Though no longer iambic, this conserves alternation of accent. See Gasparov, *A History of European Versification*, p. 127. Similarly, the tenth-century octosyllabic *Passion du Christ* shows oxytonic 'e' assonance between Latin and French: '"crucifige, crucifige!" | crident Pilat trestuit ensems' (Karl Bartsch, *Chrestomathie de l'ancien français*, 10th edn (Leipzig: Vogel, 1910), p. 8). The oxytonic rhyme in our hymn also suggests the presence of oxytonic accent within the Latin verse-line e.g. *propheticis oraculis; miscuit substantiae*.

31. This line-final accent is of course incompatible with a quantitative reading.

32. Though the manuscript containing this text (now Munich, Bayerische Staatsbibliothek, MS Clm 4660) is thought to have been largely copied around 1230, some of its contents date from as early as the tenth century. The text is given in Helen Waddell, *Medieval Latin Lyrics* (Harmondsworth: Penguin, 1962), p. 254.

33. Lote, *Histoire du vers français*, I, 97. See the final accented syllable of the first two lines of the *Eulalia* given above.

34. *La Passion du Christ*, in Bartsch, *Chrestomathie de l'ancien français*, p. 6.

35. A brief analysis of this text figured in Roger Pensom, 'Rythme et sens', *Poétique*, 167 (2011), 53–72 (pp. 66–68). Unlike its forerunner, the discussion that follows situates the text at a critical juncture in the emergence of French verse.

36. For example, in 'un amour insensé', the countertonic accent of *insensé* is deleted, and in 'joli chat' the word-accent on *joli* is displaced leftward to give 'joli chat'. When juxtaposed, the accents of low-frequency monosyllables both stand: 'une fleur blanche'.

37. A famous example from Baudelaire's sonnet 'La Beauté': 'Car j'ai, pour fasciner mes dociles amants, | De purs miroirs [...]' (Baudelaire's punctuation).

38. The text is that given in *Les Séquences de Sainte Eulalie*, ed. by Roger Berger and Annette Brasseur (Geneva: Droz, 2004).

39. *La Séquence de Sainte Eulalie* survives in a single manuscript, Bibliothèque municipale de Valenciennes, ms. 150. The text is readable online in the manuscript itself, thanks to Wikipedia, together with a translation.

40. To conform to the historical norm these would be accented *Eulalia* and *anima*. Together with the *clemencia* of l. 29, this would set the couplet at odds with the oxytonic final syllable of each of the remaining twenty-six lines.

41. The move from one *laisse* to the next is signalled by a change in assonance, i.e. the final tonic vowel of the verse-line. In *laisse* 1 it is [u], as in *amur* and *prut*, and switches in *laisse* 2 to [nasal a], as in *Abraham* and *tant*. Lines with an 'epic cesura', i.e. a supernumerary syllable in fifth position, are marked *.

42. The inversion of syntax in *perdut ad* (101) is emphatic.

43. This is a feminine *laisse*, in which the extra-metrical eleventh syllable of each line is [ə]. Masculine and feminine *laisses* alternate apparently randomly in this text, 38 per cent being feminine. The wholesale masculinity of 'Aeternus orbis conditor' and of *Sequence de Sainte Eulalie* is avoided by poets from the twelfth century onward by alternation of masculine and feminine rhymes. By the time of Ronsard, alexandrine couplets will alternate thus.

44. *The Life of St. Alexius in the Old French Version of the Hildesheim Manuscript*, ed. by Carl J. Odenkirchen (Brookline, MA, & Leiden: Classical Folia Editions, 1978). Texts and extracts of texts in this and the following chapter are representative of author and/or genre.

45. Cornulier, *Art poëtique*, p. 62, n. 71, and Fabb and Halle, *Meter in Poetry*, p. 151.

46. In the ninth-century manuscript of the *Eulalia*, the text is presented in pairs of whole lines written continuously across the page, each line being marked by an initial capital. See Lote, *Histoire du vers français*, IV, facing p. 120. In the oldest known manuscript of the *Vie de Saint Alexis* (Hildesheim, Dombibliothek, St. God. Nr 1), the text is written continuously, as prose, but each strophe begins with an illuminated capital, and the end of each line is indicated by a point. (See *The Life of St. Alexius*, ed. by Odenkirchen, p. 91.)

47. In the sample analysed below, 7 only of 250 verses (3 per cent) showed a matching of 'ə's in fifth and twelfth positions. In contrast, line-final [ə] is maintained strictly throughout each feminine *laisse*.

48. For the origins of the alexandrine see Gasparov, *A History of European Versification*, pp. 130–31.

49. *Est* is tonic being on a syntactic boundary.

50. * marks irregular syllable count.

51. *Le Siège de Barbastre*, ed. by J. L. Perrier (Paris: Honoré Champion, 1926) , p. 1.

52. *La Chanson de Roland*, ed. by Whitehead; Jean Racine, *Phèdre*, in *Théâtre complet*, ed. by Rat.

53. A full account of this work is to be found in Pensom, *Accent and Metre in French*.

54. In a personal communication, August 1978.

55. A glance at the frequency-tables available on the website *1000 Most Common French Words* (<http://french.languagedaily.com/wordsandphrases/most-common-words> [accessed 19 February 2010]) confirms these distributions.

56. *Le Chanson de Roland*, p. 5.

57. See the concluding paragraphs of the Introduction.

58. As noted above, the analyses are based on he analyses are based on a sample of 716 major hemistichs from *La Chanson de Roland* and 1000 first hemistichs from *Phèdre*.

59. Racine, *Phèdre*, I.3, in *Théâtre complet*, ed. by Rat, p. 550.

60. In Racine, the noun phrase, for example 'père généreux', 'ami loyal', plays an important role in intensifying affective rapport with the spectator. In the whole of *Phèdre*, I count 539 instances of such noun phrases: of these 7 only show clear juxtaposed accents, that is 0.13 per cent. One must conclude from the rarity of noun phrases of the types (...01) (1) and (...01) (10) that the language of Racine's tragedies excluded leftward displacement of accent (e.g. 'crayon vert', 'amant doux' etc.). See n. 36 above.

61. For the transition to modern French see Peter Rickard, *A History of the French Language* (London: Hutchinson, 1974), pp. 102–03.

62. Ibid., p. 61, for further details.

63. Pope, *From Latin to Modern French*, p. 82.

64. This and the following examples are drawn from the posthumous volumes of Georges Lote, *Histoire du vers français*, IV.

65. From Corneille's *La Veuve*, cited by Lote, *Histoire du vers français*, IV, 199.

66. A sample of this style of performance can be found on the CD *The Spirits of England and France 2* (Hyperion, CD A66773, 1995) in which Gothic Voices under Christopher Page perform Gace Brulé's 'De bien amer grant joie atent'.

67. *Cansos de Trobairitz*, performed by Hesperion XXI in *Cansos de Trobairitz*, directed by Jordi Savall (Virgin Classics CD, remastering of 1978 recording no. 7243 5 61310 26).

68. One minim = two crotchets; a dotted minim = three crotchets.
69. Gustave Reese, *Music in the Middle Ages* (London: Dent, 1941), pp. 207–08.
70. Dr David Fallows, in a personal communication of October 1982.
71. Roger Pensom, 'Performing the Medieval Lyric', *Performance Practice Review*, 10 (1997), 212–21.
72. The collection known as the 'Chansonnier Cangé' found in Bibliothèque de France, ms. fr. 846, and edited by Jean Beck in *Les Chansonniers des troubadours et des trouvères*, 2 vols (New York: Broude Bros, 1964).
73. By Garsenda de Forcalquier (b. 1170): a debate between mistress and lover. She wants to know why he is so timid: he explains that he is overwhelmed by her prestige and prays that she will accept his deeds in the absence of words.
74. Accents in bold. Misplaced accents in bold and italic.
75. Chansonnier Cangé, fol. 41$^{r–v}$.
76. While 'trochaic' rhythm is incompatible with the decasyllable, it is frequently encountered in settings of the undivided seven-syllable line (1010101).
77. Runs of three atonic syllables in italics.
78. For an analysis of the relative incidence in prose and verse of runs of atonic syllables, see Pensom, 'Accent et syllabe', pp. 354–61. This account finds that in two passages with the same number of words, the verse-passage showed eleven runs of atonic syllables and the prose passage fifty-nine. While the former showed two runs of more than three syllables, the latter showed twenty-eight with ten of more than four syllables.
79. Obvious scribal errors in the manuscript have been silently corrected. Musical notation in the manuscript comprises long and short notes (*longæ* and breves). Accent is thus represented in terms of duration rather than intensity. Accent in French generally is expressed on three parameters: pitch, intensity and duration; the latter before a full stop. For further observations see Pensom, *Accent and Metre in French*, pp. 50–51.
80. Lote, *Histoire du vers français*, IV, 137.
81. Ibid., p. 140.
82. High-priority words which are atonic here are in italics.
83. This case is by no means exceptional. Lote himself cites a 'dactylic' song, which, if scanned 'iambically', generates a surplus of word-accent violations, see Lote, *Histoire du vers français*, IV, 20.
84. An editor might well delete the personal pronoun here: in Old French the distinctive morphology of the verb-forms makes it redundant. Compare l. 13, *qu'ai esprouvé*.
85. Chansonnier Cangé, folio 31a.
86. The notation followed is the transcription provided by Leo Schrade, in Guillaume de Machaut, *Oeuvres complètes*, ed. by Leo Schrade (Editions de L'Oiseau Lyre: Monaco, 1977), III, 37. Vowels accented in violation of linguistic word-accent are in bold and italics. For detailed discussion of Machaut as poet and composer see Elizabeth Eva Leach, *Guillaume de Machaut* (Ithaca, NY: Cornell University Press, 2011).
87. Leach, *Guillaume de Machaut*, prints a full transcription of the triple *ballade* 'De triste cuer' (pp. 104–07) which again shows persistent coincidence of atonic word-final [ə] with bar-accent.
88. See Guillaume de Machaut, *Musikalische Werke*, ed. by Friedrich Ludwig, 4 vols (Leipzig: Breitkopf und Härtel, 1926), I.
89. Atonic runs in italics.
90. Proclitic *t'ont* accented.
91. Quoted, with references, in D. P. Walker, *Music, Spirit and Language in the Renaissance* (London: Variorum Reprints, 1985), p. 58.
92. For example, written: 'Mon oncle est un homme avare'; spoken: [mõ. nõ. klɛ. tœ̃. nom. ma. va:R].
93. Jean Palsgrave, *L'Esclaircissement de la langue francoyse* (Paris; [n.pub.], 1530).
94. Lote, *Histoire du vers français*, IV, 105.
95. Pierre Ronsard, *Art poétique*, in *Œuvres completes*, ed. by Gustave Cohen, 2 vols (Paris: Gallimard, 1950), II, 999.

96. Lote, *Histoire du vers français*, IV, 113–14.

97. And here they are with Lote's scansion based on his idea of linguistic accent:

Je veux aymer ardante**ment**	00010001
Aussi **veux**-je qu'égale**ment**	00100001
On m'**ayme** d'une am**our** ard**ante**	010001010

98. Cited by Lote, *Histoire du vers français*, IV, 128.

99. Further biographical and historical details can be found in Lote, *Histoire du vers français*, VI, Chapter 2.

100. Jean-Baptiste Lully, *Alceste, reconstituée et réduite pour piano et chant par Théodore de Lajarte* (Paris: Théodore Michaelis, [n.d.]).

101. Further discussion of Lully's recitative with full music examples can be found in Jean Duron, 'L'Instinct de M. de Lully', in *La Tragédie lyrique*, ed. by Patrick F. Van Dieren and Alain Durel (Paris: Cicero, 1991), pp. 65–119. This essay and others in the collection are a rich source of technical and background information on opera and the stage under Louis XIV, much of which is still relevant for the opera of Rameau.

102. See the earlier reference to Zipf's Law in the Introduction, n. 2.

103. See James Anthony, *French Baroque Music: From Beaujoyeulx to Rameau* (London: Batsford, 1974), p. 78.

104. For example, on the final [ə] of paroxytones, e.g. *femme*, or on the pretonic syllable of oxytones, e.g. *intêret*.

105. For clarity we print quavers for semiquavers.

106. * indicates an illicit form.

107. Jean-Bapstiste de Lully, *Thésée*, ed. by Théodore de Lajarte (Paris: Théodore Michaelis, [n.d.]).

108. The composer's accents are in bold while atonic runs identified by our criteria are italicised.

109. Like ours, Lully's response to Quinault's text thus avoids juxtaposed accent in *heureux sort*. To place *bien* in an accented position would change the meaning from *bien heureux* to *bienheureux*. Hence the *accent d'insistance* on the possessive, comes very much from the domain of *parole*, as does Lully's reading of Quinault's *j'arme son propre père* as *j'arme son propre père*. This last hemistich alternates regularly by our criteria.

110. Henceforth 'marked' means 'accented', and 'unmarked' means 'unaccented'

111. For our purposes, the strength of the accent is immaterial. Though some will be stronger than others, alternation only requires the perceptible difference implied by our notation.

112. In his musical notation, Lully is ratifying the provision of our model not only for the normal countertonic accent in polysyllables but also for its deletion when juxtaposed to an accent of higher informational priority. This deletion expresses the language's general tendency to avoid juxtaposed accents.

113. Other solutions are of course possible. For example, in a group of two quavers, the second loses prominence through alternation. If it is then followed immediately by a pair of semiquavers, the head semiquaver of this group loses prominence being shorter than the preceding quaver. Thus the group composed of the second quaver and the two semiquavers is atonic.

114. i.e., we find 10 exceptions in the total 188 words of the quoted passages, all of which are atonic clitics or prepositions which the composer has accented.

115. Jean-Philippe Rameau, *Hippolyte et Aricie*, ed. by Sylvie Bouissou (Kassel: Bärenreiter, 2010).

116. Although we see here lines of nine and eleven syllables, these do not necessarily contravene Cornulier's 'loi des 8'. The nine-syllable lines are both analysable as 4 + 5 and the eleven-syllable line as 5 + 6.

117. For the historical and cultural context of this and other Rameau operas see David Charlton, *Opera in the Age of Rousseau* (Cambridge: Cambridge University Press, 2015), pp. 76–92.

118. Where we identify an unaccented run and Rameau does not, we italicise, while marking Rameau's accent.

119. Where Rameau finds an accent and we do not, the relevant vowel is in bold and italic.

120. Line 6, *A Thésée, à son fils, ces jours sont odieux*. The dotted crotchet on *sont* makes the composer's intention quite clear. This avoidance of the plain 'iambic' solution, *ces jours sont odieux*, gives an affective function to the displaced accent.
121. Atonic runs in italics.
122. The accented countertonic appears *only* if its syllable is preceded by an atonic syllable, that is for example in *les immolez* but not in *le fier Hippolyte*. This is a consequence of the language's tendency to avoid juxtaposed accents within the phrase and conforms to Zipf's Law.
123. As elsewhere, in ll. 5, 9, 15, 24 etc., this position is defined as unaccented by a preceding semiquaver rest.
124. See also in the second extract, ll. 1 *Inexorable*, 10 *égale*, 11 *récompense* and 17 *Pirithoüs*.
125. For further historical detail see Donald Jay Grout, *A History of Western Music* (London: Dent, 1962), pp. 429–39.
126. Christoph Willibald Gluck, *Alceste*, ed. by Hans Vogt (Kassel: Bärenreiter, 1957).
127. Our model suggests *Réponds-moi* which would give an alternating hemistich. This is the only instance in the two extracts in which Gluck contradicts our scansion.
128. The monosyllables are: *tu, des, ma, ton, Tu, Je, cet, ma, dont, je*.
129. In this example bold shows correspondence between word-accent and musical accent.
130. As earlier, atonic runs identified by our criteria are italicised.
131. These seventeen examples indirectly illustrate the strong tendency to promote alternation of accent by avoiding juxtaposition of accent. While *horribles lieux, funèbres accents, pâle clarté* and *éternelle nuit* show the affective force of the preposed adjective, we find no collocations such as *profonds antres*, effrayant bruit*, affreux lieux**. In Racine's *Phèdre* there are 539 such nominal phrases of which eleven only (2 per cent) show accents on adjacent high-priority monosyllables (e.g. *champs libre, oeil morne*).
132. 'C'est ainsi que le français tend à éviter la succession immediate de deux accents' (Paul Garde, *L'Accent* (Paris: PUF, 1968), p. 94).
133. These exceptions show that there is nothing mechanical about Gluck's accenting of clitics in the other examples.
134. See Joël-Marie Fauquet, 'Berlioz and Gluck', in *The Cambridge Companion to Berlioz*, ed. by Peter Bloom (Cambridge: Cambridge University Press, 1999), pp. 199–201.
135. Grout, *A History of Western Music*, p. 550. For background and the qualities of *Les Troyens* see James Haar, 'The Operas and the Dramatic Legends', in *The Cambridge Companion to Berlioz*, ed. by Bloom, pp. 92–94.
136. Text from Hector Berlioz, *Les Troyens* (Paris: Choudens Fils, 1892).
137. As before, runs of three atonic syllables by our criteria are italicised.
138. The first syllable of *ennui* is under the first of a pair of quavers, suggesting the usual avoidance of juxtaposed accents by leftward displacement of the word-accent.
139. The accents on *soeur, # implorer* are separated by a syntactical boundary ('#') and thus not juxtaposed.
140. In this and other examples these are in bold italics.
141. The Fauré songs cited appear in Gabriel Fauré, *An Album of Twenty Songs* ([n.p.]: Edward B. Marks Music Company, [n.d.]), pp. 17–21, 34–38 & 39–47.
142. Our accent on *Qui* implies a syntactical boundary, i.e. *Qui, dans les halliers, te cueille* where *Qui* is group-final. See n. 35 above.
143. The high frequency of occurrence of this adjective reduces its informational value and hence its prosodic profile.
144. In more popular registers, the accenting of atonic syllables, including word-final 'ə', is common. In Charles Aznavour's 'Il faut savoir' we hear 'Il **faut** sa**voir**, coute que **coute**, | Garder toute sa dignité', and in Jacques Brel's 'Les Flamandes', 'Les Flamandes dansent sans rien dire, | Sans rien dire aux Dimanches sonnants'.
145. Three hundred years before Leconte de Lisle, Bonaventure des Périers had written the following verses, with regular alternation of accent using two metrical solutions:

Caresme prenant, c'est pour vray le diable.	01001 # 00101
Le diable d'enfer plus insatiable.	01001 # 00101
Le plus furieux, le plus dissolut,	01001 # 01001
Le plus empeschant la voie du salut.	01001 # 01001
Le diable qui soit au profond manoir,	01001 # 00101
Où se tient Pluton, ce roi laid et noir.	00101 # 01001
C'est le débaucheur des malings esprits	00101 # 00101
Qui souz forte main sont liez et pris.	00101 # 00101

(Quoted in Louis Kastner, *History of French Versification* (Oxford: Clarendon Press, 1906), pp. 100–01).

146. See for example Fauré's creation of a 'trochaic' hemistich above in *Salua la fleur.*

147.
De la musique avant **toute** chose	0001001010 9 + ə
Et pour cela préfère L'Impair.	000101001 9

As against, say, a 6 + 6 line such as 'Mes volages humeurs, plus stériles que belles'. Here, in Agrippa d'Aubigné's 'L'Hyver', the even syllable-count allows a fourfold repetition of 001.

148. Cornulier, *Théorie du vers*, p. 93.

149. Cornulier, *Art poëtique*, pp. 97–105.

150. Of these seventeen lines, two show rhythmically identical hemistichs (12 per cent).

151. An *accent d'insistance* on **vous**, in contrast to *je*.

152. As before, runs which are atonic by our criteria are italicised.

153. The informational value of the noun *mains* is reduced by its semantic redundancy in the context of *déchirez*.

154. In a bar consisting entirely of quavers or of semiquavers, the first of each pair is relatively accented, which guarantees the maintenance of a sense of recurring pulse. This basic regularity can however be overridden: for example in 'J'arrive *tout cou*vert', the accented vowel in *arrive* is under a full crotchet followed by a quaver on the ə, followed by a pair of semiquavers on *tout cou*. Here the progressive diminution of note-values overrides the normal alternation of accent; the quaver following the crotchet is perceived through the contrast of length as unaccented as is the semiquaver which follows the quaver. As we have seen in Rameau and Gluck, this makes possible the setting of runs of three atonic syllables.

155. As before 'a group of quavers' is the equivalent of a whole crotchet in a bar of say 4/4, and 'a group of semiquavers' equals a whole quaver.

156. See n. 112 above. As in 'crotchet + quaver', the first semiquaver in 'quaver + semiquaver + semiquaver' is perceived as atonic through contrast of length with the preceding note-value.

157. See *Songs of Claude Debussy: A Critical Edition*, ed. by James R. Briscoe, 2 vols (Milwaukee: Hal Leonard Corporation, 1993), II, 113–17.

158. The brisker the tempo, the stronger the sense of 'one accent per bar'.

159. Debussy begins each of these atonic runs at the head of the bar but 'damps' the potential accent with a '[p]' over the first quaver.

160. David Mus, in a personal communication.

161. Ronsard, *Poèmes*, p. 112. Sonnets L and LI from *Sonnets pour Hélène*.

162. For details see Gouvard, *Critique du vers*, pp. 10–11.

163. For Lote this change originated in a revolt by poets and dramatists against the tradition of arhythmic declamation which had dominated the French stage (see *Histoire du vers français*, IV, 283–92).

164. See n. 112 above.

165. *The Poem of the Cid*, ed. by Ian Michael, trans. by Rita Hamilton and Janet Perry (Harmondsworth: Penguin, 1975), p. 22.

166. See Gasparov, *A History of European Versification*, p. 135.

167. Atonic runs in italics. Only one line is without one; two lines have two runs.

168. The syllable-count is maintained by a Spanish 'poetic licence' which permits suspension of synaloepha. This, together with permitted dieresis of the diphthong (e.g. *süave*, normally a

monosyllable), and syneresis (e.g. *poeta*, normally a disyllable), suggests a subsisting instability in Spanish syllable-count. It is often up to the reader to deduce the poet's intention. Most readers faced with uncertainty will locate a verse-line which can show none of these 'licences' and use it as a model.

169. Gustavo Bécquer, *Rimas*, no. LII, in *The Penguin Book of Spanish Verse*, ed. and trans. by J. M. Cohen (Harmondsworth: Penguin, 1956), p. 319. As in Italian, synaloepha (i.e. the linking of vowels across word-boundaries) is normal, e.g. 'env**uelto**entre la s**á**bana d**ee**spumas'.

170. Accents on syllables 4 and 10.

171. Gasparov, *A History of European Versification*, p. 102.

172. See Gasparov, *A History of European Versification*, p. 124. For example, Leopardi's famous lines: '[...] Così tra questa | immen**sità** # s'annega il **pen**sier mio: | e il na**ufragar** # m'è dolce in qu**esto** m**are**' ('L'Infinito', in *Canti*, ed. by John Humphreys Whitfield (Manchester: Manchester University Press, 1967), p. 63).

173. In our thirty-five lines from the *Alexis*, six (17 per cent) showed rhythmically identical hemistichs: similarly five of our twenty-five lines (20 per cent) from the *Siège de Barbastre*. In our sample from Corneille, the count was two out of seventeen lines (12 per cent). See n. 149 above. There may be a historical-cultural trend here.

CHAPTER 2

Accent and French Poetic Art

C'est l'alternance fixe qui est le premier principe de notre
versification. L'isosyllabie, le syllabisme, n'en est que la
conséquence.

PAUL VERRIER[1]

Verrier's insight is not supported by the evidence needed to justify it. We have been
busy so far looking for this missing evidence; what we have found can be summarised
as follows. Our review of French verse in the historical record, in synchronic analysis
and in the evidence from music indicates that all such verse is marked by constraints
on the distribution of accented syllables within the verse-unit. The question arises: are
these constraints a feature of verse only or of the language generally? An answer should
be found in a comparative analysis of samples of verse and prose.[2]

As a trial, two randomly selected passages in modern French of similar lengths, the
first from Racine's *Phèdre* (254 words) and the second from Le Sage's *Gil Blas* (259
words), were marked with oxytonic/paroxytonic word-accent as we have defined it on
the basis of our historical survey: the verse-passage showed one instance of juxtaposed
accents to the seven which appear in the prose passage. Furthermore, while the accents
in the verse are separated by a syntactic boundary, six of the seven cases in the prose
occur within the phrase. This analysis also confirmed the relative rarity of runs of more
than two atonic syllables in verse as opposed to prose: while the verse-passage showed
twenty such runs of which five have more than three syllables, the prose passage shows
fifty-eight of which twenty-seven have more than three syllables.[3]

This result challenges the currently prevalent view that the distribution of accent
within the verse-unit is due to chance or to the general properties of the French language. Alternation of accent, as we conceive it, requires the relative rarity in verse
of both juxtaposed accents and long runs of atonic syllables, which rarity this study
confirms. If atonic runs and juxtaposed accents are thus constrained in verse, who does
the constraining? If not the language then it must be the poet. Why then does the poet
do this? Because the poet's business is to create meaning through the ordering of the
raw materials furnished by his or her native language with respect to the categories of
similarity and difference:

Cerise *cuve* de *candeur*	01010001
Digi*tale* cri*stal* soyeux	00100101
*Ber*gamotte *ber*ceau de miel	00100101
*Pen*sée im*mense* aux yeux du *paon.*[4]	10010101

In these verses of Eluard, the phonetic form shows in the ordered recurrence of equivalent phonetic units which occur normally without order in French. Whether we name individual instances 'alliteration' ('*c*uve de *c*andeur') or 'rhyme' ('Digi*tal*e cri*stal*'), the principle is the same: the recurrent elements are ordered; by alliteration at the head of matched words, and rhyme at their ends. In the last line the repeated nasal vowel is coupled with a word-accent.

The word-accent of French is similarly subject to ordering, the middle lines of the quatrain showing the same distribution of word-accents. As we have seen, French prose shows a relatively unordered distribution of word-accents, just as it shows an unordered distribution of phonetic units. The creation of equivalences in the arrangement of these language-elements is the work of the poet who, though using language, is working from outside it.

The concept of 'equivalence' is not simple because the recognition of 'similarity' supposes that of 'difference'. Our perception of the similarity/identity of 'c' and 'c' depends on our recognition of the difference between 'c' and the other members of the set of all consonants in French. Likewise, our perception of the matching of the accent-distributions in our quatrain's middle lines implies our recognition of the difference between 00100101 and each of the other possible combinations of 0 and 1. Thus our perception of equivalence arises from a dialectic of similarity and difference, and this perception is a precondition of our sense of meaning arising from formal organisation.

Our hypothesis as previously stated is that the ordered alternation of word-accent within the verse-unit has two functions: firstly, it facilitates the perception of recurrent syllabic count via the summation of two- and three-syllable feet within the verse-unit. Our model for alternation posits: (a) oxytonic and countertonic word-accent as demonstrated in the evolution of French accent from Latin; and (b) constraints on juxtaposed accents and runs of atonic syllables as demonstrated by our synchronic analysis of verse-texts in Old French and modern French. These two factors combine to provide a basis for the justification of Verrier's assertion quoted above.

The question then remains: why are French poets interested in alternation? What is the relevance of the formal organisation of accent in French verse to the semantic values of the poetry itself? An answer is found in the second phase of our hypothesis which concerns the role of accent as raw material for the creation of meaning. We will proceed as we did in making predictive scansions to be tested by the judgement of our composers. Now however it will be our readers who will put these scansions to the test. In studying the accentual structure of individual texts, we will be learning something non-trivial about the semantic values created by these structures.

One of the clear conclusions of our *Chanson de Roland-Phèdre* analysis is that the constraints producing alternation of accent survive unchanged from Old French into modern French. This implies that verse written within that time-span will be shaped by the same constraints. On the evidence found so far, a rule-governed relation between accent-distribution and syllable-count is conserved, despite intervening linguistic and cultural change. Surprising though it may seem, this invariant obliges us to expect in the rhythmic organisation of a Baudelaire sonnet the same tendency to avoid colliding accents and atonic runs that we would predict in a trouvère song. What will vary unpredictably from poet to poet as time passes will be the relation between the accentual structure of the verse and its semantic content. It is here that the unique quality of a poet's voice is to be heard.

If alternation of accent in French verse is historically a constant, the chronology of a general survey of this verse will be indifferent: we could as well start today and work backwards. But history being what it is, meaning is not ahistorical. So, just as we followed word-accent from Saint Ambrose to Racine, we shall follow the writing of French verse from the thirteenth century to the twentieth. The choice of texts is varied but stays with notable names; the charge that they have been chosen with a view to justifying our theory can only be answered by inviting readers to try out our theory on texts of his or her own choosing.

The Thirteenth Century: Thibaut de Champagne

Thibaut de Champagne, King of Navarre, was writing within the lyric tradition of the trouvères for whom music was an integral component of their art. We have briefly noted the problems encountered by modern performers in inferring the rhythm of this verse from the non-mensural notation which accompanies it in the manuscript tradition. We will sidestep this difficulty and limit ourselves to exploring the possible relevance of accentual structure on the semantic values of the verse.[5]

The following song is in decasyllables with cesura/accent at the fourth syllable. The rhyme-scheme of the second strophe follows that of the first and the fourth that of the third. The fifth strophe is an orphan with respect to rhyme-scheme, though the concluding *envoi* picks up one of its rhymes:

	Seigneurs, sachiez; qui or ne s'en ira	0101 # **0**11001
	En cele terre, ou Deus fu morz et vis	0101 # 010101
	Et qui la croiz d'Outremer ne prendra[6]	0101 # 001001
	A peines mès ira en Paradis.	0101 # 010101
5	Qui a en soi pitié ne remembrance[7]	0101 # 010101
	Au haut seigneur doit querre sa venjance	0101 # 01**00**01
	Et delivrer sa terre et son païs.	0101 # 01**00**01
	Tuit li mauvais demorront par deça,	1001 # 001001
	Qui n'aiment Dieu, bien, ne honor, ne pris;	0101 # 100101
10	Et chascun dit: 'Ma fame, que fera?	0101 # 010101
	Je ne leroie a nul fuer mes amis.'[8]	1001 # 001001
	Cil sont cheoit en trop fole atendance,[9]	1001 # 001001
	Qu'il n'est amis, fors que cil sanz doutance,	0101 # 001001
	Qui pour nos fu en la vraie croiz mis.	1011 # 001011
15	**Or** s'en iront cil vaillant bacheler	1001 # 001001
	Qui aiment Dieu et l'oneur de cest mont,	0101 # 001001
	Qui sagement vuelent a Dieu aler;	0101 # 100101
	Et li morveus, li cendreus demorront.	**000**1 # 001001
	Avugles est, de ce ne dout je mie,	0101 # 010101
20	Qui **un** secors ne fet Dieu en sa **vie**,	0101 # 001001
	Et por si **pou** pert la gloire del mont.	**000**1 # 101001
	Deus se lessa por nos en croiz pener	1001 # 010101
	Et nos dira au jor ou tuit venront:	0101 # 010101

	'Vos qui ma croiz m'aidastes a porter	1001 # 01**00**01
25	Voz en iroiz la ou mi angre sont	1001 # 100101
	La me verroiz et ma mere Marie.	1001 # 001001
	Et vos, par qui je n'oi onques aïe,	0101 # 001001
	Descendroiz tuit en Enfer le parfont.'	00**11** # 001001
	Chascun cuide demorer toz haitiez	1010 # 101001
30	Et que jamès ne doie mal avoir;	**0001** # 010101
	Ensi les tient Anemis et pechiez;	0101 # 001001
	Que il n'ont sens, hardement, ne pooir.	0101 # 001001
	Biau sire Deus, ostez nos tel pensee,	0101 # 101001
	Et nos metez en la vostre contree	**0001** # 001001
	Si saintement que vos puissons veoir!	0101 # 010101
	Douce Dame, Roïne coronee,	1010 # 010101
	Prïez pour nos, Virge beneüree,	0101 # 100101
	Et puis après ne nos puet mescheoir.[10]	0101 # 100101

[My lords: know that he who will not go to the land where God died and lived, and who will not in the Holy Land take up the Cross, will scarcely come to Paradise. He who pities and remembers the Highest Lord must avenge him and free his land and his country.

All cowards will stay at home. They love neither God, honour nor renown. Each says: 'What will my wife do? I certainly can't abandon my friends'. Such men have fallen into foolish delusion. There is no friend indeed save He who was put on the True Cross.

Indeed it is those brave young men who love God and honour in this world who wisely wish to go to God, and the snivelling, worthless remnant will remain behind. He is without doubt blind who not even once in his life fights on God's side. For so little, he loses his worldly reputation.

For us, God allowed Himself to suffer on the Cross and will say to us on that day when all come before him: 'You, who helped me bear my Cross, you will go where my angels are; there you will see me and Mary my Mother. And you others, from whom I never had help, will all go down into deepest Hell'.

Each one thinks he will always be healthy and free of affliction; thus in the grip of Satan and sin they lack all wit, courage and power. Dear Lord God, free us from such thoughts and bring us to your country with your saints, that we may see You!

Sweet Lady, royal Queen, pray for us, blessed Virgin, for then no harm can come to us.][11]

Of these seventy-six hemistichs, sixty-six alternate (87 per cent) and ten are 'irregular' by our criteria: four of these have juxtaposed accents and seven have runs of three atonic syllables. Do these irregularities have any role in the creation of meaning?

The juxtaposed accents in the first line make an unmistakeable call to action in a *ballade* proclaiming a Holy War: in *qui or ne s'en ira* the intercalated adverb *or* [now!] with the resulting collision of accents, insists on the urgency of the call and the nullity of those who refuse it. The brief relaxation of tension with the 'anapests' of l. 3 gives sharp relief to the return of the 'iambic' pulse in the next line with its pitiless reminder of the fate of the 'fainéant', the forfeiting of Paradise. What could become monotony in the 'iambic' rhythm instead surprises with the accented *a* of l. 5. The syntax gives this normally atonic verb a special significance: qualified by the intercalated *en soi* [in himself], its group-final accent underlines the *true* belief which must be there in the heart of the Christian warrior.[12] The proclisis in the 'overflow' of *remembranc(e) →* *Au haut seigneur* deletes the final [ə] of *remembrance* keeping the idea of the Spiritual Vassal and his Heavenly Lord all in one breath. The syntactic parallelism of ll. 6 and 7 (*doit querre* + complement [...] = *Delivrer* + complement) gains emphatic force by being coupled with a rhythmic equivalence (010001 = 010001) *and* with the internal rhyme-pair *querre/terre*, whose accents occupy symmetrical sites on the rhythmic grid.[13] Though these tiny features might well pass unnoticed by the silent reader, the attentive listener will instantly recognise their critical importance for the thrust of the poem.

The line-initial accent of the second strophe (1001) censures 'faith-breakers' for their refusal of the call to arms. Its force derives from the breaking of the pattern established so far by the series of first hemistichs (0101). Similarly, the four balanced accents of l. 8 give way to the more insistent accentuation of l. 9 (five accents), whose vehemence is pointed by colliding accents at the 'cesura'. And the rude intensity of the paired accents of the final line stands out against the regular alternation of the preceding lines. The *Qui* and the *fu* here, normally atonic, are both at a syntactic boundary and thus carry a group-accent:

> Qui # por nos # fu # en la vraie croiz # mis #.[14]

Por nos achieves semantic prominence as an 'insert', separating subject and verb, as does *la vraie croiz*, displaced leftward between auxiliary verb and participle, and creating a climactic collision of accents. The startling compression of this line condenses all that is fervent, absolute, in the belief of the Christian warrior. The strophe as a whole expresses an idea from scripture whose importance is as much political as religious. The future Crusader must be ready to abandon everything to follow his Lord:

> If any man come to me, and hate not his [...] wife [...], he cannot be my disciple. And whosoever doth not bear his cross, and come after me, cannot be my disciple.[15]

In l. 16, the 'iambic' rhythm of *qui aiment Dieu* brings the pre-eminence of love into focus against the 'anapests' of the preceding line. In l. 17 the intercalation of the adverb between subject and verb brings about a collision of accents at the 'cesura', throwing the deliberately 'volitive' sense of the verb into prominence: for the true knight, this is an act, not a mere intention. In contrast, the first hemistich of l. 18 evoking the 'spineless cowards', is the first since l. 7 to show a run of three atonic syllables and also the single line in the *ballade* with only three accented syllables. In ll. 19–20, the syntactical inversion of the direct object, *un secors*, gives its *un* the value of a numeral by accenting it, an accent doubtless made stronger by a semantic *accent d'insistance*.

In strophe 4, the measured words of Christ to the faithful (ll. 24–26), showing no fewer than three line-initial accents, seal the doom of faithless cowards. In l. 25, the emphatic *Vos* excludes by implication the latter, promising the true knights Paradise. The juxtaposed accent at the cesura in *#la ou mi angre sont* insists on the uniqueness of that heavenly place reserved for the faithful knight: it is there and *there only* that he will see Jesus and his Mother. The fate of the 'faithless' is pitilessly marked by the colliding accents of *Descendroiz tuit*, where the force of 'All' at the 'cesura' emphasises the inflexibility of the divine decree — no exceptions.

The four ll. 29–32, in which the fate of the unsuspecting sinner is outlined, are interrupted by a prayer whose anguish is registered by a juxtaposed accent at the 'cesura':

> Biaus sire **Deu**s, # **ostez nos** tel pensee.

In the imperative *ostez nos*, the normal accent on the verbal inflexion (*vos ostez*) is juxtaposed to the accented indirect pronoun and thus displaced leftward.[16] The accent on *nos* — that is 'we, the valiant knights' — sets *nous* apart from *il*, the 'fainéants' of the previous line. In the next line, the accented disjunctive *nos* throws into relief the possessive pronoun/adjective in *la vostre contree*. This line ends with an attenuated syntactical boundary, the adverbial *Si saintement* of l. 35 modifying the *metez* of the foregoing line. In this overflow, the absence of pause sharpens the urgency already aroused by imperatives and accent-patterning. The *vos* in *que vos puissons veoir* attracts an accent both syntactically, because of the emphasis implied by its leftward displacement, and semantically because it represents God.

The envoi is addressed to the Mother of Christ: the line-initial accent makes a further supplication, its emphasis carrying us into a plea whose fervour appears in the juxtaposed accent at the 'cesura' of the penultimate line. The indispensable nature of the Virgin's intercession is affirmed in the final line, where the syntactic boundaries *puis* # *après* # imply that only once this intercession is made can the believer be sure of salvation.

The Fourteenth Century: Philippe de Vitry

We have already met Philippe, Bishop of Meaux (1291–1361), as innovator in the musical notation of the *Ars Nova*. The European reputation of this poet and mathematician was remarked by Petrarch himself. We would not be surprised to find a preoccupation with rhythm in the verse of a man much concerned with the accurate notation of rhythm in music. The following poem, 'Le Dit de Franc Gontier', was widely known and copied in his time and, later, parodied by François Villon in his *Testament*. In it, the Narrator comes upon a rustic pair enjoying a country dinner in their portable shelter:

	Soubs **feui**lle vert, sur herbe delitable,	0101 # 0101010
	Lez **ru** bruiant et près clere fontaine,	0101 # 0010010
	Trouvay fichee une borde portable.	0101 # 0010010
4	Illec mengeoit Gontier o dame Helaine	0101 # 0101010
	Fromaige frais, lait, bu**rre**, fromagee,	0101 # **11**01010
	Craime, ma**ton**, pomme, noix, prune, poire,	1001 # 1**011010**
	Civot, oignon, escalongne froyee,	0101 # 1010010[17]
8	Sur crouste bise, au gros sel, pour mieulx boire.	0101 # 0010010
	Au gourmer burent, et oisi**llon** harpoient	0101(0) # 0101010
	Pour resbaudir et le dru et la drue,	0101 # 0010010
	Que par amours après s'**entre**baisoient[18]	100101 # 10010
12	Et **bou**che et nez, polie et bien barbue.	0101 # 0101010
	Quant orent pris le doulz mès de nature,	*0001* # 0010010
	Tantost Gontier, haiche au col, au **bois** entre	0101 # 1010**110**
	Et dame Helaine si met **toute** sa cure	01010 # 0010010
16	A ce buer qui cue**uv**re dos et ventre.	0101 # 0101010

	J'oÿ Gontier en abatant son arbre	0101 # 0101010
	Dieu mercier de sa vie seüre.	1001 # 0010010
	'Ne say', dit-il, 'que sont piliers de marbre,	0101 # 0101010
20	Pommeaux luisants, murs vestus de painture;	0101 # 1010010
	Je n'ay paour de traïson, tissue	0101 # 0101010
	Soulz beau semblant, ne qu'empoisonné soye	0101 # 0010010
	En vaisseau d'or: je n'ay la teste nue	0101 # 0101010
24	Devant tirant, ne genoil qui se ploie.	0101 # 0010010
	Verge d'huissier jamais ne me deboute,	1001 # 0110010
	Car jusques la ne m'esprent convoitise,[19]	1001 # 1010010
	Ambicion, ne lescherie gloute;	0101 # 0101010
28	Labour me paist en joyeuse franchise;	0101 # 0010010
	Moult j'aime Helaine et elle moy sans faille,[20]	0101 # 0101010
	Et c'est assez. De tombel n'avons cure.	0101 # 0010010
	Lors je di: 'Las! Serf de court ne vaut maille,	1011 # 1010010
32	Mais Franc Gontier vault en or jame pure'.[21]	0101 # 0011010

[Beneath green leaves, on sweet grass, beside a loud stream and near a clear spring, I found set up a portable cabin. In it Gontier and Dame Helaine were eating: curds, milk, butter, cheese, cream, junket, apples, nuts, plums, pears, chives, onion, shallots, on brown bread with coarse salt, all the better to drink!

They drained the cup, and the birds made music to rejoice the lover and his mistress; who afterwards, for pure love, kissed each other's mouth and nose, smooth skin against rough beard. When they had finished their good country food, straightway Gontier is off to the woods, axe on shoulder, and Dame Helaine busies herself laundering shirts and smalls.

While he was chopping down his tree, I heard Gontier thanking God for his steady life. 'I wouldn't', he says, 'know a marble pillar if I saw one; neither shining ornaments nor painted walls; I fear no treachery hidden behind a smile nor being poisoned by drinking from a golden cup. I take my hat off to no tyrant nor do I bend my knee.

'Never am I turned away by the doorkeeper's staff: neither desire, ambition, nor greedy appetite would bring me to that. A free man's joyful labour feeds me; Helaine I love indeed and she me without doubt, and that's enough. The grave can look after itself. As for me, the courtly slave is not worth ha'pence: but Franc Gontier is worth pure gold.']

Of these sixty-four decasyllabic hemistichs, fifty-seven alternate accent (89 per cent), six showing juxtaposed accents and one a run of atonic syllables. The rhymes are all feminine and the rhyme-scheme ABAB CDCD can subdivide the strophe, offering the potential surprise of the appearance of the new C rhyme. In strophe 1, the ABAB unit opens and closes with completely 'iambic' lines, while the unrhymed second and third lines which they enclose are rhythmically equivalent (both 0101 # 001001). This gives an intriguing formal ambiguity to the quatrain: with respect to rhythm, the rhyming lines contrast, while the non-rhyming ones are equivalent.

The move to the C rhyme coincides with a rhythmic irruption, colliding accents at the 'cesura' and on *lait, burre*. The frequency of food-words is now matched by the increased incidence of accent, continued in line-initial accent on *Craime*, double accent at the 'cesura', *maton # pomme*, and colliding accents on *noix, prune*. Accent has a further emphatic function in overdetermining rhyme/vowel-harmony in *frais*, *lait* and *Craime*, and alliteration in *frais* and *fromagee*, and in *pomme*, *prune* and *poire*. One of the effects of the accent on the vowel is a more marked articulation of the preceding consonant,[22] resulting in a coupling of the idea of the 'abundance' of eatables with the 'frequency' of marked alliterating consonants. As a quantitative measure of this formal abundance, both ll. 5 and 6 have six accents as opposed to the alternating count of 4 and 5 in ll. 1–4. In the last two lines of the strophe, the transition from 'eating' to 'drinking' coincides with a progressive decline in accent-frequency, l. 6 has six accents, l. 7 has five and l. 8 four.

Strophe 2 begins again with an 'iambic' line, this time sporting a supernumerary vowel at the 'cesura'. Though this latter was a feature of the decasyllable of the Old French epic, it is absent from the thirteenth-century trouvère lyric as it is from the decasyllables of Guillaume de Machaut, Philippe's contemporary. Its presence here may well connote 'old-fashioned', in keeping with the poem's tongue-in-cheek re-run of the ancient topos 'simple country, good; sophisticated city, bad'. The lovers drink from the same cup, gladdened by bird-song, and the reciprocity of the shared cup is affirmed by the metrical/syntactic symmetry of *et le dru et la drue*, a hemistich foregrounded by the contrast between its 'anapests' and the prevailing 'iambic' rhythm. Modern readers may be struck by the egalitarian significance of this vision of relations between the sexes, developed in:

> Que par amour après s'**en**trebaisoient [...]

where true affection, seemliness (they embrace *after* eating) and reciprocity are united, not without humour. Not that sexual difference passes unremarked:

> [...] s'entrebaisoient
> Et bouche et nez, polie et bien barbue.

Both 'smooth' and 'fully bearded', although which is what is not clear. Again, the C rhyme punctuates the action. Their wholesome dinner finished, the pair return to their gendered labours. After the accentually tranquil:

> Quant orent pris le doulz **m**ès de nature,[23]   *0001* # 0010010

we hear:

> Tantost Gontier, h**ai**che au c**ol**, au b**ois en**tre,   0101 #1010110

which, with the bumpy irregularity of its second hemistich and its six accents, two at the 'cesura' and two juxtaposed, enact the 'energy?' of these gestures.[24] As we turn to his partner, the accentual burden lifts:

> Et d**a**me Hel**ai**ne si met t**ou**te sa c**u**re   01010 # 0010010

only to settle down in an 'iambic' line:

> A c**e** b**ue**r qui c**ue**uvre dos et v**en**tre.[25]   0101 # 0101010

Though this line has the full complement of 'iambic' accents, their even distribution contrasts tellingly with the stressful irregularity of the corresponding rhyme-line *haiche au col, au bois entre*, where in this Middle French, the aspiration of *haiche*, the *enchaînement* of [ha□ok□l] and the *liaison* and colliding accents of [bw□zãntrə] demand effort from the reciter's articulation. There is clear evidence of the coupling of the formal opposition 'accentual irregularity' ≠ 'regular alternation' with the semantic opposition 'Gontier, male', ≠ 'Helaine, female'.

In contrast to the first line of strophe 3, the direct complement, *Dieu* in l. 18 is stressed through leftward displacement, giving the only line-initial accent in the strophe and the third of three in the poem. These relatively rare events are, correspondingly, informationally significant. In:

'Ne **say**' dit-**il**, 'que **sont** piliers de marbre,
Pommeaux luisants, murs vestus de painture';

the accent on *sont*, due to its emphatic leftward displacement, tells us that Gontier has absolutely no truck with these inessentials, even if he evidently does know exactly what they are. His ironic *Ne say que* gives juxtaposed accents at the 'cesura' of l. 20 the force of a 'contemptuous dismissal?' of such trash, in a 'list' whose tone is the antithesis of that of the 'euphoric' country foodstuffs of strophe 1. The level assurance of the 'iambic' measure in:

Je n'**ay** paour de traïson, tissue
Soulz **beau** semblant, [...]

is disturbed in:

[...] ne qu'empoisonné soye
En vaisseau d'or.

The word *empoisonnée* is already affectively charged when the syntactical inversion 'thematises' the word-accent by throwing it back onto the countertonic.[26] In the second hemistichs of the last four lines of this strophe, the alternation of rhyme CDCD is coupled with second hemistichs which alternate rhythmically: for C, 0101010; and for D, 0010010. This coupling concerns categories which are, as in ll. 1–4, purely formal, rhyme with rhythm, there being no sign of the coupling of similar or contrasting semantic values.

Line 25 shows the semantic force of accent in a line-initial stress and in the intensified word-accent on *jamais* procured again by syntactic inversion. Since in Middle French *ne* before the verb suffices to mark negation, the presence of auxiliary adverbs, *jamais*, *point*, *mie*, is always emphatic. This emphasis is here compounded by leftward displacement. The quality of normal word-accent is thus modified to create a semantic value ('insistence?'), by an increase in intensity and pitch. The line-initial accent in l. 26 marks a syntactical boundary:

Car # jusque la # ne m'esprent convoitise.

Though the accent-count of l. 27 is still the standard five of the 'iambic' decasyllable:

Ambicion, ne lescherie gloute;

it is free of juxtaposed accents, having returned to 'strict alternation' (0101 # 0101010). In the following line:

Labour me paist en joyeuse franchise;   0101 # 0010010 the accent-count falls to four, in a line whose second hemistich is the first wholly 'anapestic' one of the strophe, connoting 'lightness of heart?'.

Just as we found evidence of coupling in Thibaut de Champagne's song, so we have found it here, enriching our awareness of the affective force of a poetry which could be written off as a catalogue of commonplaces. In this final strophe, what does the reader/listener experience in the relation between accent-distribution and sense, between the formal and the semantic? What is there that is 'objective' in the contribution of each of these levels to the structure of the poetry?

In the penultimate strophe, we found overall one line-initial accent, one 'cesura' with juxtaposed accents, both these in different lines, and within the hemistich, no colliding accents. No line in this strophe had more than five accents. What is clear is that, in this context, the two opening lines of this final strophe are accentually deviant: l. 25 shows *both* line-initial accent and juxtaposed accent within the hemistich, and l. 26 shows *six* accents of which one line-initial and two juxtaposed at the 'cesura'. These two lines contrast in turn with the following two, which revert to the 'normal' accent-distribution of the previous strophe, the verb-less l. 27 with 'iambic' alternation, and l. 28 with the reduced accent-count of an 'anapestic' hemistich. Accentual pressure continues to decline with the atonic run and three accents of l. 30. So much for the formal, but what is happening semantically?

The negative syntax of strophe 3 is sustained as Gontier counters and denies the force of the temptations of court-life. Rejection of its 'immorality' and its 'dread of the Law' in ll. 25 and 26 is coloured by the 'violence' implicit in the 'dysphoric' verbs *deboute* and *esprent*. But in l. 28, with the completion of the ABAB rhyme-cycle, breaks a new dawn:

> La**bou**r me **pai**st en joy**eu**se fran**chi**se.

The disappearance of negative syntax and sudden presence of 'euphoric' language coincide with the lowest accent-count of the strophe so far: the closing B rhyme *franchise* is the moral and political antonym of its rhyme-partner, the servitude of *convoitise*. The all-sufficing mutual love of the country-dwellers is reasserted, and their acceptance of their mortality is quietly confirmed in l. 30, a line with only three accents:

> Et c'est assez. De tombel n'avons cure.[27]

The poem ends with a bang: in a flurry of strong, irregular accentuation, the narrator rejects the servitude of 'court life' (negative syntax) and positively proclaims the 'gold-standard' of Franc Gontier's 'simple existence'.

The Fifteenth Century: François Villon

Like that of Philippe de Vitry, the poetry of Villon is a poetry of commonplaces: proverbs, place-names, slang, even the eight-syllable eight-line stanza, are the common property of his fellow versifiers. For us, this might mean that it is trivial, but not for Villon. What we all share is, for us, diminished by its familiarity. The poet's job is to wake us up to its revelatory strengths. The medieval alchemists' quest was for the Philosopher's Stone which transmutes everything into gold: but this Stone looked so like any other stone that we are still looking for it. Accordingly, Villon's *Testament* takes the hackneyed form of a mock will, in which he bequeaths this or that to whomever. All these bequests are jokes. To his adoptive father, he leaves the *Romance of the Devil's Fart*; to Jehan Perdrier, he leaves — nothing! And the same to Jehan's brother. To others he wills the famous lyrics which enrich his testament. Here is his *double ballade* for those lovers whose reward is 'Pour une joye cent doulours' (l. 624).

	Pour ce, amez[28] tant que vouldrez,	01011001
	Suyvez assemblées et festes,	010010010
	En la fin ja mieulx n'en vauldrez	00101001
628	Et n'y romperez que voz testes.	001010010
	Folles amours font les gens bestes:	100100110
	Salmon en ydolatria,	01010101
	Sanson en perdit les lunectes.	010010010
632	Bien eureux est qui riens n'y a!	10010101
	Orpheüs, le doulx menestrier,	00101001
	Jouant de fluctes et musectes,	010100010
	En fut en dangier d'un murtrier	01001001
636	Chien Cerberuz à quatre testes.	100101010
	Et Narcisus, ly beaulx honnestes,	010101010
	En ung parfont puis s'en noya	00011001
	Pour l'amour de ses amouretes.	001001010
640	Bien eureux est qui riens n'y a!	10010101
	Sardana, le preux chevallier,	00101001
	Qui conquist le resne de Crestes,	001010010
	En voulut devenir moullier	00100101
644	Et filler entre pucellectes;	001001010
	David ly roys, saiges prophetes,	010110010
	Crainte de Dieu en oublia,	10010101
	Voyant laver cuisses bien fetes.	010110010
648	Bien eureux est qui riens n'y a!	10010101
	Amon en voult deshonnourer,	01010101
	Faignant de menger tartelectes,	010010010
	Sa seur Thamar et defflourer,	01010101
652	Qui fut chose moult deshonnestes;	001001010
	Herodes — pas ne sont sornectes! —	010100010
	Saint Jehan Baptiste en decola	01010101
	Pour dances, saulx et chansonnectes,	010101010
656	Bien eureux est qui riens n'y a!	10010101
	De moy povre je vueil parler:	01100101
	J'en fuz batu comme à ru telles,	100100110
	Tout nu, ja ne le quiers celer.	01100101
660	Qui me fist maschier ces groselles,	101010010
	Fors Katherine de Vausselles?	010100010
	Noël le tiers est,[29] qui fut la,	01011001
	Mitaines à ces nopces telles	010001010
664	Bien eureux est qui riens n'y a!	10010101
	Mais... que ce jeune bachelier	10010101
	Laissast ces jeunes bachelectes?	010101010

	Non! et le deust on vif brusler	10010101
668	Comme un chevaucheur... d'escrinnectes!	001010010
	Plus doulces luy sont que civetes;	010010010
	Mais touteffois fol s'y fya:	01011001
	Soient blanches, soient brunetes,	101010010
672	Bien eureux est qui riens n'y a!³⁰	10010101

[On this account, love to your heart's content! Go to parties and banquets. All said and done, you will be no better off and all you'll break is your head. Mad love makes beasts of men: Solomon ended up worshipping idols, because of it Samson lost his peepers. Lucky is he who has nothing to do with it!

Orpheus, the sweet minstrel, playing flutes and bagpipes, because of love, fell prey to Cerberus, a murderous four-headed dog; and Narcissus, the fair and virtuous, drowned himself in a deep well for the sake of his loves. That man is better off who has nothing to do with it!

Sarda, that valiant knight, who conquered the realm of Crete, wanted to become a woman and spin yarn among girls; David the King, wise prophet, forgot his fear of God when he saw shapely thighs being washed. Lucky is he etc.

Because of love, Amon (on the pretext of eating little cakes) decided to despoil and ravish his sister Tamar, a very wicked deed. Herod, (and I'm being quite serious here), cut off John the Baptist's head for dances, hops and ditties, Lucky is he etc.

And now a word about poor me: for the sake of love I was beaten like washing by a stream; quite naked; I tell the embarrassing truth. And who made me chew these gooseberries but Katherine de Vaucelles? Noel was number three there; what a beating that was! Lucky is he etc.

But should this young chap leave these lasses alone? Not on your life! Not even if they were to burn him alive like men that ride on women's purses.³¹ To him they are sweeter than perfume. But all the same, a fool did trust them; be they blonds be they brunettes, lucky is he etc.]

Here Villon revisits 'La Querelle des femmes', the contemporary debate concerning the virtue or otherwise of women, that had inspired the *Champion des dames* of Martin Le Franc, a forerunner of Villon. Even a quick glance at this *ballade* reveals the hoariness of the subject-matter, a tally of classical and biblical menfolk ruined by women. If some modern critics are to be believed, the treatment is as tired as the subject-matter: Villon is for them a 'Médiocre versificateur [...] pratiquant le style de la disharmonie ou de la dissonance'.³² Have these critics, doubtless in search of the poetic Philosopher's Stone, really found nothing but another pebble?

Of the *ballade*'s forty-eight octosyllabic verse-units, thirty-seven alternate regularly (77 per cent). Five verse-units show a run of three atonic syllables and six show juxta-posed accents within the syntactic unit, one verse-unit showing both. But this patchwork of literary commonplaces pulsates with rhythmic life. Marot, a poet of the generation following Villon's, admired in the latter 'la quantité de ses syllabes [...] ses coupes tant féminines que masculines'.³³ Whatever Marot meant by 'quantité', it is clear that he refers to the formal properties of the verse, probably accent and the internal division of the verse-unit. The *ballade* has no title in the manuscripts and nothing in the text warns the listener of the transition from the *huitains*, the standard eight-line octosyllabic unit of the *Testament*, to a *ballade*-structure with its own repeated rhyme-scheme. In one major witness (the first known printed edition, of 1489), the first line answers the last one of the preceding *huitain* with an ironic metrical parallelism:

| Pour **ung** plaisir **mi**lle dou**leurs** | 0101 # 1001 |
| Pour **ce**, a**mez tant** que vou**drez**. | 0101 # 1001 |

Though the octosyllable has in principle no fixed 'cesura', twenty-two of the forty-eight verse-units in this *ballade* have a syntactical boundary after the fourth syllable. A mid-line break in the octosyllable is not a formal requirement but a stylistic choice, which takes us back to Marot's compliment concerning the division of the verse-line in Villon.

The four accents of the first line, of which two are given prominence by the mid-line break, are followed by a line with one accent less and a repeated *liaison*-consonant: [s☐i.ve.**za**.sã.ble.ə.**ze**.f☐.təs]. Together with the repeated [ə], whose acoustic weakness enhances the perceived intensity of the preceding accent, the *phonetic* equivalence [z] = [z] energetically overdetermines the *semantic* equivalence of *assemblees* = *festes*. This redundance foregrounds the purely rhythmic value of the verse: compared to l. 625 with its irregular accentuation and internal pauses, this line is free of internal boundaries. *Assemblees et festes* is further overdetermined by the rhythmic equivalence 001 = 0010, evoking, in this context, the lilt of triple-metre dance. Line 629 carries an initial accent on *Folles*, a word of thematic importance throughout the *Testament*; its full negative sense is confirmed by the colliding accents on *gens bestes*. Emphasis is achieved through the coupling of accentuation and sense in the synonyms *Folles* = *bestes* (compare *assemblees* = *et festes*) with metrical irregularity. The C non-rhyme abruptly changes gear: leaving the language and concerns of everyday life, we are back in the *Old Testament* with Solomon where a learned polysyllable *ydolatria*, in a line whose mock pomposity, confirmed by its wholly 'iambic' measure, is instantly punctured by a lively three-accent line, leading us rapidly to the rhyme-word, *lunetes*, straight from the world of picturesque slang.[34] The wryly moralising refrain is weighted by a line-initial *accent d'insistance* and a return to four accents.

The second strophe sets a deliberately 'low-register' tone with the *rime pauvre*, *vouldrez/menestrier*, where, strictly speaking, each of the accented 'e's should have a different timbre.[35] The *faux naïf* manner of this strophe's handling of classical commonplaces reaches parody in ll. 635–36, where the relation between syntax and metre approaches incoherence: the noun phrase *murtrier/Chien* straddles the line-end on the eighth syllable of l. 635, which, if *murtrier* is an adjective, moves its accent leftward to the first syllable. We thus have a masculine line in which the final accent falls on the seventh syllable, an exceptionally violent rupture of the verse-structure. This metrical shock gives the mock horror of the poet confronted by a cardboard monster. With the C non-rhyme of l. 648, leaving the measured calm of an 'iambic' line, the listener trips and falls into the Well of Narcissus. He or she has run into the obstacle of the juxtaposed accents of *parfont puis* where the coupling of a fatal image and an extreme metrical irregularity gives the listener a start.[36]

The third strophe again falls into two groups of four lines so that the pagan world is set against that of scripture. The opposition is marked by the 'profane' ≠ 'sacred' alternation in the couplet-rhyme *pucelletes* ≠ *prophetes* and by metrical alternation: the first quatrain is made up of lines with three accents and the second with four. The tale of 'Sardana', in l. 639, prolongs the lighter measure of:

Pour l'amour de ses amourectes,

with three-accent lines lacking 'cesura', all begun with an 'anapest'. But David demands a more serious treatment. In lines of *four* accents, his name and quality are announced in a more solemn rhythm: in l. 645 the very first 'iambic' half-line of the strophe closes on what sounds like a 'cesura', where juxtaposed accents foreground the words *roy* and *sage*. Unlike the lines of the first quatrain, each of these last four shows *both* a word-boundary *and* a syntactical boundary after the fourth syllable. But this sudden gravity is a pretext for some very serious fun in l. 647:

Voyant laver cuisses bien fetes.   0101 # 10010

Here, though repeating exactly the formal structure of l. 645:

David ly roys, saiges prophetes,   0101 # 10010

with which it also rhymes, the affective impact of accentually prominent *cuisses* surprises us by its membership of the semantic series which characterises Sardana: *moullier/filles/pucelletes*, all of which share the semic element feminine. A *formal* equivalence, 0101 # 10010 = 0101 # 10010, is thus coupled with a *semantic* opposition: 'sacred' $\neq$ 'profane', *simultaneously* contrasting and identifying the Man of God and the Pagan. Though as we have noted, there is, properly speaking, no 'cesura' in the octosyllable, the creation of a syntactic limit after the fourth syllable gives a resource to the poet who seeks variety within the limited and over-familiar framework of the octosyllabic *huitain*.

The ironic tone of the poet's re-telling of the biblical story of Amon and Tamar again owes something to contrast at the rhythmic level. The regular 'iambic' rhythm of l. 649 is interrupted by l. 650, an aside whose 'chatty colloquialism' is due to the switch from four accents ('iambic') to three ('anapestic') being overdetermined by an abrupt register-alternation of serious *deshonnourer* with the diminutive/familiar *tarteletes*, both in rhyme-position. While the next line takes up the syntax and rhythm of the first line together with its rather po-faced tone, l. 652:

Qui feut chose moult deshonnestes   001001010

reverts to the 'anapestic' familiarity of l. 649.

Though we know that formal configurations have, *in se*, no fixed semantic value, passages like this do suggest that there is something significant in the contrast between a line of four accents and one of three. Objectively the time taken to recite each one may be the same, yet the coupling of formal and semantic values may give rise to perception of *qualitative* differences between them. A corollary of Zipf's law suggests that, statistically, accent correlates with information; that is, more accents equals more information.[37] This in turn means that a line with more information needs more attention. So, the work we have to do in processing the information in a given line affects our perception of it. A line needing less work may seem 'lighter', 'quicker', than one needing more. The complex of factors conditioning the contrast of sense and mood between ll. 649 and 650 may therefore include the perception of a change of pace, the sententious 'heaviness'/'slowness' of the first line giving way to the gossipy 'lightness'/'quickness' of the second. Through this magical interaction of quantity and quality, the poet transforms the lead of the commonplace into his own gold. Thus the run of atonic syllables in l. 653:

> Herodes, — pas *ne sont so*rnectes! — ,

stands out against the four-accent lines as a 'gossipy aside?', butting in on a moralising catalogue.

The first C rhyme of each strophe so far has a 'dysphoric' value: *ydolatria, noya, oublia, decola*, while the penultimate line of the fourth strophe (l. 655) condenses the 'catalogue' format of the *ballade* in a merry *stretto*:

> Pour dances, saulz et chansonnectes,

where the phonetic anaphora [s→s→z→□→s] is coupled with the semantic overlap of the nouns. The *ballade*'s ironic ceremonial is now abruptly broken into by the insistent voice of the testator himself in l. 657:

> De moy, povre, je vueil parler: 01100101
> J'en fus batu comme a ru telles.   10010011

The accented disjunctive pronoun at the syntactic boundary is juxtaposed to the signature-adjective of the testator, *povre*, also on a boundary. This metrical transgression is compounded in the next line with most unusual juxtaposed accents at the rhyme which, moreover, *is not* a rhyme, since it breaks the rhyme-patterning of the *ballade* with *tarteletes* ≠ *telles*. So here, what should be a defining property of the *ballade* serves only to make more outrageous the unexpected intrusion of the speaker, rudely elbowing out of the way the great figures of legend and history with his tale of personal humiliation. The strophe itself is a wholesale formal and semantic violation of the norms established by the *ballade*. It is behaving just like common-or-garden *huitains* in those parts of the *Testament* which are not explicitly lyric. The 4 + 4 subdivision of the strophe which has prevailed this far, is here abolished by an emphatic BB mid-strophe couplet, its line-initial accent spitting out an accusation against a female bully. At the semantic level, the *effet de réel* of these gritty autobiographical allusions presents an equally violent contrast to the commonplaces of the biblical and classical traditions. The resulting presence of a rowdy, transgressive 'Villon' is unmistakeable.

With the return of the B rhyme in the final strophe, we take up again the rudely interrupted tenor of our *ballade*. The initial accent on *Mais* followed by the subjunctive *laissast* underlines the incredulity of the speaker — who still sounds like the emphatic *moy* of the previous strophe. The initial accents of ll. 665 and 667 proclaim the irresistibility of love. The 'iambic' rhythm of the first three lines and the unruly 001010010 of l. 668 gives way, in l. 669, to an 'anapestic' dominant:

> Plus doulces luy sont que cyvetes.   010010010

This line strikes this reader as the heart of the strophe, a view which may be justified by the line's formal properties: rhythmically it is marked out by the alternation 'iambic' ≠ 'anapestic' and, at the semantic level, by its 'euphoric'/'erotic' simile which presents an arresting contrast to the 'dysphoric violence' of *vif bruler*. The line's lower accent-count, rhythmic balance and 'euphoric'/'erotic' connotation highlight it as a moment of 'anapestic' repose in a predominantly 'iambic' strophe, which consists so far of incredulous query and vehement exclamation. But the real wonder of this line lies in its syntax: first there is the obvious contrast of its inverted syntax with the normal ordering of the preceding lines. Less obvious are the subtle effects of this trick, which the listener feels before he can consciously identify them: the inversion of verb and complement, while accenting the former also intensifies the accent on the latter. The resulting force of both adjective and verb is affectively crucial, bringing an elegiac tenderness to the sense;[38] a mood abruptly banished by the no-nonsense of l. 670:

> Mais **toutefoys**, fol s'y **fya**: 0101 # 1001

whose opening 'iambic' half-line halts at the 'cesura' which, with its juxtaposed accents, had earlier, in l. 645, carried the connotation 'grave formality?':

> David ly **roys**, **saiges** prophetes.   0101 # 10010

In this hilarious vaudeville, Villon reconciles eternal opposites. The celebration of sexual love stands here as ever in irreducible contradiction with its condemnation.

We find in Villon an aesthetic familiar to readers of our present age. Since Rimbaud and Mallarmé poets have increasingly preferred a language closer to the *paubres motz*, the 'everyday words', of certain of the troubadours, of whom Villon, unlike the Meschinots and Crétins of his time, is the true successor. The commonplace in his words and expressions is transformed in a poetry which reveals the mystery of the familiar and the banality of beauty.

The Sixteenth Century: Joachim du Bellay

From the late fifteenth century onward, the influence of the Italian language and its poetry was increasingly felt in France.[39] The Italian sonnet, whose origin lay in the *ballades* of the trouvères and troubadours, became for French poets the preferred vehicle for the condensed expression of idea and emotion. Joachim du Bellay (1522–60) spent four years in Italy in the service of his cardinal uncle. On his return, he published two collections of sonnets, the *Antiquitéz de Rome* and the *Regrets*, the first alternating sonnets in decasyllables and alexandrines, and the second entirely in alexandrines. The alexandrine, available in French since its use in the twelfth-century *Roman d'Alexandre*, had been typically an epic metre. Villon wrote no alexandrines, his preferred stanza being the *huitain* and his set-piece *ballades* being in either octosyllables or decasyllables. With the impact on syntax of the evolving relationship between word-accent and group-accent, evidently French after 1500 became more comfortable with the smoother symmetry of the 6 + 6 format. The earlier sonnets of Ronsard, du Bellay's influential colleague, are decasyllabic, though later he preferred the alexandrine. In parallel, the sonnets of du Bellay's early *L'Olive* (1550) are decasyllabic, in contrast to the alexandrines of the later *Regrets*. We take two examples, the first from *L'Olive*, and the second from the *Regrets*:

XIX

	Deja la nuit en son parc amassoit	0101 # 001001
	Un grand troupeau d'etoiles vagabondes,	0101 # 01010
	Et pour entrer aux cavernes profondes	**0001** # 0010010
4	Fuyant le jour, ses noirs chevaux chassoit.	0101 # 010101
	Deja le ciel aux Indes rougissoit,	0101 # 010101
	Et l'**Aulbe** encor' de ses tresses tant blondes	0101 # 0010010
	Faisant gresler mile perlettes rondes,	0101 # **1001010**
8	De ses thesors les prez enrichissoit:	**0001** # 010101
	Quand d'occident, comme une etoile vive,	0101 # **0001010**
	Je vy sortir dessus ta verde rive,	0101 # 010101(0)
11	O fleuve mien! une Nymphe en rient.	0101 # 001001
	Alors voyant cete nouvelle Aurore,	0101 # **0001010**
	Le jour honteux d'un double teint colore	0101 # 010101(0)
14	Et l'Angevin & l'Indique orient.[40]	0101 # 001001

[Already night was gathering in its park a great flock of wandering stars and, fleeing daylight, was ready to enter deep caverns, driving on its black horses. Already the Indian sky was reddening, and Dawn still with her blond tresses, showering down a thousand tiny pearls, adorned the meadows with her treasures. When from the west, I glimpsed emerging on your green shore, O my dear stream a laughing Nymph. Then, beholding this second Dawn, shame-faced day dyes with double hue the east of both Anjou and India.]

The possible alternating distribution of accents on the first hemistich of these fourteen decasyllables are 0101 and 1001. Here, eleven first hemistichs show 0101 and no initial accents. The six syllables of the second hemistich make possible four distributions: 010101, 001001, 100101, 101001, of which three are realised here:

# dessus ta verde rive	010101	(6)
# aux cavernes profondes	001001	(4)
# mile perlettes rondes	100101	(1)

Of the total twenty-eight hemistichs, four show a run of three atonic syllables and there is no juxtaposition of accents within the phrase. Thus 86 per cent show alternation by our criteria.

The second hemistichs of the first quatrain alternate 001001 and 010101; this confers rhythmic equivalence on lines with contrasting rhymes, and creates rhythmic dissonance between lines which rhyme but whose semantic values contrast. In ll. 2 and 3, which rhyme, we note the semic opposition 'light' ≠ 'darkness' in the pair *étoiles* ≠ *cavernes*, while the rhymed ll. 1 and 4 contrast on both rhythmic and semantic levels: the expression *en son parc* in l. 1 sets the notion 'sheep' ('peaceful') against the *noirs chevaux* of l. 4, where the preposing of the adjective foregrounds its negative connotation. Lines 1 and 4 on the A rhyme are thus rhythmically and semantically dissonant, and ll. 2 and 3, on the BB couplet, are equally so.

Rhyme here is thus a fragile guarantor of formal unity; its integrating potential is neutralised by dissonance at the levels of rhythm and sense throughout the quatrain. In Thibaut de Champagne, Philippe de Vitry and Villon, we noted the possibility of creating non-lexical meaning by the coupling of rhythmic and semantic units, something completely absent here. Du Bellay is intent rather on *dislocating* sense and rhythm in their relation to rhyme. What looks on the page like a conventional quatrain with a predictable ABBA rhyme-scheme, surprises the listener with an unexpected sense of menace and confusion.[41]

Though the second quatrain reiterates the expected ABBA rhyme-scheme, in it the rapport of form and sense is completely reorganised. Firstly, the sense of return induced by the syntactic equivalence of ll. 1 and 5 is upset by a rhythmic chiasmus in the second hemistichs:

$$1.\ 001001 \quad \rightarrow \quad 5.\ 010101$$
$$2.\ 0101010 \quad \rightarrow \quad 6.\ 0010010$$

As the reader proceeds, in marked contrast to the first quatrain, the equivalence of the second hemistichs of ll. 5 and 8 is abundantly overdetermined: rhythmically, 010101 = 010101; in rhyme-position, phonetically, [ru□i = ri□i], where the anaphoric [r] which begins each of the words forming the richer leonine rhyme is prominent at the onset of an accented vowel, and [□] = [□], though respectively voiced and unvoiced, have the same articulatory position. Semantically *rouge* and *riche* both connote 'rich'. The second hemistichs of ll. 5 and 6 couple the gender opposition of *ciel*/masculine ≠ *Aulbe*/feminine with the rhythmic contrast 010101 ≠ 001001. In the context of *tresses tant blondes*, the lesser accentual density of 001001 connotes 'gentle' as opposed to the 'strong' accentual density of the previous line. In l. 7, the reassuring 'iambic' first hemistich leaves the listener open to the surprise of a verse-unit with an initial accent:

mile perlettes rondes.   100101

This first and only initial accent in a second hemistich overdetermines the hyperbole of the metaphor. This intensity, dissipated in the atonic run of l. 8, finally relaxes into the 010101 of its l. 5 rhyme-partner.

In the first line of the first tercet, after the steady beat of the 'iambic' first hemistich, from the neutral ground of an atonic run, rises a startling new idea — 000101 — *comme une étoile vive*, a metaphor which abolishes the opposition 'living' ≠ 'inert' . The impact of this paradoxical *étoile* is in part due to the contrast of its accentual structure with the semantic vacuity of the atonic *comme une* which precedes it. Generally, the correlation of accent and informational density finds its obverse in a run of unaccented syllables. The idea of 'emergence of something from something', suggested formally here, is named outright in the 'iambic' opening of the next line: *Je vy sortir*, its 'suddenness' underlined by the aspectual contrast of the first and only past definite tense of the sonnet with the descriptive imperfects of the first two stanzas. The sustained 'iambic' pulse of the line, carried over by the line-final synaloepha (*riv*[ə] *O fleuve mien!*) throws into relief the contrasting 'anapests' of the 'living star' — *une Nymphe en rient*. The lovely strangeness of this climactic moment arises in the empty space of the D rhyme which is not a rhyme. The rhythmic contrast in these lines between the 'iambic' *Je* and the 'anapestic' *Nymphe*, is a complex anaphor of the contrast between ll. 5 and 6, where the opposition 'iambic' ≠ 'anapestic' was coupled with the opposition *ciel*/masculine ≠ *Aulbe*/feminine. The poet has become an actor in the mystery of this new day. The first line of the second tercet restates the rhythm and the metaphorical surprise of its fellow in the first tercet, although with muted effect. The sonnet ends with ironic humour in the conjoining of the 'familiar' and the 'exotic': the every day *Angevin* is sturdily 'iambic' and the exotic *Indique orient* 'anapestic'.

Now we turn to our second example, from the *Regrets*:

	De-vaulx, la mer reçoit tous les fleuves du monde	010101 # 101001
	Et n'en augmente point: semblable à la grand'mer	010101 # 010011
	Est ce Paris sans pair, ou l'on void abysmer	*000*101 # 001001
4	Tout ce qui là dedans de toutes parts abonde.	100101 # 010101
	Paris est en sçavoir une Grece feconde,	101001 # 001001
	Une Rome en grandeur Paris on peult nommer,	001001 # 010101
	Une Asie en richesse on le peult estimer,	001001 # 001001
8	En rares nouveautez une Afrique seconde.	010101 # 001001
	Bref, en voyant (De-vaulx) ceste grande cité	100101 # 001001
	Mon oeil, qui paravent estoit exercité	011001 # 010101
	A ne s'emerveiller des choses plus estranges,	010101 # 010101
12	Print esbaïssement. Ce qui ne me peult plaire,	100101 # 001001
	Ce fut l'estonnement du badaud populaire,	010101 # 001001
	La presse des chartiers, les procez, & les fanges.[42]	01*0001* # 001001

[My dear De-vaulx, the sea receives all the rivers of the world and grows no bigger: and like the great sea is this peerless Paris wherein are swallowed up all the riches of all the world. Paris in learning is a fertile Greece; for grandeur it can be called another Rome; for wealth an Asia, for prodigious novelties a second Africa. In short, De-vaulx, at the sight of this great city, my eye, customarily indifferent to even stranger things, was struck with astonishment. What could not please me was the amazement of the gaping crowd, the throng of carters, the law-suits and the filth.]

As opposed to the decasyllable, the syllabic equivalence of the two hemistichs of the alexandrine allows the same rhythmic variety to each. All alternating accent-distributions are represented: 010101, 001001, 101001, 100101. Two hemistichs show a run of three atonic syllables and one has phrase-internal accents juxtaposed. Thus of the twenty-eight verse-units, twenty-four alternate regularly (86 per cent).

In l. 1, the juxtaposed accent on *tous* establishes the hyperbolic tone prolonged in the accented *tout* and *toutes* of l. 4. In l. 2, the juxtaposed accents of etymological *grand'mer* colliding with the initial accent of l. 3 confirm the hyperbolic character of the quatrain. In addition, the enjambement of ll. 2 and 3 forces the *enchaînement* 'grand'me [r→ Est]' which maintains impetus by deleting the line-final pause. The inversion of syntax (CVS as opposed to SVC) gives accentual relief to *Est*, continuing the hyperbolic tone by the juxtaposition of line-final and line-initial accents, a configuration paralleled in the juxtaposition of accents between ll. 3 and 4:

> [...] ou l'on void abysmer
> Tout ce qui là dedans [...].

The semantic value 'hyperbolic' suggested by these colliding accents emerges in contrast with the predominance of strict alternation of accent in this sonnet. Although *est* is normally atonic, here it is on a syntactic boundary resulting from the intercalation of an adverbial complement, and thus carries a group-accent:

Paris[43] est # en sçavoir # une Grece feconde.[44]   101001 # 0010010

'Anapestic' rhythm dominates the quatrain: the *Paris* of the first hemistich is identified, one by one, with Greece, Rome, Asia and Africa, as each one takes up the same rhythm: *une Grece feconde = Une Rome en grandeur = Une Asie en richesse = une Afrique seconde*. The 'identification' is enforced by the coupling of rhythmic and syntactic equivalences.

The move to the new rhyme of the first tercet coincides with a dramatic line-initial accent in l. 9. Both the 'anapestic' rhythm and the sense of *ceste grande cité* echo those of the hemistichs which earlier evoked the rivals of Paris. In l. 10, *Mon oeil*, subject of the SVC clause completed in the first line of the second tercet, is followed by a long, intercalated relative clause. The sense of 'urgent enthusiasm' in the accented *Bref* is continued in juxtaposition of accents:

Mon [oeil, qui] # paravent # estoit exercité.

The accented *qui*, accompanied by the sense of 'suspense' as we await its verb, gives us the 'astonishment' of the narrator. The trite regularity of the 'iambic' l. 11 with its formulaic *nil admirari*, is swept aside by the spectacle of the great city.

The 'surprise' of the poet's conversion from Roman *nil admirari* to his Parisian 'enthusiasm' is thus expressed by a series of formal contrasts: at the semantic level, it is *ne s'émerveiller* ≠ *esbaïssement*; syntactically, by the alternation 'brief main clause' (*Mon oeil [...] Print esbaïssement*) ≠ 'long intercalated subordinate clause'; grammatically, we have the aspectual contrast 'imperfect tense' (*estoit*) ≠ 'passé simple' (*Print*),[45] and rhythmically, between ll. 11 and 12, 010101 # ≠ 100101 #.

The final lines take us from 'exaltation' to the tawdry reality of the city's daily life. Following the revelatory 'shock' of the three accents of *Print esbaïssement*, the lower accent-count of each of the remaining hemistichs, their runs of atonic syllables and the 'monotonous' 001001 of all three of the second hemistichs of the second tercet, all add up to a decline in rhythmic tension: the semantic opposition 'exaltation' ≠ 'depression' is thus coupled with a pronounced rhythmic contrast.

In these sonnets of du Bellay, the shift from 4 + 6 to 6 + 6 leads to a freer treatment of the relationship between word-accent and syntactic accent. While in our italianate sonnet from *L'Olive*, alternation of accent was obtained simply through word-accent, the intimate, conversational register of our sonnet from the *Regrets* uses the fuller resources of the spoken language. The intercalated vocatives of ll. 1 and 9, the insistent anaphora of accented *tous*, *Tout* and *toutes* in the first quatrain, the adverbial inserts of ll. 5 and 10, the suspension of syntax in ll. 9 and 10, the 'astonished' grammatical/ aspectual contrast of *estoit* and *Print* in the tercets and the dumbfounded 'halt' in midline 12, all these are features of a discourse in which the formal properties of verse persuade language to give colloquial expression to excited emotion.

Critics will object that these instances are ad hoc moves to guarantee the sustained alternation of accent in our scansion, but 'the proof of the pudding is in the eating'. If we read the sonnets aloud to see first what the language prompts us to do, it will then become clear that though accent-placement in French verse must meet the requirements of phonology and syntax, the resulting configurations may be subject to marginal interference by the semantic structures of the text, as in the repetitions of *tout* and the *estoit/Print* alternation.

The Seventeenth Century: La Fontaine

Two hundred years before the *vers libristes*, Jean de La Fontaine was, like many of his Middle French predecessors, blithely ignoring the supposed 'constraint' of fixed syllabic count. His *Fables* are loved by readers for their spontaneity and freshness. But when we read La Fontaine, are we reading verse? While the poet was writing, the language specialists of Port-Royal were pronouncing: 'La structure (du vers français) ne consiste qu'en un certain nombre de syllabes', a verdict to be tirelessly reiterated by proponents of isosyllabism down to the present.

By this criterion, much of La Fontaine's verse is not verse at all. His cocktails of alexandrines, deca-, octo- and heptasyllables often provide nothing recurrent for the French reader to get hold of. The silence provoked by this scandal was at last broken by Maya Slater who, in 2000, drew attention to the crucial importance of accent-distribution within the phrase for an adequate reading of the *Fables*. On the relation between versification and meaning in this poetry, she writes:

> La Fontaine's consummate mastery of verse makes it a flexible instrument for expressing nuances of meaning which echo the sense of the words themselves. [...] Stress can be manipulated with great subtlety to contribute to stylistic excess. [...] The effect is difficult to pin down, as French versification analysis does not fully acknowledge nuances of stress variation within a line of verse.[46]

This declaration of the interdependence of prosodic form and meaning in La Fontaine poses the challenge we are now taking up. Though Slater offers no analysis to support her contention, our theory makes it possible to test it on the page. La Fontaine is a critical witness in the debate between isosyllabists and accentualists, and two contrasting *fables* may help us understand how and why his verse manages to survive a persistent heterosyllabism. and yet remain verse. Firstly, 'Le Corbeau et le renard':

	Maître Corbeau, sur un arbre perché,[47]	1001 # 001001	10
	Tenait en son bec un fromage.	01001001	8 + ə
	Maître Renard, par l'odeur alléché,	1001 # 001001	10
	Lui tint à peu près ce langage:	01001001	8 + ə
5	Hé bonjour, Monsieur du Corbeau.	10101001	8
	Que vous êtes joli! Que vous me semblez beau!	101001 # 100101	12
	Sans mentir, si votre ramage	001*00001*	8 + ə
	Se rapporte à votre plumage,	001*00001*	8 + ə
	Vous êtes le Phénix des hôtes de ce bois.	01*0001* # 01*0001*	12
10	A ces mots, le Corbeau ne se sent pas de joie;	001001 # 100101	12
	Et pour montrer sa belle voix,	*00010101*	8
	Il ouvre un large bec, laisse tomber sa proie.	010101 # 100101	12
	Le Renard s'en saisit, et dit: Mon bon Monsieur,	001001 # 010101	12
	Apprenez que tout flatteur	0010101	7
15	Vit au dépense de celui qui l'écoute.	10010 # 0010010	10 + ə
	Cette leçon vaut bien un fromage, sans doute,	*0001* # 01001001	12 + ə

Le Corbeau honteux et confus,   00101001   8
Jura, mais un peu tard, qu'on ne l'y prendrait plus.[48] 01*0001* # 010101   12

This familiar fable begins with the reassuring regularity of a nursery rhyme: l. 1 is syllabically, rhythmically and syntactically symmetrical with l. 3, as is l. 2 with l. 4. The protagonists are introduced as a rhythmically equivalent pair, each with an ironically dignifying initial accent (1001 = 1001). In l. 5 the voice of the Fox breaks in with an octosyllable in which the dominance of binary rhythmic units **10101001** overdetermines the contrast 'narrative voice' ≠ 'direct speech' where the 'narrative voice' had spoken in exclusively *ternary* units: 1001 # 001001 | 001001001 | 1001 # 001001 | 01001001 | 10101001. Line 6 shows the Fox moving from a deferentially conversational octosyllable to the rhetorical overkill of an alexandrine whose exaggerated symmetry tells us all we need to know about the Fox's intentions. The syntactic parallelism and punctuation of this line invite ironically emphatic phrase-internal accent:

Que vous êtes joli! que vous me semblez beau![49]

Here the poet exploits the generic connotations of the contrasting metres, octosyllable ≠ alexandrine: the first of these is a 'simple' metre without 'cesura', much used in popular narrative poetry, while the second, whose complex structure permits antithesis or parallel, is associated with the 'grand' register of dramatic verse.

In ll. 7 and 8, the alexandrine's hyperbolic eulogy gives way abruptly to prosaic octosyllables again. This pair of lines presents the low-key, tongue-in-cheek protasis of a conditional sentence whose (unfulfillable) apodosis in l. 9 maintains the runs of atonic syllables. This change of mode, from exclamation to logical inference, is marked by the first runs of atonic syllables with their suggestion of 'prosiness'.[50] Lines 7 and 8 are rhythmically equivalent in a way which gives us the sly Fox's logical cast of mind, his inferential powers being further suggested by the 'if → then' relation between the couplet's rhyme-words whose phonetic similarity, he hints, imply a material analogy. This is of course an exercise in persuasion in which the Machiavellian Fox bends to his will a witless Crow dominated by vanity. The victim's capitulation, in l. 10, is immediate and unconditional:

A ces mots, le Corbeau ne se sent pas de joie.   001001 # 100101[51]

In an ecstasy of flattered *amour propre*, he prepares to sing. Line 11, a subordinate phrase with a run of three atonic syllables, throws the full accentuation of the alexandrine main clause into relief:

Et pour montrer sa belle voix   *00010101*
Il **ou**vre un large bec, laisse tomber sa proie.   010101 # 100101

In l. 12, the juxtaposed accents at the 'cesura' perform the surprise of the dropped cheese. Anyone coming fresh to the story and hearing the first hemistich of l. 12 might well have expected the Crow to start singing. But no, we had forgotten the cheese! And it is the shock of the juxtaposed accents which reminds us.

The first hemistich of l. 13, with its two accents, contrasts with the three accents of the second hemistich of l. 12:

Il **ouv**re un large bec, laisse tomber sa **proie**	010101 # 100101	
Le Renard s'en saisit, et dit: Mon **bon** Monsieur	001001 # 010101	

Since, in this preceding hemistich, each of the three accents marks a lexical item of low frequency of occurrence, while in the latter only two are thus marked, the resulting difference in semantic density may be perceived as a difference in tempo; that is, the following hemistich, *Le Renard s'en saisit*, is perceived as moving more rapidly than the first. Here is a formal/semantic representation of the Fox's 'pounce on the cheese'. The immediate reversion to an 'iambic' three-accent second hemistich recovers semantic density: the Fox has collected his wits.

The Fox's homily to the Crow gets some of its preacherly tone from the reversion to the dominant regular alternation of accent in ll. 13–16: # 01010 | 0010101 | 1001 # 001001 | *000*101 # 001001. This sequence of *vers irréguliers* shows clearly the integrating function of alternating accent. After a pair of alexandrines, the unexpected earliness of the rhyme in l. 14 tells the listener of an abrupt switch to a trenchant seven-syllable line, the lordly *Apprenez* of the Fox marking the foregoing *Mon bon Monsieur* as a condescending sneer. The final line, with the narrator's tart interjection, tails off in two runs of three unaccented syllables, the contrast with the regular alternation of accent in the preceding lines announcing the bathos of the Crow's feeble rejoinder.

Does the absence of sustained recurrence of syllabic count leave a listener hearing rhymed prose? The number of times that this fable has been learned by heart and recited suggests that remembering it is not difficult. Anyone reading the first four lines aloud cannot fail to sense that their rhythmic structure has an unmistakeable shape which sticks in the mind. If verse in its beginnings was primarily mnemonic, La Fontaine's fable is unmistakeably verse. But here is an even more irregular one, 'Les Grenouilles qui demandent un roi' (Book III, 4):

	Les Gren**ou**illes, se lass**ant**	001*0*001	7
	De l'état Démocratique,	00101010	7
	Par leurs clam**eur**s firent t**ant**	*000*1001	7
	Que Jup**in** les soum**it** au pouvoir Monarchique.	001001 # 0010010	12
5	Il leur tomb**a** du Ciel un Roi t**out** pacifique:	*000*101 # 0**11**0010	12
	Ce **Roi** f**it** tout**efois** un tel bruit en tombant	0**11**001 # 001001	12
	Que la **gent** maré**cageuse,**	00101010	7
	Gent fort sotte et fort peureuse,	**111**01010	7
	S'alla cacher sous les **eaux,**	0101001	7
10	Dans les **jon**cs, dans les ros**eaux,**	0010*0*01	7
	Dans les **trou**s du mar**é**cage,	00101010	7
	Sans oser de longtemps regarder au visage	001001 # 0010010	12
	Celui qu'elles croyaient être un gé**ant** nouveau;	010010100101	12
	Or c'était un Soliveau,	1*000*101	7
15	De qui la gravité f**it peur** à la première	010101 # 010*0*010	12
	Qui de le **voir** s'aventur**ant**	10010101	8
	Osa bien quitter sa tanière.	101010010	8
	Elle **approcha,** mais en tremblant.	01010*0*01	8
	Une **autre** la suiv**it,** une **autre** en fit aut**ant,**	010*0*01 # 010*0*01	12
20	Il en **vint** une four**mi**lière;	001001010	8
	Et leur **troupe** à la **fin** se rend**it** familière	001001 # 0010010	12

	Jusqu'à sauter sur l'épaule du Roi.	*0001* # 001001	10
	Le bon Sire le souffre, et se tient toujours coi.	001001 # 001001	12
	Jupin en a bientôt la cervelle rompue.	010101 # 0010010	12
25	Donnez-nous, dit le peuple, un Roi qui se remue,	101001# 01*00010*	12
	Le Monarque des Dieux leur envoie une Grue,	001001 # 0010010	12
	Qui les croque, qui les tue,	00*100010*	7
	Qui les gobe à son plaisir,	001*0001*	7
	Et Grenouilles de se plaindre;	00*100010*	7
30	Et Jupin de leur dire: Eh quoi! votre désir	001001 # 01*0001*	12
	A ses lois croit-il nous astreindre?	001010010	8
	Vous avez dû premièrement	*00*010101	8
	Garder votre Gouvernement;	01*000*101	8
	Mais, ne l'ayant pas fait, il vous devait suffire	101001 # *0001*010	12
35	Que votre premier roi fût débonnaire et doux:	*000*101 # 010101	12
	De celui-ci, contentez-vous	01010101	8
	De peur d'en rencontrer un pire.[52]	010101010	8

In l. 1, the poet punctuates to divide a seven-syllable line, which can have no 'cesura', by way of introducing his protagonists: humble creatures (whose metre is the humble heptasyllable) burdened by self-government, who clamour for a ruler.[53] Jupiter answers their prayer, descending in the contrasting majesty of an alexandrine to give them a King.[54] The untidy measure of their complaint and supplication, with its atonic runs and overflow, is answered in the ordered formality of an authoritatively end-stopped verse-line whose alternating rhythm is perfectly balanced around its 'cesura': 001001 # 001001, a striking coupling of accentual, metrical and semantic contrasts. The narrative continues in alexandrines, but now the the generic contrast between the 'demotic' heptasyllable and the 'regal' alexandrine is beginning to blur. The rhythm of l. 5, disturbed by an atonic run and colliding accents, moves away from the formal balance of l. 4 towards something more like ordinary speech.[55] In l. 6, colliding accents and an intercalated adverb *toutefois*, together with another insert, this time the adverbial *en tombant*, hold up the forward movement of the syntax, which at this point is incomplete. This progressive distancing of the register from that of l. 4 creates a colloquial intimacy, albeit achieved by subtle management of syntax and accent-distribution: intercalation, colliding accents, deferring of syntactical closure.

Thus the 'down-graded' alexandrines of ll. 5 and 6 lead back naturally to the workaday heptasyllable, with yet more colliding accents in the still suspended syntax of l. 8. The rhythmic anaphora of the series *sous les **eaux**, Dans les **joncs**, dans les roseaux, Dans les trous*, with its structure of 'same + different' suggests, with the idea of the 'same activity in different places', the 'trying this, trying that' of the frogs' aimless panic. The precipitate activity indicated by the punctual preterite *S'alla cacher* gives way to the 'state of fearful anticipation' given in the non-finite duration of *Sans oser de longtemps*, where the intercalated adverbial phrase makes us wait for the fearful dependent infinitive. The contrast 'panic activity' ≠ 'fearful stillness?' is coupled with the transition from 'irregular heptasyllable' to 'ordered alexandrine'.[56] This switch is brought home to readers by their having to wait for the couplet-rhyme *visage* to arrive in an unexpectedly longer line.[57] This line is not only longer but also incomplete: its syntax again prolonging our 'wait' for the cause of the dread until the *Celui* at the head of l. 13. The poet might well have written for example 'Leur **Roi**, qu'elles croyaient être un géant nouveau' but instead he chose a semantically empty pronoun to figure the frogs' nameless dread. Though no edition punctuates here, this dramatic crux demands a marked boundary between the accented *Celui* and the subordinate clause. Until this point, the text has *enacted* the fearfulness of the frogs, whereas the clause that follows *explains* it. They thought he was another giant; no, he was a lump of wood. Now the transition back from alexandrine to heptasyllable enacts the bathos, the reader surprised again, but this time by a rhyme that arrives too soon. The tongue-in-cheek punning on *gravité* of l. 15 sets the tone of the narrating voice for the effects of the lines that follow. The first mud-dweller to dare approach Him, 'ventures out' with the 'hesitancy?' of a line interrupted by syntactical boundaries and the consequently marked accents (l. 16):

> Qui # de le **voir** # s'aventur**ant**

where the unmarked order of the syntax would be 'Qui s'av**en**tur**ant** de le **voir**'. The participle leads to a decisive finite verb in the following line:

> **O**sa bi**en** quitter sa tani**è**re   101010010

which verb is given relief by its oxytonic accent being displaced to the left by the intercalated emphatic adverb. This 'exceptional daring?' prompts a response. The alexandrine of l. 18 mobilises the metre's potential for symmetry but not this time for grandiloquence. The humour here is in the gulf between the elevated connotation of the metre and the 'hesitant fearfulness?' of the mud-dwellers. An unusually marked 'cesural' pause between syntactically independent verb + subject phrases gives us yet again the idea of 'diffidence, hesitation?'. The structure of the verse-line itself is a metaphor for the verb *suivit* since the second hemistich 'imitates' the first, syntactically, rhythmically and semantically. Then everybody piles in, in a 'cesura'-less octosyllable whose anapestic 'forward rush' contrasts hilariously with the tip-toeing circumspection of its forerunner.[58] These frogs, who cannot manage a democratic polity, are temperamentally helpless followers.

This sudden 'rush' settles in l. 21 into the stress-free equilibrium of an alexandrine whose rhythm echos that of l. 4:

> Et leur tr**ou**pe à la f**in** # se rendit famili**è**re.

But the 'ideal' form of the rhythmically and syntactically symmetrical alexandrine is 'down-graded' by the mundane connotations of *troupe* and *familière*. Any doubts concerning the poet's supreme awareness of the possibilities of heterosyllabism are dispelled in the decasyllable of l. 22: here, the surprise foreshortening (on *sauter*) of the expected alexandrine's first hemistich, is the perfect formal expression of 'irreverent familiarity?'.[59] In l. 23, the alexandrine returns, but now the rhythmic 'sameness' of its hemistichs ironically evokes the 'wooden immobility?' of the divine 'Soliveau'.

Meanwhile, back on Olympus, Jupiter is at his wits' end. The importunity of the mud-dwellers is driving him to such distraction that the normally high-frequency verb *a* of his l. 24 alexandrine acquires an accent through the intercalation of *bientôt*, the intensity of his irritation being expressed through the 'accelerating' effect of the 'anapestic' second hemistich in contrast to the 'iambic' measure of the first.[60] The remonstrations of the froggy mob are reported in a now vehemently untidy alexandrine with initial accent in the first hemistich and a run of atonic syllables in the second. But in l. 26, the voice of the King of the Gods is heard in a return of the grave, judicial measure of l. 4, whose balanced rhythm and lofty register is itself a reproof to the complaining ingrates of the disorderly previous line. Their doom is sealed. The hammer-blows of the rhythmic equivalence of the three heptasyllables which follow underscore the inevitable connection of wrong-doing and suffering. Though Jupin's final judgement moves from an alexandrine to a pair of octosyllables, the register of his speech remains lofty, formal, the syntactical inversion in line 31 re-inforcing accent on *lois* and the incredulous *croit-il*. While this line alternates accent, the less formal 'if only' asides of octosyllables 32 and 33 relax into runs of three atonic syllables. Regal reproof returns with the alexandrines of ll. 34 and 35, though even these show informality in overflow and atonic runs. The 'suddenness' of the couplet-rhyme in the penultimate line sharpens the shock of the metrical alternation of octosyllable with alexandrine and the remarkably sustained 'iambic' rhythm of the final lines insists on the finality of Jupiter's judgement.

In our text, we find eighteen runs of three atonic syllables and one case of colliding accents in fifty-two verse-units. of which 65 per cent alternate accent by our criteria. Detailed description of the accent distributions in this verse is clearly indispensable to the full realisation of its semantic values. We find corroboration for our description of La Fontaine's rhythms in Lully's settings of Quinault, both artists being cultural and linguistic contemporaries of our poet. In these settings we noted not only the thoroughgoing oxytonic and countertonic accentuation of words within the phrase but also the interplay of accent-patterning with the sense of Quinault's libretto. In isosyllabic verse from the thirteenth century onward, we have seen such accent-patterning dedicated to the creation of meaning. La Fontaine, though dispensing with recurrent syllabic count in many of his fables, finds in such patterning the possibility of formal ordering for his verse, exploiting the potential for interplay between rhythm and sense for the creation of non-paraphrasable meaning whose subtlety is a constant and surprising delight for his readers.

In short, *either* accent within the verse-unit is nothing more than a random distribution derived from the poet's native French, *or* the accentual structure of that language has been transformed through conscious ordering into a rich source of meaning.[61] We are experiencing, through the poet's formal ordering of linguistic accent, a projection of meaning on to the 'sensorium' of the reader. Since the *Fables* are clearly intended to be read aloud, it is above all to the *body* of the reader/listener that these texts address their minutely organised changes of register and tempo. All sensory perception, be it auditory, visual, tactile or olfactory, is perception of a change of state in the ground of what is perceived. The rhythm of the poet's verse, his ordering of linguistic accent, arouses potential motor activity in the body of the reader/listener, re-creating the poet's experience of his world. The silent reader feels only a faint 'neural echo' generated by the subaudible reflex movement of the organs of speech. We are studying here the nature of the non-eidetic sensations we receive from poetry through the interaction of its syntactic, semantic and accentual-metrical structures. Some of these are slowness, speed, acceleration and de-acceleration, as well as density, diffuseness, roughness or smoothness, weight or lightness, balance or imbalance. In other words experiences otherwise caused by changes of state in the ordinary objects of our perception as we perceive them through sight, hearing, touch and smell, and also through the innervation of our bodies' surfaces and deeper structures. As in the 'Housman test' for poetry ('the prickling on the back of the neck'), that we are able to feel these things while reading or listening to poetry means that these somatic events are triggered by formal structures in poetic 'language', if we understand by 'language' a semiological system that includes formal codes (accent, metre, rhyme and so on).

Poetry like that of La Fontaine surely makes the utmost use of these resources. His free verse, while deploying canonical verse-units, relies for its characteristic effects on similarity or contrast between accentual configurations in neighbouring verse-units, often of different lengths. The *vers libre* of the nineteenth century, while abandoning the former, retained the latter. La Fontaine thus remains required reading for anyone wanting to understand better the poetry of Laforgue and of French *vers libristes* of the twentieth century.

The Eighteenth Century

In any anthology of French poetry, the pages devoted to this century will be relatively few. How many readers, if asked to name an eighteenth-century French poet who excited them, could reply without hesitation? Only the name of André Chénier might come up. Though he died in 1794 under the guillotine, his kinship with his Romantic successors is striking. His poetry is indeed inspired by classical models, but it is his committed intensity that marks him off from his contemporaries.[62]

Here are passages from two poems: the first, on a classical theme, shows Chénier's pedigree; the second, an extract from *Ïambes*, written while he was in prison awaiting execution, is a 'report from the front', grimly familiar to any twenty-first-century political prisoner.

In this passage from 'L'Aveugle', the blind Homer, a guest in Syros, repays his hosts by recounting the battle between the Lapiths and the Centaurs:

	Quand Thésée, au milieu de la joie et du vin,	001001 # 001001
	La nuit où son ami reçut à son festin	010001 # 010001
	Le peuple monstrueux des enfants de la Nue,	010101 # 0010010
	Fut contraint d'arracher l'épouse demi-nue	001001 # 010101(0)
5	Au bras ivre et nerveux du sauvage Eurytus.	011001 # 001001
	Soudain, le glaive en main, l'ardent Pirithoüs:	010101 # 010101
	'Attends; il faut ici que mon affront s'expie,	010101 # 0001010
	Traître!' Mais avant lui, sur le Centaure impie,	100101 # 0001010
	Dryas a fait tomber, avec tous ses rameaux,	010101 # 001001
10	Un long arbre de fer hérissé de flambeaux.	011001 # 001001
	L'insolent quadrupède en vain s'écrie; il tombe,	101001 # 010101(0)
	Et son pied bat le sol qui doit être sa tombe.	001101 # 0010010
	Sous l'effort de Nessus, la table du repas	001001 # 010001
	Roule, écrase Cymèle, Évagre, Périphas.	101001 # 010101
15	Pirithoüs égorge Antimaque, et Pétrée,	010101 # 001001(0)

	Et Cyllare aux pieds blancs et le noir Macarée,	001011 # 0010010
	Qui de trois fiers lions, dépouillés par sa main	101101 # 001001
	Couvrait ses quatre flancs, armait son double sein.	010101 # 010101
	Courbé, levant un roc choisi pour leur vengeance,	010101 # 0100010
20	Tout à coup, sous l'airain d'un vase antique, immense,	001001 # 0101010
	L'imprudent Bianor, par Hercule surpris,	101001 # 001001
	Sent de sa tête énorme éclater les débris.	100101 # 001001
	Mais d'un double combat Eurynome est avide,	001001 # 0010010
	Car ses pieds agités en un cercle rapide	001001 # 0010010
25	Battent à coups pressés l'armure de Nestor.	100101 # 010001
	Le quadrupède Hélops fuit. L'agile Crantor,	010101 # 101001
	Le bras levé, l'atteint. Eurynome l'arrête.	010101 # 0010010
	D'un érable noueux il va fendre sa tête,	001001 # 0010010
	Lorsque le fils d'Égée, invincible, sanglant,	*000101* # 001001
30	L'aperçoit, à l'autel prend un chêne brûlant,	001001 # 101001
	Sur sa croupe indomptée, avec un cri terrible,	001001 # 0101010
	S'élance, va saisir sa chevelure horrible,	010101 # 0101010
	L'entraîne, et, quand sa bouche ouverte avec effort	011001 # 010101
	Crie, il y plonge ensemble et la flamme et la mort.[63]	100101 # 001001

This alexandrine recreation of Homer breathes in long paragraphs. Of the sixty-eight verse-units here, eight show atonic runs of three syllables and five show accents juxtaposed within the phrase. This leaves fifty-five verse-units (81 per cent) which alternate regularly. While the exhilarating violence of battle is heard in the verse-rhythm, the tumult is set against the alternating norm found in French verse since the thirteenth century.

As we have seen, to qualify as alternating, the rhythm of the hemistich must be one of the following: 010101, 001001, 100101 or 101001. All are represented here. Of 010101, we find twenty instances and of 001001 twenty-six, of the others four and five respectively.

Lines 1 and 2 give no hint of the terrible events to come. From their low accent-count, either with repeated 001 or with an atonic run, the move to three accents coincides with an abrupt switch from 'euphoric' semantic value — *joi, vin, festin* — to the 'dysphoric' *monstrueux* of l. 3. There is thus a coupling of semantic and rhythmic values, the semantic opposition 'euphoric' ≠ 'dysphoric' being overdetermined by the rhythmic opposition 'two accents' ≠ 'three accents'. Line 4 brings further 'dysphoria' with *arracher* and the following *épouse demi-nue* in a three-accent hemistich. Our suspicion that 'rape' is imminent is swiftly confirmed in an enjambement which brings the surprise of a line shortened by the proclisis of its final [ə] with the initial *Au* of l. 5. This violation of the alternation of masculine and feminine rhymes prepares the further shock of a colliding accent on the transferred epithet in *bras ivre*, the correlation 'dysphoric' = 'three accents' being maintained.[64]

Line 6 brings the intervention of the King of the Lapiths: Theseus's bosom friend, Pirithous, the offended bridegroom-to-be. This is the first line to be entirely 'iambic'. Its six accents mark semantically critical lexemes: in its initial adverb *Soudain*, the word-accent coincides with a lengthening group-accent; *glaive* is a weapon, and the word-accent on *l'ardent*, emphasised by its position before the noun, will have a raised value on the pitch parameter. The name *Pirithoüs*, with its group-final accent, is informationally critical: it confirms our suspicion that it is indeed the Battle of the Lapiths and Centaurs that we are about to hear. The group-final accent of the opening imperative of l. 7 heralds a line which continues the theme of three accents. One of these, on *ici*, has a semantic force: the King will brook no delay in exacting his vengeance. This accent is marked both by the adverb's leftward displacement *and* its position at the 'cesura'. Pirithoüs's shout of *Traître!* in the next line, raises the stakes with a line-initial accent. In l. 10, symmetrical with [bra.zivʀ] in l. 5, the colliding accents of *long arbre de fer* force the unvoiced *liaison*-consonant in [lɔ̃.kaʀbʀə], where the plosive [k] forms the emphatic onset of the accented vowel in *arbre*. The force of the accent is further increased by the closing and abrupt opening of the airway in the articulation of the plosive [k].

As in *l'ardent* above, the accents in *L'insolent* in l. 11 are given articulatory prominence by the preposing of the adjective, distinguished once again by the raised pitch of the vowels. The 'cesura' is weakened by the *enchaînement*, in *quadrupède en vain* ([kadʀyp◻. dɑ̃. v◻.]) where the sixth syllable is accented but the word-boundary follows the seventh, leading the ear forward to the foregrounded accent on *vain*. This is the first line in the passage without a word-boundary at the 'cesura'. It finishes with two strong group-final accents: *s'écrie: il tombe*, separated by an awkward hiatus which forces the reciter to pause just before the 'fall'. Again, proclisis deletes the [ə] of *tomb(ə)*, carrying us forward into the next line. Just as in *bras ivre* and *long arbre*, the colliding accents in *Et son pied bat le sol* are overdetermined at another level of organisation. In *bras ivre* the accents coincided with a rhetorical figure, in *long arbre*, the overdetermination was phonetic; here, in the verb *bat*, the onomatopoeic initial plosive literally enacts its sense, the effect of the juxtaposed accent on the vowel.

In l. 13, Nessus turns the tables: his effort is matched by that of the reciter in managing the collision of accents which encumber the 'overflow' into the next line:

> [...] la table du repas→Roule [...].[65]

Just as the idea of the abrupt 'suddenness' of the table's motion is given by the deletion of the line-boundary and the resulting clash of accents, so the idea of the *speed* of the 'rolling table' is given by deleting the word-boundaries both after *Roule* and at the 'cesura'. In l. 14, the table does not stop once it has crushed Cymèle, it is already flattening Évagre:

> [ʀou. le.kʀa.zə. si.m◻ # le.va.gʀə [...]]

It is the idea of being 'carried forward' that this line has in common with l. 11:

> L'insolent quadrup◻ # [dɑ̃. vɛ̃.].

The brute fact of the irregular 'cesura' has no meaning of its own. For example, in the following:

> Le paysage amica # lɔ̃kɑ̃d◻sɑ̃ # tekutə*

any relation between form and sense is hard to imagine. Though formal structures have no inherent semantic value, they can through coupling acquire a sense resistant to paraphrase. In l. 15 *enchaînement* again keeps the line moving by blurring word-boundaries:

[pi.ʀito.y..se.goʀ. □ã.ti.ma. ke. pe.tre.]

The normally atonic *Qui* at the head of l. 17 has a group-accent, the first of four in the hemistich overdetermining the hyperbolic sense of *trois fiers lions*. In l. 18, the exact syntactic equivalence of the two hemistichs, verb + possessive + numeral + noun = verb + possessive + numeral + noun, is coupled with the rhythmic equivalence 010101 = 010101. Exceptionally, there is further equivalence in the distribution of word-boundaries: $2 + 1 + 2 + 1 = 2 + 1 + 2 + 1$.[66] The semantic value of this virtuosic super-equivalence represents the 'irresistible destructive power?' of Pirithoüs. In l. 20:

Tout à coup, sous l'airain d'un vase antique, immense,

the lower accent-count of the 'anapestic' first hemistich with the pause between its brief adverbial phrases contrasts with the higher accent-count and uninterrupted phonetic unity of [va.zã. tik.kim.mã.sə.]. The accentually 'lighter' *Tout à coup* contrasts with the semantic value 'weight' implied by the sense of *airain* strengthened by the 'cesural' accent, and by *immense* with its ponderous 'double consonant' and matching group-accent.[67] In parallel, the first hemistich's adverbial phrases, separated by a pause, contrast with the 'single object' suggested by the unbroken phonetic unity of [va.zã. ti.kim.mã.sə]. 'Battle' + 'weight' + 'object': the *vase* becomes a weapon.

In a shift in tempo, the three accents of the first hemistichs of ll. 21 and 22, ll. 23 and 24 are entirely 'anapestic'. In l. 25, their sustained forward rhythm is broken by a line-initial accent in *Battent à coups pressés*. The impact of the tonic vowel in *Battent* is reinforced by the 'metaphorical' value of the plosive onset (compare *pied bat* in l. 12) and also by an effortful break in phonation forced by the 'doubling of the 'tt' resulting from the *enchaînement* in *Batt(en) tà*, i.e. [bat□ əta]. The poetic strategy which creates excitement through the alternation of tension and release is made even more evident by the next line. Here, the listener, enjoying the momentary respite of a 'regular' 'iambic' hemistich, *Le quadrupède Hélops*, is galvanised by what happens at the expected 'cesura'. There *is* no 'cesura'. What was to be the first syllable of the second hemistich receives a group-final accent:

Le quadrupède Hélops (#?) fuit.

The listener sustains thus a double shock: the defeat of his 'cesural' expectation, plus a metrically transgressive collision of accents, enact the 'unexpected abruptness?' of the centaur's flight.

In *L'entraîne, et*, the final climactic couplet suspends movement on a colliding pair of lengthened group-final accents, then moves forward over a 'cesura' eclipsed by *enchaînement*:

[...] quand sa bou # □uverte avec effort

to a line-initial accent on *Crie*. The final collision of lengthened accents in *effort/Crie* again suspends forward movement. Then the verse rushes forward over a 'cesura' again attenuated by *enchaînement*: [i.li.pl □̃.□ã.sã # bl.e.la. flam.me.la.m□ʀ.] into a hemistich whose two accents shock with the victim's hideous death.

Now to a final composition by Chénier, written from prison in 1793, 'Saint-Lazare' (*Iambes*, VIII):

	On vit; on vit infâme. Eh bien? Il fallut l'être;	010101 # 0101010
	L'infâme après **tout** mange et dort.	01001**1**01
	Ici même, en ses parcs, où la mort nous fait **paî**tre,	001001 # 0010010
	Où la hache nous tire au sort,	00100101
5	**Beaux** poulets sont écrits; maris, a**man**ts sont dupes;	101001 # 0101010
	Caquetage, intrigues de sots.	00101001
	On y **chan**te; on y **joue**; on y **lève** des jupes;	001001 # 0010010
	On y **fait** chansons et bons mots;	00101001
	L'un **pou**sse et fait bondir sur les **toits**, sur les vitres,	01*0*001 # 0010010
10	Un ballon tout gonflé de **vent**,	00100101
	Comme **sont** les **dis**cours des sept **cent** plats belîtres,	001001 # 00**11**010
	Dont Barère est le plus savant.	00100101
	L'autre **court**; l'autre **saute**; et **brail**lent, **boi**vent, **rient**,	001001 # 0101010
	Politiques et raisonneurs;	10100101
15	Et sur les **gonds** de **fer** soudain les portes crient;	*000*101 # 0101010
	Des juges tigres nos seigneurs,	01010*0*01
	Le pourvoy**eur** paraît. Quelle sera la proie	010101 # 100101(0)
	Que la hache appelle aujourd'hui?	00101001
	Cha**cun** frissonne, é**coute**; et cha**cun** avec **joie**	010101 # 001001(0)
20	Voit que c'est n'est pas encore lui...[68]	100*0*1001

Of these thirty verse-units, four show a run of three atonic syllables and two show juxtaposed accents. Thus, twenty-four alternate regularly (80 per cent). The alternation of alexandrine and octosyllable is found elsewhere in Chénier's poems, for example, in 'Le Jeu de Paume', one of the few published in his lifetime. In 'Saint-Lazare', the alternation between feminine alexandrine and masculine octosyllable is coupled with alternating rhyme ABAB CDCD... . Though such coupling concerns only formal features, and has no intrinsic semantic value, the opening lines show it being put to work. Compared for example with the AABB couplets of 'L'Aveugle', the first B rhyme here *is not* a rhyme until its match in l. 4. The poet thus has a difference with which to work. As we hear the first two lines, further differences strike us: at the formal level, the alexandrine alternates strictly in 'iambic' rhythm. Its hemistichs are rhythmically and syntactically symmetrical and their syllable-counts identically partitioned. In stark contrast the undivided octosyllable, with its mixed rhythmic units and juxtaposed accents, could be prose. Meanwhile, at the semantic level, l. 1 shows rhetorical features: there is anaphora in the first hemistich and implied apostrophe (*Eh bien?*) in the second. The 'punctual' connotation of the past definite *fallut* marks a 'high' register, while the down-to-earth indefinite present of *mange et dort* belongs to a colloquial one.

In short, the historical and generic contrast of the two metres is exploited by Chénier, as it was by La Fontaine. The alexandrine with its connotation of 'seriousness, gravity', maintained from the later *chanson de geste* down to the theatre of Corneille and Racine, produces its meanings in colloquy with the 'demotic' and 'serviceable' octosyllable. In these two lines, as often in La Fontaine, the dramatic effect of the exchange is to bring magniloquence down to earth. This asserting of the primacy of the everyday has a moral significance for the reader reflecting on the human context in which these verses were written.

In l. 3, the regular 'anapests' of the alexandrine contrast sharply with the regular iambs of l. 1. With the relaxation of a reduced accent-count, the poet ironises on the topos we met in du Bellay's sonnet, that of the shepherd and his flock, for in this reminiscence of 'pastoral' ideality, Death is the shepherd: 'Et in Arcadia ego'. Syntax is crucial since it highlights the key themes: *parcs* and *paître*, with enhanced accent; the former at the 'cesura' and the latter at the line-boundary confirm the reference to the pastoral topos, only for *mort* to subvert it. In l. 5, though the 'cesura' is marked and the hemistichs are opposed rhythmically, this contrast is not overdetermined; it is the semantic world of l. 2 which now prevails. The colliding accents on *la hache nous tirer au sort,* | *Beaux poulets* dramatise the paradoxical coexistence of imminent death with unconcerned normality. The ironic insistence of the line-initial accent on *Beaux* proclaims its triviality: love-letters, cuckolds, betrayal: life awaiting execution is life as it always was. *Maris* and *amants*, semantically contrasted but rhythmically equivalent, are in the same boat. In l. 6, the synaloepha creates *enchaînement* ([ka.kə.ta. ◻◻̃ tʀi.]), insisting on the common 'turpitude' of the accented nouns. By l. 7 the 'solemnity' of the initial 'iambic' alexandrine has completely vanished. The ironising rhythmic monotony of the line is forced on our attention by the overdetermination of the repeated syntactic unit (*on y* + verb) by the 001 rhythmic cell. In each instance, the semantically redundant atonic *on y* leads to a verb whose word-accent is reinforced by group-accent, making the line into a grim waltz. This is echoed in l. 9 with the 001001 of *sur les toits # sur les vitres*, enacting the 'dancing' bounce of *Un ballon tout gonflé* (001001).

The scene now turns political with a sarcastic jibe at the Convention Nationale under the Terror; the bitter humour of the transition being enhanced by the persistent rhythm of the ball 'bouncing' into the domain of political debate:

Un **ballon** tout gonflé [...]	001001
Comme **sont** les dis**cours** [...].[69]	001001

In the second hemistich, the force of the accent on *plat* is heightened both by juxtaposition to *cent* and by preposition to its noun.[70] In the first hemistich of l. 13, the rhythm takes us back to the carefree activities of the common prisoners in l. 7. In the second hemistich, a switch from 'anapestic' to 'iambic' marks off political and professional prisoners. As the verb-number moves from the anonymous 'singular' to the 'plural', from monosyllabic *court* and *saut(e)* to the disyllabic *braillent, boivent* and *rient* of the *politiques et raisonneurs*, the contrasting accentual structures of these verbs are a *rhythmic* expression of the *semantic* opposition between 'physical' and 'intellectual/social' activity.

Whatever social distinctions may separate the prisoners, the fear of death unites them. The dreaded moment arrives. In:

Et sur les **gonds** de fer # soud**ain** #

the impending terror is intensified by the breath-stopping intercalation of the adverb.[71] At last the portals groan. But then another wait: who will come in? Further inversion of syntax delays the advent of the messenger of death. The verb *paraît*, just like line-final *crient*, comes at the very last moment, at the group-final 'cesura' of l. 17. The terrible question is posed and the 'social solidarity' of the third-person plural gives way to singular lonely fear of *Chacun frissonne, écoute*. This fearful anticipation, underlined by the return of the 'heavier' 'iambic' pulse, is mercifully relieved by the reversion to the 'lighter' 'anapests' of *et chacun avec joie*. The anaphora of this *chacun* is more intense being on a syntactic boundary, *chacun # avec joie #*. Then the overwhelming relief of reprieve bursts out in the colliding accents of *joi(e)/Voit*,[72] strengthened by the rhyme.

Though Chénier's verse on the page looks very much of its time, the ear is constantly surprised by its individual voice. Certainly the 6 + 6 of the alexandrine stays close to the 'classical' model: in a random sample of 250 of his alexandrines, we find that the 'cesural' syllable is nearly always tonic and followed by a word-boundary. Boileau's rule, that breaks in the sense and metrical divisions should coincide, is usually followed;[73] but Chénier can have other ideas too:

> Les belles **font** aimer; elles **aiment**. Les belles
> Nous charment **tous**. Heureux qui **peut** être aimé d'elles![74]

Here the 'cesural' accent and word-boundary are in place, but the line-boundary falls illicitly within the verb phrase: *Les belles* (#?) *Nous charment tous*. Because *belles* is thus not group-final, it is not slowed down by lengthening. We are carried rapturously forward into a line in which the golden rule is broken: the major syntactical boundary ('cesura'?) is at the fourth syllable, giving the division 4 + 8. 'Subject → verb' enjambement can be found also in Victor Hugo and Rimbaud, but Chénier's double infraction is extreme even by their standard.

In our passage from 'L'Aveugle', we found our poet again piling up infractions to great effect:

> Sous l'effort de Nessus, la table du repas
> Roule, écrase Cym☐ # le.va.gʀə. Périphas,
> Pirithoüs é.gor. # ☐ã.ti.ma.ke. pe.tre.[75]

Here the 'subject → verb' enjambement, *repas → Roule*, is coupled with juxtaposed accents and followed by a 'cesura' whose statutory word-boundary is deleted by *enchaînement* ([si.m☐ # le.**va**.gʀə [...]]). Moreover, in 'Pirithoüs é.gor. (#?) ☐ã.ti.**ma**.ke' there can be no syntactical boundary between verb and object. Similarly in:

> Le quadrupède Hélops (#?) fuit[76]

there is double violation of the 'cesural' rule: there can be no boundary between subject and verb and, if this is a 7 + 5 alexandrine, there will be a juxtaposed accent on positions 6 and 7.

Throughout we have noted the informational richness that Chénier derives from juxtaposed accents. In 'L'Aveugle', we found *bras ivre*, *long arbre*, *pied bat* and *trois fiers* within the hemistich, and *repas/Roule*, *surpris/Sent* and *effort/Crie* at the line-end: in all these instances accentual structure is semantically overdetermined. In 'Saint-Lazare', *sort/Beaux* and *joie/Voit* sum up the contradictions and violent emotions of the prisoners' lives.

The Nineteenth Century

The sonnets of Joachim du Bellay owed their form to Petrarch, but it is the personal tenor of his mature poetry that distinguishes him from Petrarch and from Ronsard, his more brilliant contemporary. The discursive proclivity of the eighteenth century turned French minds away from such demanding lyric forms. It was only as the prestige of *la raison* gradually gave way to that of feeling that the sonnet again found a voice. French poets Émile Deschamps, Hugo, Nerval, all occasionally turned to it, but it was above all Charles Baudelaire who understood its power in crystallising what is intense and otherwise unutterable in human feeling and thought. In the eighty-five poems of his *Spleen et Idéal*, thirty-eight are sonnets, of which we will discuss two of the most familiar, numbers XII and XVII. Firstly, number XII, 'Bohémiens en voyage':[77]

La tribu prophétique aux prunelles ardentes	001001 # 0010010
Hier s'est mise en route, emportant ses petits	010101 # 001001
Sur son dos, ou livrant à leurs fiers appétits	001 # 001001001
Le trésor toujours prêt des mamelles pendantes.	001001 # 0010010
Les hommes vont à pied sous leurs armes luisantes	010101 # 0010010
Le long des chariots où les leurs sont blottis,	010101 # 001001
Promenant sur le ciel des yeux appesantis	001001 # 010101
Par le morne regret des chimères absentes.	001001 # 0010010
Du fond de son réduit sablonneux, le grillon,	010*001*001 # 001
Les regardant passer, redouble sa chanson;	010101 # 010*001*
Cybèle, qui les aime, augmente ses verdures,	010*001* # 010*001*
Fait couler le rocher, et fleurir le désert	001001 # 001001
Devant ces voyageurs, pour lesquels est ouvert	010101 # 001001
L'empire familier des ténèbres futures.[78]	010101 # 001001

Of the sonnet's twenty-eight verse-units, here, four show in a single strophe a run of three atonic syllables and none show juxtaposed accents within the phrase, meaning that twenty-four show alternating accent by our criteria (86 per cent).

The rhythmic contrast between the 001001 of the first line and the 010101 of the first hemistich of the second correlates with a semantic contrast: the 'anapestic' symmetry of the hemistichs, evoking a people gifted with visionary prescience, is suddenly interrupted by a switch to an 'iambic' rhythm and to an entirely different register. The move from 001001 ('anapestic') to 010101 ('iambic'), with its increase in accent-count,[79] makes us *feel*[80] the contradiction between the 'elevated'/'euphoric' and the 'mundane'/'dysphoric', between the 'visionary dignity' of the gypsy and the wearisome business of moving camp. So we find a coupling being created between a *semantic* and a *formal* contrast, that is a 'relationship between relationships'.[81]

This coupling discharges an aesthetic shock as the 'formal' elements acquire a semantic value.[82] The idea of the 'mundane' is expressed through the 'halting' break in l. 3:[83]

[...] # emportant ses petits	# 001001
Sur son dos, # ou livrant à leurs fiers appétits.	001 # 001001001

This unexpected 'halt' is coloured by a condensed coupling: the perceived 'weight'

of the accent, due to group-final lengthening, is overdetermined by the 'mundane'/
'dysphoric' sense of *sur son dos*, with its 'dysphoric' connotation of 'arduous labour'.
In the remainder of the line:

[...] ou livrant # à leurs fiers appétits #

the accent on *livrant* falls on the normally 'cesural' sixth syllable, while that on *fiers* is
intensified by the pre-position of the adjective. The syntactical boundary at the 'cesura'
gives rise to a pause before the intercalated phrase which follows. Preposed *fiers* lends
contrastive 'vehemence' to:

à leurs fiers appétits #

and the *liaison* [u li.vRã. # a.lœr. fjɛR. zap.pe.ti. #] sustains phonation, thus adding
'urgency' to *appétits*, in marked contrast to the pauses at syntactical boundaries in
Sur son dos #, where Baudelaire punctuates, and *livrant #*, also on a boundary.[84]
The regular 'anapests' of l. 4, arranged symmetrically around the regular 'cesura',
foreground the rhythmic equivalence of *trésor* and *mamelles* whose accented vowels
fall in identical positions within their respective hemistichs. This formal similarity
is offset by a recurring semantic contrast, *trésor* belongs to the 'elevated'/'euphoric'
register established in l. 1 and *mamelles pendantes* to the 'mundane'/'dysphoric'
of l. 2. What is more, this relationship within the line also exists at the level of the
strophe: *prunelles ardentes* (l. 1) is the phonetic, rhythmic and syntactical equivalent
of *mamelles pendantes* while contrasting with it with respect to the same opposition,
'elevated'/'euphoric' ≠ 'mundane'/'dysphoric'. We thus have a coupling horizontally
within the line and another vertically within the strophe.[85] There is nothing surprising
about the 'double nature' of the *bohémien*, who is commonly seen by 'decent citizens'
as both 'mysterious' and 'banal', but what may be surprising is the role of rhythmic
organisation in intensifying the affective impact of this enigmatic contradiction.

The second strophe begins with a restatement of the 'mundane'/'dysphoric' theme
with its 'iambic' tread:

Les hommes vont à pied #.   010101 #

In its echo of:

Hier s'est mise en route #   010101 #

the parallelism between sense and rhythm is now making a 'metaphor' of this latter.
Indeed, in the following l. 6 we find again:

Le long des chariots #.[86]   010101 #

While the first two of these 'iambic' hemistichs are foregrounded against the dominant
'anapestic' rhythm, the central couplet of the second strophe bring the opposites
together in a chiasmus:

(A) Le long des chariots   (B) ou les leurs sont blottis,
(B) Promenant sur le ciel   (A) leurs yeux appesantis

with B = B both being 'anapestic', A = A both being 'iambic'. Furthermore, l. 7
shows a further coupling of contrasts: while *ciel* in an 'anapestic' hemistich is 'ele-

vated'/'euphoric', *yeux appesantis* illustrates the text's correlation of 'iambic' and 'mundane'/'dysphoric'. In [lœʀ.zj□.zap.pə.zã.ti] the semantic value *peser* is overdetermined by *enchaînement*, in which the persistent anaphora of [z] in *appesantis* recalls the 'laborious?' connotation of *mise en route* and *vont à pied*.[87]

The first tercet takes us by surprise with a change of mood. There is unexpected rhythmic relaxation in l. 9, the first in the sonnet to show a sequence of three unaccented vowels. Metrical 'relaxation' takes the form of the marked displacement of the 'cesura':

Du fond de son réduit sablonneux, # le grillon.   010001001 # 001

Though the sixth syllable is accented, there can be no 'cesural' pause: *réduit sablonneux* is a noun phrase which can have no internal boundary.[88] The effect of this long, inverted adverbial phrase is to 'squeeze' the eventual subject, the 'cricket', into a 'confined space' between two syntactical boundaries at the line-end, thus creating, for the eye as well as for the ear, a 'metrical metaphor' for *son réduit*. In the last two lines of this tercet, the reality of intra-phrasal word-accent is affirmed in the parallelism between *redouble sa chanson* and *augmente ses verdures* where rhythm, syntax and sense join in a triple equivalence to suggest 'abundance' in this 'desert' (*sablonneux*). This 'biblical' feel of the rhetorical figure is sustained in the second tercet where a further parallelism is condensed into a single line of surpassing loveliness:

Fait couler le rocher et fleurir le désert.   001001 # 001001[89]

Here the line may demand the avoidance of hiatus, a 'hiccup' at the 'cesura', which we get if we read the line as [fe.ku.le.lə.ʀ□.□e.e.flœ.ʀiʀ.lə.de.zɛʀ.]. The interdiction of hiatus in classic verse would require [fe.ku.le.lə.ʀ□.□e. ʀe.flœ.ʀiʀ.lə.de.zɛʀ.] with linking by *liaison* of syntactically and rhythmically parallel phrases.[90] This adds further density to the existing parallelisms in the half-rhyme [ʀ□.□e.ʀ = de.zɛʀ.]. This, together with the anaphora of ʀ further enriches the semantic/syntactic equivalence of the two hemistichs. This *liaison* at the 'cesura' makes pause impossible, thus intensifying the sense of 'flowing movement' (*couler*?) in a line which is already unbrokenly 'anapestic'.

At the beginning of l. 13, the return of 'iambic' rhythm is coupled with *voyageurs*. This is a further anaphora of the value 'mundane'/'dysphoric' as it appeared in: l. 2, *Hier s'est mise en route*; l. 5, *Les hommes vont à pied*; l. 6, *Le long des chariots*; and l. 7, *des yeux appesantis*, each instance being coupled with an 'iambic' pulse. This development of the 'iambic'/'dysphoric' theme is countered by that of its 'anapestic'/'euphoric' counterpart in: l. 1, *La tribu prophétique aux prunelles ardentes*; l. 4, *Le trésor toujours prêt*; and l. 7, *Promenant sur le ciel*.

But in l. 12, *Fait couler le rocher et fleurir le désert*, we find a thrilling surprise in the conjunction of opposing themes.[91] The development of the sonnet in the quatrains might strike the listener as rather like that of the classical 'sonata' in which contrasting themes are combined and transformed. In l. 12, the poetic device, a kind of 'foreshortening', has a precise analogue in fugal texture. In strict fugue, the fugal subject is first stated and then subjected to combination with itself or with other motifs. Music alone permits the simultaneous statement of two motifs, a possibility denied to linguistic forms, but the conjoining of opposites here, within the 'euphoric' anapestic hemistich,[92] produces in the listener an aesthetic 'shock' very like that experienced by the same listener in the climactic *stretto* of a fugue. In this, we hear overlapping statements of the fugal subject, one starting immediately after the other. In both the poem and the music, the 'critical mass' achieved by the bringing together of elements previously contrasted creates an aesthetic 'explosion'.

This is the climactic moment of the sonnet; the tension declines in its final lines with the segregation of the opposing themes in rhythmically contrasting hemistichs. Even so, we hear an echo of the magic of l. 12 in the return of the contrasting themes of the 'sonata'. In l. 14, the opposites, ('mundane', *familier*, e.g. *route, pied, chariots*, and 'high register', *ténèbres*, e.g. *prophétique, ardentes, trésor, ciel*), are drawn together by syntactical equivalence into a concluding *conjunctio oppositorum*, the mysterious 'union of opposites' in the tribe itself.[93]

We turn now to the second of the two sonnets, number XVII, 'La Beauté':

Je suis belle, ô mortels! comme un rêve de pierre,	001001 # 0010010
Et mon sein, où chacun s'est meurtri tour à tour,	001001 # 001001
Est fait pour inspirer au poète un amour	010101 # 001001
Éternel et muet ainsi que la matière.	001001 # 0100010
Je trône dans l'azur comme un sphinx incompris;	010001 # 001001
J'unis un coeur de neige à la blancheur des cygnes;	010101 # 0001010
Je hais le mouvement qui déplace les lignes,	010101 # 0010010
Et jamais je ne pleure et jamais je ne ris.	001001 # 001001
Les poètes, devant mes grandes attitudes,	0010 # 010101010
Que j'ai l'air d'emprunter aux plus fiers monuments,	001001 # 001001
Consumeront leurs jours en d'austères études;	010101 # 0010010
Car j'ai, pour fasciner ces dociles amants,	010101 # 001001
De purs miroirs qui font toutes choses plus belles:	0101 # 001010010
Mes yeux, mes larges yeux aux clartes éternelles![94]	010101 # 0010010

Of this sonnet's twenty-eight verse-units three show atonic runs and none show juxtaposed accents. Thus 89 per cent alternate by our criteria.

The first line shows both an internal rhyme [b□l. = m□R.t□l.] and an assonance [R□v. = pj□R]: these are equivalent in respect of accent-distribution and then of anaphora of tonic [□], which foregrounds the thematic oxymoron 'ideal' (*belle, rêve*) ≠ 'material' (*mortel, pierre*). In l. 2, the shock of the oxymoronic collocation *rêve* ≠ *pierre* is quickly followed by another, *sein* ('soft?', 'feminine?') ≠ *meurtri*, and intensified by the rhythmic equivalence of the two hemistichs:

En mon **sein** où chacun # est meurtri tour à **tour**.	001001 # 001001[95]

The shock is further intensified by the symmetrical placing of the tonic vowels of the antonyms *sein* ('tender?') and *meurtri* ('brutal?') on position 3 in their respective hemistichs. The consistently 'anapestic' rhythm is then broken by the first 'iambic' hemistich. This change in rhythm highlights the countertonic accent on the first trisyllable of the sonnet, *inspirer*. Unlike l. 12 of 'Bohémiens en voyage', the syntax forbids *liaison/enchaînement* at positions 6 and 8 but requires it at position 12: [e.fɛ. pu. Rɛ̃.spi.Re # o.po.□t # œ̃.na.mu.Re...]. The leftward displacement of *au poète*, and the consequent absence of *liaison* and *enchaînement*, give unmistakeable syntactic prominence to Beauty's favourite, and the 'commanding voice' of the Goddess is heard in a sustained *enchaînement enjambant*: [œ̃.na.mu. #? ʀe.t□ʀ.n□.le.my.□ #]. Here, the relative syntactic independence of the second hemistich permits an interruption of phonation. The hiatus created by the dieresis [my.□] is followed by a *further* hiatus [my.□. # □.si ke. la. ma.tj□.ʀə], and the prolonged 'silence' following the accented [my.□ #] becomes a 'metaphor' for the meaning of the word itself.[96]

The four accents of l. 5 mark lexical items with complex semantic values: *trône* and *azur* are members of the 'ideal' paradigm, while *sphinx*, like *pierre* and *meurtri*, is a member of 'material'. The second hemistich takes up the rhythm and syntax of its analogue in l. 1, *comme un rêve de pierre* (001001) = *comme un sphinx incompris* (001001), the rhythmic equivalence suggesting the *semantic* equivalence of the noun phrases: that is, *Je*, *un rêve de pierre* and *un sphinx incompris* all refer to the same thing, *la beauté*. The 'materiality' of the *sphinx* was affirmed in l. 2:

> Et mon *sein* où chacun # s'est *meurtri* [...].

The 'feminine/comforting' connotation of *mon sein* collides with the 'painful' connotation of *meurtri* to create the the complex value 'bruising embrace?' (*sein* + *meurtri*), in which 'euphoric' and 'dysphoric' are conjoined.[97] Line 6 juxtaposes an 'iambic' hemistich to an 'anapestic' one; in the first, the verb *J'unis* tells us that the proper of 'La Beauté' is the 'union of opposites', *un coeur de neige* ('dysphoric') ≠ *la blancheur des cygnes* ('euphoric').[98] This opposition will be neutralised by a triple equivalence: (a) semantic, *neige* = *blancheur* (*blanc* being a semic component of *neige*); (b) phonetic, [kœʀ] rhymes with [blɑ̃□œʀ]; (c) isotopic, the relevant accented vowel falls in each instance on position 4 of the hemistich. Our growing sense of the poem's enactment of the 'conjunction of opposites' is encouraged by the *enchaînement* produced by the [□] which begins both hemistichs: [□y.ni.zœ̃.kœʀ. də. n□. # □a. la. blɑ̃.□œʀ. de. si□ə]. This anaphor of [□] gives unbroken phonation, 'uniting' the semantically dissonant hemistichs. At the same time, the consonant-distribution is subject to phonetic constraint: [□] is the voiced equivalent of [□] and [z] is the voiced equivalent of [s]. Thus, the two hemistichs are simultaneously marked by difference and by equivalence: the first shows only the voiced forms, [□] and [z], while the second shows only unvoiced forms, [□] and [s]. This alternation implies another: the greater effort required in 'voicing' overdetermines the 'dysphoric' semantic value [□y.ni.zœ̃. kœr], while the lesser effort required by the phonation of unvoiced consonants overdetermines the 'euphoric' value [la. blɑ̃.□œʀ. de. si□ə]. In this latter group, the unvoiced consonants mark in each instance the onset of a tonic vowel.

The first hemistich of l. 7 takes up the rhythm of its analogue in l. 6 — *J'unis* = *Je hais* — but this rhythmic equivalence itself embodies a semantic contrast: *unir* ≠ *haïr*. This latter is phonetically overdetermined by [□y.ni] ≠ [□ə.□] where the aspirated hiatus of the latter underlines its sense with a 'vehement' contraction of the diaphragm. The emphasis on 'immobility' (compare *pierre*, *sphinx*, *monuments*) recurs in the stasis of l. 8, where 'change' is denied semantically by negative verbs and formally by the rhythmic/syntactic 'sameness' of the hemistichs.

The first line of the first tercet has its actual 'cesura' (accent + syntactical boundary) unexpectedly at position 3. Though *devant* at position 6, has word-accent, here there can be no syntactical boundary.[99] Whereas the analogous effect in l. 9 of ' Bohémiens en voyage' gives the 'cricket' a 'low profile', here, *Les poètes*, a verbal subject at the head of the line, is foregrounded. But only briefly: the 'anapest' of *Les poètes* is immediately overwhelmed by the eight syllables and four accents of [de.vã.me.gRã:də.za.ti.ty.də]. The accent of intensity on the nasal vowel of *grandes* has an added pitch-value standing before its atonic [ə]. This 'big' accent overdetermines the *semantic* value of *grandes*, and this, with the contrasts of syllable-count, (three syllables ≠ eight syllables), and rhythm, (001 ≠ 010101010), marks the subaltern status of poets and the supreme authority of 'La Beauté'. In the next lines, there is rhythmic alternation: l. 10 is entirely 'anapestic', the first hemistich of l. 11 is 'iambic'. In a parallel semantic 'alternation?' *Que j'ai l'air* connotes '*désinvolte?*' while the semantic value of *consumeront* connotes 'laborious?', its semantic value being overdetermined by its status as a 'weighty' tetrasyllable rare in verse, and by its two accents.

   In the second tercet, the 'weight' of the 'iambic' first hemistich is increased by the higher values of intensity and pitch in group-final *J'ai*, while the 'docility' of the poets is heard in the lower accent-count of the 'anapestic' second hemistich. Line 13 is metrically irregular in that position 6 is occupied by *font*, a verb with high frequency of occurrence and hence atonic. It follows that, as in l. 9, the 'cesura' (?) moves to the line-internal syntactic limit, this time at position 4:

   De purs miroirs # qui font toutes choses plus belles.

The pre-positioning of the adjective steps up its accent with a rise in pitch, while the anaphora of [R] in the accented syllables [pyR. mi. Rwar] gives an 'audio-visual' analogue of the implied semantic value 'reflection'. Is this the relation between the two parts of the line? The two segments contrast at several levels: rhythmically, *De purs miroirs* is 'iambic' while the rest of the line is dominantly 'anapestic' (00101001). Then semantically, the pre-posed adjective in *De purs miroirs* is 'high-register' while the rest of the line, with its neglected 'cesura' and *accent d'insistance* on *toutes*, borders on the 'colloquial'. The arresting irregularity of the 'cesura' (?) takes us from one world to another. In l. 14, [me.zjø.me.laR.□ə.zjø #[100] o.klaR.te. ze.t□R.n□l.lə], hemistich 1 has three tonic vowels, of which the repeated tonic, 'closed' [zjø] contrasts with the tonic 'open' vowel of the pre-posed adjective [laR.□ə], the *only* 'open' vowel in the hemistich. So the prominence of *larges* is due to multiple overdetermination of its semantic value (compare *grandes* in l. 9). Phonetically, by the acoustic quality of the 'open' [a], which is 'larger' (i.e. more resonant) than the 'closed' [ø]. Syntactically, it achieves prominence through being pre-posed, and prosodically, by the enhanced intensity and pitch of its accent. In hemistich 1, the element *yeux* is a member of the paradigm series *sein* + *coeur*, that is, the 'organic/material' components of 'La Beauté'. On the other hand, *clartés éternelles* of the second hemistich joins the 'transcendent/immaterial' series of the sonnet: *belle, rêve* + *éternel* + *azur* + *purs*. This semantic contrast is coupled first with the rhythmic alternation 010101 ≠ 001001, and second with phonetic contrast: hemistich 2 has unvoiced plosives [k] and [t] while hemistich 1 has none. Throughout, the interplay between semantic, rhythmic and phonetic levels of organisation results in the 'semantisation' of formal components: rhythmic alternation contrasts 'heavy' (three accents) with 'light' (two accents) while phonetic contrast (see l. 6) opposes 'greater effort' to 'lesser effort'.

In contrast to *Les Fleurs du Mal*, which is essentially classical and isosyllabic, the prose poems of *Le Spleen de Paris* illustrate Baudelaire's idea of 'une prose poétique, musicale, sans rythme et sans rime'. Born before Baudelaire died, Jules Laforgue (1860–87) explored the possibilities of a verse which was not necessarily isosyllabic. Already in the seventeenth century, Corneille and La Fontaine had been writing poems whose lines could vary in length, though their metres were mainly those of the tradition: the alexandrine, the decasyllable, the octosyllable. The cultural restlessness of the 1880s brought a revolt against the philosophical naturalism and poetic conservatism of the Parnassian poets, with whom Baudelaire had sympathised.[101] The first signs of a new way of writing can be found in Rimbaud's *Illuminations* (1886); in 'Marine', the brief verse-like layout is nevertheless rhymeless and syllabically irregular. For Gouvard:

> Les textes de ces auteurs [i.e. of 'post-classical' poets from Laforgue onwards] offrent en effet des variations formelles beaucoup plus fréquentes et beaucoup plus variées que les oeuvres composées pendant la période dite 'classique', et ne peuvent être décrites de manière satisfaisante avec les concepts propres à la versification traditionnelle.[102]

For him the disappearance of isosyllabism, and hence of formal metrical equivalence, implies that 'le vers libre n'aurait rien de métrique et ne nous intéresserait guère' (Gouvard, *La Versification*, p. 296). Since we are testing the hypothesis that rhythm in French verse has a metrical function, we need not join Gouvard in despair. Our theory of rhythm allows precisely for the construction of formal equivalences that for our critic are not available in heterosyllabic verse.

In sharp contrast to Baudelaire, here is the opening section of a poem by Jules Laforgue which illustrates his move from isosyllabism and strophe to rhymed free verse, 'L'Hiver qui vient':

	Blocus sentimental! Messageries du Levant!...	010101 0101001	13
	Oh, tombée de la pluie! Oh, tombée de la nuit!	101001 101001	12
	Oh, le vent!...	101	3
	La Toussaint, la Noël et la Nouvelle Année,	001001 *000*101	12
5	Oh, dans les bruines, toutes mes cheminées!...	10010 100101	11
	D'usines...	010	3
	On ne peut plus s'asseoir, tous les bancs sont mouillés;	*000*101 101001	12
	Crois-moi, c'est bien fini jusqu'à l'année prochaine,	010101 *000*101	12
	Tant les bancs sont mouillés, tant les bois sont rouillés,	101001 101001	12
10	Et tant les cors ont fait ton ton, ton taine!	010101 0101	10
	Ah! nuées accourues des côtes de la Manche,	101001 01*0*001	12
	Vous nous avez gâté notre dernier dimanche!	*000001* 001001	12
	Il bruine;	01	2
	Dans la forêt mouillée, les toiles d'araignées	*00010* 010101	12
15	Ploient sous les gouttes d'eau, et c'est leur ruine.[103]	100101 0101	10
	Soleils plénipotentiaires des travaux en blonds Pactoles	01010101 0010101	15
	Des spectacles agricoles,	0010101	7

	Ce soir un soleil fichu gît au haut du coteau,	0100101 101001	13
	Gît sur le flanc, dans les genêts, sur son manteau,	1001 *0001 0001*	12
20	Un soleil blanc comme un crachat d'estaminet	001 *1000*10101	12
	Sur une litière de jaunes genêts,	*0001* 0101	8
	De jaunes genêts d'automne	010101	6
	Et les cors lui sonnent!	00101	5
	Qu'il revienne.	001	3
25	Qu'il revienne à lui!	00101	5
	Taïaut! Taïaut! et hallali!	101 101 0101	10
	O triste antienne, as-tu fini!...	0101 1001	8
	Et font les fous!...	0101	4
	Et il gît là, comme une glande arrachée dans un cou,	0011 001001001	13
30	Et il frissonne, sans personne!...[104]	*0001*001	8

In a letter to Gustave Kahn, the poet wrote as follows about this poem: 'J'oublie de rimer, j'oublie le nombre de syllabes, j'oublie la distribution des strophes, mes lignes commencent à la marge comme de la prose'.[105] The reader, forced onto the back foot, will decide how disingenuous this is. Certainly, rhyme seems the only real survivor of the poet's abandonment of classic verse-form. In most of the text, irregular syllable-count together with persistent parataxis (absence of syntactic connection), fix attention on the compensating relation between semantic and prosodic values. As paraphrase becomes increasingly impossible, the sense is in the form. Though syllable count is irregular, lineation is preserved through return to the left-hand margin.

The first six syllables of l.1 will be instantly perceived as an accentually regular alexandrine hemistich. Though initially prolonging the 'iambic' rhythm, the second half of the line ends by breaking both the syllable count and the rhythm. This line is, as it were, a 'declaration of intent': it effectively condenses the history of the poet's relationship with classical verse-forms. While his earlier *Complaintes* had been anchored in the alexandrine and the octosyllable, the *Derniers vers* is finding new ways of creating poetic forms.

These forms, unlike extra-linguistic isosyllabism, arise naturally from the properties of language itself. In l.1, accentual equivalences are coupled with semantic ones. Though each half-line shows a complex contrast, the half-lines are themselves equivalent: [*Blocus* ('denotative') ≠ *sentimental* ('connotative')] = [*Messageries* ('denotative') ≠ *Levant* ('connotative')].[106] But within this symmetry are nested further structures: *Blocus* = *Messageries* with respect to military/technical connotation while contrasting in number of syllables and accents. *Sentimental* = *Levant* with respect to 'affective' connotation while contrasting likewise. *Blocus* ≠ *Levant* with respect to connotation, though they are equivalent with respect to syllable count and accent. *Sentimental* ≠ *Messageries* with respect to connotation, though they are identical in syllable count and accent distribution. Parataxis is foregrounding the ordering of the line in accordance with prosodic and semantic intent.

Once again, accent-distribution within the verse-unit is fundamental to the creation of meaning. The conventional story that accent in French verse is uniquely group-final would make the structures of this line both invisible and inaudible.[107] The poet is using the prosodic resources of his language (i.e. group-accent and oxytonic and countertonic word-accent) to transcend the two-value logic of 'common-sense': difference coincides with similarity.

The challenge of l.1 finds respite in the simpler equivalences of l. 2, a model alexandrine, whose rhythmically/syntactically identical hemistichs monotonously overdetermine the wintry equivalence of rain and darkness, the polysemy of *tombée* finding further difference in similarity. Since, until l. 5, the poet has avoided word-final [ə] within the line, *bruinəs* and *toutəs* present a conundrum to the reader.[108] Though register, via the rhyme *Levant* = *vent* and the alexandrine regularity of ll. 2 and 4, prompts the realisation of [ə] here, the line is still a syllable short. Parataxis again suggests through connotation the group-final antinomy of *bruines* ≠ *cheminées* (Wet ≠ dry; chill ≠ 'comfort?') But the potential 'cosiness?' of *cheminées* is abruptly cancelled by a return with *D'usines* to the ironic juxtaposition of contradictories of *Blocus* ≠ *sentimental*.

The classic form of the rhymed alexandrine strophe of ll. 7–10 with regular 'cesura', is undercut by the deliberate banality of its register. Word-accent is critical in l. 9 where group-accent alone would leave the verb-subjects withot prosodic relief, thus obscuring the thematic alternation 'Culture' ≠ 'Nature' implicit in *bancs* ≠ *bois*, and blurring the alternation 'literal' (*bancs mouillés*) ≠ 'metaphorical' (*bois rouillés*), in which Nature is abruptly assimilated to industrial culture. This surprising dissonance is coupled with the consonance of rhythmically/syntactically equivalent hemistichs, 101001 = 101001. [ə] is absent from these four lines, but we are faced by the problem of its realisation in the following couplet. Line 11 is a full alexandrine with 'cesura', its 'poetic' diction prompting syllabic value for the [ə] in *côtəs*. Yet again, irony intrudes: the 'poetic' *nuées accourues* collide with the colloquial register of the following alexandrine line with its exceptional *langue de tous les jours* run of *five* atonic syllables.[109] As the drizzle falls in l. 13, we move again from culture to nature. The *bancs mouillés* are now *la forêt mouillée* and the spiders' sodden webs sag with the weight of adjacent accents at line-end and line-head:

> [...] les toiles d'araigné(es/Ploient [...].

This is the only instance in our text of a return to the left-hand margin which interrupts an elementary syntactic unit, in this case a subject + verb phrase.[110] The fifteen syllables of l. 16 pick up the 'iambic' rhythm of l. 1 together with the theme of *Levant'*, only for its grandiloquent mythologising to collapse paratactically into the bathos of l. 17.[111] A register-contrast is once more coupled with a rhythmic equivalence: *des travaux en blonds Pactoles* = *Des spectacles agricoles*, 0010101 = 0010101. In l. 18, the awkwardness of juxtaposed *fichu* and *gît*, words drawn from violently contrasting registers, is compounded by their colliding accents, the hiccup of a hiatus in *au haut* and a jingling rhyme with *coteau*.[112]

The structure of l. 19 again seems motivated by phonetic considerations. The accented vowels descend from high palatal [i] through medial [ã] and [□] to closed frontal [o] with the rhyme. The colliding accents of *Un soleil, blanc* force the contrast between *blanc* and the 'golden sun' of l. 16 and continue the idea of a register *dégringolade* in the move from the 'mythic' *blonds Pactoles* to the 'consumptive' *crachat d'estaminet*. In the opposite direction, the rhyme *crachat d'estaminet/jaunes genêts* takes us from the culture of *cheminées/D'usine*, *bancs mouillés*, *rouillés*, *agricoles* and *estaminet*, to the nature of *pluie*, *vent*, *bois*, *forêt*, *toiles d'araignées* and back to *jaunes genêts*, where the glory of *blonds Pactoles* finds a muted echo in the preposed adjective. It would be impossible to feel the impact of these thematic structures without the prominence given to their lexical components by word-accent within the phrase, a prominence denied by those for whom phrase-final accent is the only prosodic point of reference where accent is concerned.

Though the role of rhythm as an organising principle in French verse is currently discounted by French theorists, Laforgue is remarkable in the history of French verse for the importance he explicitly attached to it. In commenting on a fellow poet he writes: 'Corbière ne s'occupe ni de la strophe ni des rimes [...] et jamais de rythmes, et je m'en suis préoccupé au point d'en apporter de nouvelles et de nouveaux'.[113] In these forty verse-units of 'L'Hiver qui vient' we find ten runs of three atonic syllables, one of five and one juxtaposed accent within the phrase, 70 per cent alternating according to our criteria. In the opening strophe, the syllabic ideality of the classic alexandrine is subjected to variation:

Blocus sentimental! Messageries du Levant!...	010101 # 0101001	6 + 7
Oh, dans les bruines, toutes mes cheminées!...	10010 # 100101	5 + 6

In each of these lines, one hemistich is canonical and the other is not: nevertheless, alternation of accent, the unifying principle, assures cohesion throughout. The full gamut of alternating combinations available to the six-syllable verse-unit is utilised:

Blocus sentimental!	010101
Oh tombée de la pluie!	101001
La Toussaint, la Noël	001001
toutes mes cheminées!	100101

In l. 16, when the poet finally moves into anisosyllabic free verse, alternation of accent remains dominant with five runs of three atonic syllables. In ll. 16–18:

Soleils plénipotentiair(es) des travaux en blonds Pactoles	010101 # 0010101
Des spectacles agricoles,	0010101
Ce soir un soleil fichu gît au haut du coteau,	0100101 # 101001

rhyme and accentual patterning are semantically and formally critical. The heroic 'iambic's of *Soleils plénipotentiaires* gives way to the gentler 'anapest' of *des travaux en blonds Pactoles*, whose rhythm is mockingly echoed in *Des spectacles agricoles*. Line 18 falls naturally into a subject + verb structure, with *gît* thrown into relief by colliding accents. The progressive 'degradation' of the setting sun is expressed semantically by the replacement of 'active' '*travaux*' by '*gît*', with its connotation of 'passive moribundity', and rhythmically by the progressive breaking down of the 'strong' 'iambic's of *Soleils plénipotentiaires*, first by the intrusion of 'anapests' and then by the atonic runs of l. 19.[114] In l. 20 accents around a syntactic boundary foreground the 'failing sun': '*Un soleil # blanc* comme un crachat d'estaminet'. In *blanc*, the 'pallor' of the sickly Sun is paired with the 'tubercular' connotation of *crachat*. After the increased frequency in ll. 16–21 of 'anapests' and atonic runs, the return of a pure 'iambic' l. 22 halts the decline. The repeated sound of horns (00101, 001, 00101) calls the Sun back to life. Is the lamentation over? Alas, no:

Et il gît là, comme une glande arrachée dans un cou.	0011 # 001001001

The fatal insistence of colliding accents accompanies the *glande arrachée*, sister-image of the *blanc crachat*: organic, perishable and disgusting.

In the *Derniers vers*, we find ample evidence of the shaping function of rhythm in a poetry which, to the conservative eye, may seem lacking in shape. While in Baudelaire's sonnets a unique voice sums up and transcends an ancient tradition, readers of Laforgue recognise the characteristic sound of twentieth-century poetry, and not only in French.

The Twentieth Century

Since by 1900 the isosyllabic strophe, whenever used, inevitably connotes 'old hat', the preferred medium is increasingly free verse. Paul Claudel (1868–1955) is always 'free'; Paul Valéry (1871–1945) and Charles Péguy (1873–1914) are 'isosyllabic/strophic'. Guillaume Apollinaire (1880–1918) does both. As the century moves on, so does the correlation with the frequency of the *vers libre*. Valéry was the last convinced isosyllabist, most poets before and after 1945 finding their natural voices in free verse that is nevertheless often distinguished from prose by layout, the units of discourse being marked off by white space or else an abrupt shift back to the margin.

Apollinaire's two major collections, *Alcools* and *Calligrammes*, cover the whole range from strict isosyllabism to very free verse. In his famous recording of the decasyllabic 'Le Pont Mirabeau', word-final [ə] is given syllabic value throughout; at the other end of the scale, in a recent recording, Stéphane Hessel recites 'La Jolie Rousse' by heart, without a single word-final [ə].[115]

In the following poem from *Alcools*, 'Les Colchiques', we will take two approaches. Firstly, in 'real-time'; encountering the text line by line, we may get some idea of its shape:

	Le pré est vénéneux mais joli en automne	010101 # 0010010	12
	Les vaches y paissant	010*001*	6
	Lentement s'empoisonnent	1010010	6
	Le colchique couleur de cerne et de lilas	001001010001?	12
5	Y fleurit tes yeux sont comme cette fleur-là	001010*000011*	12
	Violâtres comme leur cerne et comme cette automne	01000010000010	13
	Et ma vie pour tes yeux lentement s'empoisonne	001001 # 1010010	12
	Les enfants de l'école viennent avec fracas	0010010100101	13
	Vêtus de hoquetons et jouant de l'harmonica	0101010100101	13
10	Ils cueillent les colchiques qui sont comme des mères	01000100100010	13
	Filles de leur filles et sont couleur de tes paupières	*1*00010000100010	14
	Qui battent comme des fleurs battent au vent dément	0100001100101	13
	Le gardien du troupeau chante tout doucement	001001 # 100101	12
	Tandis que lentes et meuglant les vaches abandonnent	*000100*010101010	14
15	Pour toujours ce grand pré mal fleuri par l'automne.[116]	001001 # 0010010	12

The first line is an unmistakeable 6 + 6 alexandrine and there is no word-final [ə] to make us hesitate. But what about *vaches* in l. 2? The couplet-rhyme *automne* = *s'empoisonnent* suggests that ll. 2 and 3 are really hemistichs of a single alexandrine. So if we feel we are still in the alexandrine register, we will count word-final [ə] as syllabic and opt for [le.va.□ə.zi.p□.sã.] as a first hemistich, leading naturally into [lã.tə.mã. sã.pwa.z□.nə], where the register implied by the pre-posed adverb certainly requires the syllabic value of its [ə].[117] So far, so good. But is l. 4 an alexandrine? Comparing it with ll. 1 to 3, the reader begins to wonder: the tonic syllable of *couleur* is indeed at position 6, but there is no syntactical boundary. Its word-accent is in the middle of an adjectival phrase *couleur de cerne* which allows no pause. So, ll. 4–5:

> Le colchique #? Couleur de cerne et de lilas #   0010 #? 01010001   12?
> Y fleurit #? tes yeux sont comme cette fleur-là?   001 # 010000011   12?

The plot thickens. If we continue counting word-final [ə] as syllabic, l. 5 has twelve syllables but lacks a defining property of the alexandrine: the 'cesural' position 6 is occupied by *sont*, a verb with high frequency of occurrence and hence atonic. The only possible line-internal boundary is at position 3. This would give a 3 + 9 line, an infringement of Cornulier's 'loi des 8'. Furthermore, alternation of accent has now been completely dissipated by a run of five atonic syllables and a clash of accents in l. 6:

> Violâtres comme leur cer #? ne et comme cet automne. 0100001 # 000101   7 + 6?

The reader's growing doubts about the syllabic value of [ə] have reached a crisis: in this line, all semblance of metrical regularity has gone. Position 6 is occupied by an atonic clitic, *leur*, and the only possible 'cesural' boundary, at position 7, violates the 'rule' that such a boundary must coincide with a word-boundary. If we accord syllabic value to word-final [ə], the line moreover has thirteen syllables. And there is no alternation of accent. This is not an alexandrine. Indeed it is not metrical, and the poet knows it. By now, the literate reader, having recognised this as free verse, will have interrupted his or her reading and recapped; a re-reading of ll. 4–6, now deleting word-final [ə], gives:

> lə. kol. □i.k. ku.lœR.də.s□R.ne.də.li.la.   001 #? 01010001   11
> i.flœ.Ri.te.zjø.s□̂.k□m.s□t. flœR.la.   001 #? 0100011   10
> vjo.la,tR³ k□m.lœR.s□R. # ne. k□m.s□. t□.t□n.   01001 #? 00101   10

The poem is telling us how to read it. We know from Apollinaire's live recording of 'Le Pont Mirabeau' that he well understood the conventions governing the distribution of [ə] in syllabic verse. He knew that any reader familiar with such verse would have immediately identified the opening line as an alexandrine. That reader, by the same token, would instantly recognise l. 4 as 'irregular' and l. 5 as 'non-verse', in spite of their isosyllabism. Without word-final [ə], l. 6 alternates accent and is becoming metrically intelligible, and at the close of the strophe, l. 7 is marked by the return of the 'perfectly formed alexandrine' with the echo of *lentəment s'empoisonnent*.

In l. 8:

> Les enfants de l'écolə? viennent avec fracas

without word-final [ə], the 'post-cesural' [ə], forbidden in classical verse, will disappear, leaving a syllabically regular hemistich which also alternates accent. But the deletion of word-final [ə] leaves the second 'hemistich' a syllable short:

> [le,zã.fã,də.le.k□l. # vj□n.ta.v□k.fRa.ka.]   001001 # 10101

So while the first hemistich is now 'classical' and the second is 'free', both alternate accent. This gives to the line that 'regularity' felt in the first and last lines of the previous strophe. Line 9 follows suit:

[V□.ty.də.□.kə.t□̃. # e. □wã.də.laʀ.m□.ni.ka]   010101 # 0100101   13

Here, though the second 'hemistich' has seven syllables, again the whole line alternates. In l. 10:

[il. kœj.le. k□l.□ik # ki.s□̃. # k□m. de. m□ʀ #]^[118]   01001 # 01001

the layout is 5 + 5 with alternation of accent overall. Line 11, still without word-final [ə]:

[fij də lœʀ. fij. # e s□̃. ku.lœʀ,də.te.po.pj□ʀ]   1001 # *00010001*

looks like 4 + 8. If, on the other hand, [ə] has syllabic value, the line would be made up of 6 + 8. In both these readings, irregular 'cesura' and failure of alternation increase our sense of reading 'non-metrical verse'. The 'orphan' l. 12 with word-final [ə] gives:

[ki. bat.tə. k□m.mə.le. flœʀ #? bat.tə. to.vã de.mã.]   01*00001* #? 100101   7 + 6?

This 'cesura' implies the interruption of a verb phrase which allows no pause. This same line, minus word-final [ə] gives:

[ki. bat. k□m. le.flœʀ #? bat.to.vã.de.mã.]   01001 #? 10101^[119]   5 + 5

The the anaphora of onomatopoeic [bat]^[120] is coupled with those of syllabic count (5 → 5), and of syntax (verb + adverbial phrase → verb + adverbial phrase). The verb itself achieves further prominence in the collision of accent at the 'cesura'.^[121]

Though the couplet-rhyme joins ll. 12 and 13, there is a contrast of both sense and rhythm: 12 is 'emphatic' and is 5 + 5, while 13 reverts to the 'pastoral mode' of the opening, and the 'anapestic' six syllables of its first hemistich re-establish the alexandrine metre — a recall of the first hemistichs of strophes 1 and 2. Does the 'pastoral' aura of the 'regular' first hemistich of l. 13 call for the return of the syllabic value of word-final [ə] implied by ll. 1–3? Here are ll. 13–15:

[lə gaʀ.dj□̃. dy.tru.po. # □ã.tə.^[122] tu.du.sə,mã.]   001001 # 100101
[tã.di.ke. lã.tə^[123].ze.mœ.glã # le.va.□ə.za,bã.do.nə.]   *00010001* # 0101010
[puʀ. tu.□uʀ.sə.gʀã.pʀe # mal.flœ.ʀi.paʀ l□.t□.nə.]   001001 # 1010010

Our second approach takes a 'bird's-eye' view, comparing two possible cohesive readings of our text: version A below assumes the syllabic value of line-internal word-final [ə], and version B deletes it:

Version A

	lə.pʀe.□.ve.ne.nø. # m□.□□.li ã.n□.t□.nə	010101 # 0010010	12
	le.va.□ə.zi.p□.sã.	010001 #	6
	lã.tə.mã.sã.pwa.z□.nə.	1010010	6
	lə. kol. □i.kə. #? ku.lœʀ.də.s□ʀ.ne.də.li.la.	0010 #? 01010001	12
5	i.flœ.ʀi.te.zjø.s□̃.k□m.mə.s□.tə flœʀ.la.	001010000011	12
	vjo.la,tʀə k□m.mə.lœʀ.s□ʀ .# ne.k□m.mə.s□. t□.t□.nə	010□0010#□01010
	e.ma.vi.puʀ.te,zjø. # lã.tə.mã.sã.pwa,z□.nə.	001001 # 1010010	12

le.zã.fã. də. le.k□.lə?. # vj□n.ə.ta.vek.fʀa.ka	001001 # 100101	13
v□.ty.də. □.kə.t□̃. # e.jwã.də.laʀ.m□.ni.ka.	010101 # 0100101	13
10 il.kœ.jə le.k□l.□i.kə.? # ki.s□̃.k□m.mə.de.m□.ʀə	0100010 # 0100010	13
fijə də.lœʀ.fij? # e.s□̃.ku.lœʀ.də.te.po.pj□.ʀə	10001 # 000100010	13
ki.ba.tə.k□m.mə.le.flœʀ #? .ba.tə.to.vã.de.mã	0100001 #? 100101	13
lə gaʀ.dj□̃. dy.tru.po. # □ã.tə. tu.du.sə,mã.	001001 # 100101	12
tã.di.ke.lã.tə.ze.mœ.glã # le.va.□ə.za,bã.do.nə	*00010001 # 0101010*	14
15 puʀ. tu.□uʀ.sə.gʀã.pʀe # mal.flœ.ʀi.paʀ l□.t□.nə	001001 # 1010010	12

Version B

lə.pʀe.□.ve.ne.nø. # m□.□□.li ã.n□.t□n	010101 # 001001	12
le.va.□ə.zi.p□.sã.[124]	*010001 #*	6
lã.tə.mã.sã.pwa.z□n.[125]	101001	6
lə. kol. □i.k. #? ku.lœʀ.də.s□ʀ.ne.də.li.la.	001 #? 01010001	11
5 i.flœ.ʀi.te.zjø.s□̃.k□m.s□t. flœʀ.la.	001 #? 01*00011*	10
vjo.la,tʀ⁹ k□m.lœʀ.s□ʀ. # ne. k□m.s□. t□.t□n.	01001 #? 00101	10
e.ma.vi.puʀ.te,zjø. # lã.tə.mã.sã.pwa,z□n.	001001 # 101001	12
le.zã.fã. də. le.k□l. # vj□n.ta.vek.fʀa.ka	001001 # 10101	11
v□.ty.də. □.kə.t□̃. # e.jwã. də.laʀ.m□.ni.ka.[126]	010101 # 0100101	13
10 il.kœj. le.k□l.□i.k. # ki.s□̃.k□m.de.m□ʀ.	01001 # 01001	10
fijᵉ də.lœʀ.fij. # e.s□̃.ku.lœʀ.də.te.po.pj□ʀ.	1001 # *00010001*	12
ki.bat.k□m.le.flœʀ .#? bat.to.vã.de.mã.	01001 # 10101	10
lə gaʀ.dj□̃. dy.tru.po. # □ã.t.ᵊtu.du.sə,mã.[127]	001001 # 100101	12
tã.di.ke.lã.tə.ze.mœ.glã # le.va.□ə.za,bã.d□n	*00010001 # 010101*	14
15 puʀ. tu.□uʀ.sə.gʀã.pʀe # mal.flœ.ʀi.paʀ l□.t□n.	001001 # 101001	12

Apollinaire's poem proves a test-piece for our 'reader aloud'. Let us assume he or she is a professional who will see straightaway that, although there is strict couplet-rhyme in the text, its lines are of different lengths. Is this free verse?[128] If it is, he or she will leave out word-final [ə] but then find it is impossible to read the [ə]-less first line without realising that it is a perfect alexandrine.[129] And the implied syllabic value of medial [ə] in pre-posed *lentəment* in l. 3 makes up another alexandrine hemistich; so what to do with the [ə] of *vaches* in l. 2? This problem persists: the text shifts between the 'alexandrine regularity' of ll. 1, 7 and 15 plus the 'regular' first hemistichs of ll. 8, 9 and 13, and, at the other extremity, the unpunctuated 'prose' of l. 5.

If our reader has done his or her homework, he or she will know that if word-final [ə] has syllabic value here, then eight of the poem's fifteen lines have twelve syllables.[130] But would he or she recognise a recurrent syllable-count in ll. 4 to 6, or 10 to 12, in the absence of any real 'cesura'? The concentration of atonic runs and juxtaposed accents in these lines of version A bring it very close to prose.

To summarise: the unmistakeable alexandrine of l. 1 will prompt us to maintain the pulse by giving syllabic value to [ə] in ll. 2 and 3. This pulse is sustained in l. 4 by the initial 001001 and the accent at position 6. But the absence of the 'cesural' boundary at position 6 is the first sign of the extreme 'irregularity' which takes over in l. 5. Here, an atonic position 6, plus unpunctuated syntax and weak alternation, all indicate a 'free-verse' register in which word-final [ə] is deleted. This trend continues in l. 6 where an atonic run of four syllables leads to the 'cesural' position 6 which is occupied by the clitic *leur*, an extreme violation of the ideal alexandrine metre. If, in ll. 5 and 6, we decide to delete word-final [ə], l. 6 then would have the form 5 + 5 with sustained alternation. Order is at all events restored in l. 7, which, like l. 1, without occurrences of word-final [ə], has a syntactical boundary with group-accent at position 6 and is marked by sustained alternation of accent. The perception of 'regularity' is not due to the judgement of the reader: as in l. 1, it is forced on us by the rhythm and syntax. In the context of l. 7's alexandrine, the first hemistichs of ll. 8 and 9 will predispose the reader to reinstate word-final [ə].[131] Lines 8, 10, 11 and 12 will consequently have irregular 'cesuras', and ll. 8 to 12 will have thirteen syllables and six runs of atonic syllables. In contrast, if we read these lines *without* word-final [ə], nine of the ten hemistichs concerned alternate accent, and only two atonic runs remain; also, though syllable-count varies, ll. 8 to 11 have a clear 'cesura'.

In l. 13, we touch base once again with an evident alexandrine. A comparison of our two versions answers the question posed by our 'real-time' reading of the final lines of our poem: does the return of the 'pastoral' mode call for the correlative syllabic value of [ə]? It turns out that word-final [ə] in ll. 13 and 14 of version B is in each case 'epenthetic'; that is, it has to be there for articulation to be possible. Just as in ll. 1 and 15, where syntax and word-accent permit only one reading of the verse-line, so in l. 13 it is the phonetic structure of a word-group which guarantees the alexandrine syllable-count in the second hemistich. The repeated [t] in [# □ã.tə. tu.] generates the [ə] for 'lubrication', and in l. 14, the first word-final [ə] is required by the *liaison*. It follows that for the recitation of ll. 13 to 15, versions A and B necessarily concur.

In this 'almost sonnet', halfway between conventional verse and free verse, the poet offers possibilities to the 'reader aloud'. But this is no free-for-all: throughout, built-in constraints nudge us towards 'regularity'. It is no accident that ll. 1, 7 and 15, which remind the reader of the metrical norm, show no occurrences of word-final [ə]. It is in contrast with this 'norm' that the text's rhythmic, syntactic and syllabic deviations achieve their full effect.

Pierre Reverdy (1889–1960) can be seen as a true forerunner of recent experimenters in the art of French poetry; one thinks of André du Bouchet and David Mus. Though his words are those of the everyday, the relationship between them is not; though on the page his phrases look transparent, their conversation with each other demands a careful reader. The poet writes short pieces of continuous prose and free verse which get shape and sense from their layout on the page, such as 'Toujours là':

	J'ai besoin de ne plus me voir et d'oublier	001001010101	8 + 4
	De parler à des gens que je ne connais pas	001001*000*101	6 + 6
	De crier sans être entendu	00100101	3 + 5
	Pour rien tout seul	0101	4
5	Je connais tout le monde et chacun de vos pas	001001001001	6 + 6
	Je voudrais raconter et personne n'écoute	00100100101	6 + 5
	Les têtes et les yeux se détournent de moi	0100100101	5 + 5
	Vers la nuit	001	3
	Ma tête est une boule pleine et lourde	01001 # 101	5 + 3
10	Qui roule sur la terre avec un peu de bruit	01001010101	5 + 6
	Loin	1	1
	Rien derrière moi et rien devant	10010101	4 + 4

	Dans le vide où je descends	0010*001*	3 + 4
	Quelques vifs courants d'air[132]	001101	6
15	Vont autour de moi	00101	5
	Cruels et froids	0101	2 + 2
	Ce sont des portes mal fermées	*0001*101	4 + 3
	Sur des souvenirs encore inoubliés	00101010101	5 + 6
	Le monde comme une pendule s'est arrêté	010*00*10101	2 + 4 + 4
20	Les gens sont suspendus pour l'éternité	01010100101	6 + 5
	Un aviateur descend par un fil comme une araignée	0101010010101	6 + 3 + 5
	Tout le monde danse allégé	0011001	7
	Entre ciel et terre	00101	5
	Mais un rayon de lumière est venu	*0001*001001	4 + 6
25	De la lampe que tu as oublié d'éteindre	00100*0*10101	11
	Sur le palier	*0001*	4
	Ah ce n'est pas fini	100101	6
	L'oubli n'est pas complet	010101	6
	Et j'ai encore besoin d'apprendre à mieux me connaître.[133]	0101010101001	6 + 7

This dishevelled text nevertheless shows certain regularities. Each line begins with a capital letter and ends with a word-accent. The apparent randomness of line-length suggests general suppression of word-final [ə]. Lines 1, 2 and 5 each have no word-final [ə] and twelve syllables,[134] ll. 2 and 5 are undeniably 6 + 6, and ll. 3 and 4 are 8 + 4, all of which suggests the setting up of a metrical norm. Seven lines show runs of three atonic syllables and four have juxtaposed accents. Thus, if we except the one-syllable l. 11, eighteen lines alternate accent (64 per cent). Our aim, once again, is to look for formal relations between the rhythmic and semantic structures of the text.

The prevalence of alternating accent confirms a strong first impression that rhythm is part of meaning here. The twenty-eight returns to the lefthand margin create units whose relations with each other show significant interaction of sense and rhythm. The absence of punctuation fosters ambiguity as we find it in the transition from l. 1 to l. 2: in *d'oublier*/*De parler*, is *De parler* the complement of *d'oublier*?[135] If so, the word-accent on *oublier* is not group-final; rhythm is uninterrupted and the propositional sense clear: 'I need to forget *both* to talk to people I do not know *and* to shout without anyone hearing me': that is, to reduce the 'dysphoric' content of my experience. But if the accent on *oublier is* group-final, a very different picture appears: just like group-final *d'oublier*, both *De parler* and *De crier* then depend syntactically on *J'ai besoin*. What was both psychologically and logically coherent is now fragmented and contradictory: now it is 'I need to talk to people I do not know and to shout without being heard, alone, and for no reason at all': all of which is decidedly 'dysphoric'. In contrast with Laforgue's line-end punctuation, the return to the left-hand margin can leave open the possibility of both syntactic and semantic polyvalence.

The alexandrine in l. 5 strikes a new note both metrically and semantically: an addressee appears, the plural possessive *vos*, in a 6 + 6 line whose affirmative mood is expressed in hemistichs which are semantically (*tout le monde = chacun*) and rhythmically (001001 = 001001) equivalent. This precarious equilibrium does not last; in l. 6, it is maintained in *Je voudrais raconter* (001001) only to collapse in the negative asymmetry of *et personne n'écoute* (00101). The overdetermining of semantic values by rhythmic structure gives us in the 'anapests' of l. 5 an all-too-brief 'optimism' (001001 = 001001) which 'runs into the buffers' of the iamb of l. 6: 001001 ≠ 00101.

In l. 7:

> Les têtes et les yeux # se détournent de moi   0100100101   5 + 5

the rhythmic equivalence

> que personne n'écoute = se détournent de moi

prolongs the sense of 'defeated optimism?' with the coupling of rhythmic and semantic values. The unbroken alternation carries the sense into l. 8, where a full stop after *nuit* would imply a minor boundary after *moi*, giving the greater accentual weight to *nuit*. The phonetic and accent structure of l. 9 contributes to its sense: [ma t□. t□.tyn. bul. pl□. ne.luʀd.]. The articulatory effort required for the double anaphora of [t] anticipates the 'density/weight?' expressed semantically and rhythmically in the sense and in the juxtaposed accents of *boule pleine*, further weighted by the anaphora of tonic [u] in [bul.] → [luʀd.]. A syntactic boundary between [bul] and the following adjectival group attenuates the force of neighbouring accents. In l. 10 the value 'density/weight?' is recalled in the further anaphor of [u] in accented [ʀul], only for it to be 'modestly underplayed' by the semantic and rhythmic banality of 'iambic' [a.v□.kœ̃.pø.də. bʀ□i.], where even the full [u] of the resonant anaphor is reduced to the semi-vowel [□].

The blank space in l. 11 separates tonic [lwɛ̃] from its rhyme [ʀjɛ̃] in l. 12 and thus acquires a complex semantic value 'silent/remote/empty?' This joins the paradigm of textual elements connoting 'dysphoric'.[136] The 4 + 4 rhythmic equivalence of this line is coupled with the 'dysphoric' equivalence *Rien derrière = rien devant*. Though in l. 13, the 'dysphoric' paradigm is extended with *vide* and *descends*, l. 14 surprises with the ambiguously 'euphoric' *vifs*, emphatically pre-posed to *courants d'air* and dramatising juxtaposed accents. A further accent-clash in *air/Vont* between ll. 14 and 15 steps up the urgency with the line-initial accent of the first 'trochaic' measure of the text, but the flat 'iambic' rhyming of *cruels et froids* in l. 16 now assigns *vifs* to the 'dysphoric' paradigm.[137] The sense of ll. 17 to 20 takes us back to the *oublier* of l. 1: the *portes mal fermées* imply a failed attempt to shut something out. Is there a ghost of restored equilibrium in the couplet-rhymes of ll. 17 to 20, and in the 6 + 4(?) of l. 19 and the 6 + 5 of l. 20?

A heavenly visitant descends in the long picture-line of 21. The mood turns 'euphoric' with the juxtaposed accents of *Tout le monde danse* but is 'sauf moi' implied? Some 'light' is restored through a paradoxically redemptive act of 'forgetting' in l. 25 and hope is reborn with the astonished affirmation of l. 27. Our protagonist discovers that with the recovery of memory comes a renewed need of self-knowledge. In the final l. 29, the intercalation of *encore* restores to accentual prominence the narrator's first person in a line whose regular 'iambic' alternation sustains the reviving confidence of l. 28, *L'oubli n'est pas complet*. That ll. 27 and 28 are the only ones here to be syllabically equivalent is surely not chance, such balance being, after much restless heterosyllabism, a metaphor for 'repose'.

It is clear that the role of rhythmic structure declines as the poem develops. In much modern poetry organisation is predominantly semantic, the overlapping of semantic fields making it possible for the poet to locate 'meaning' that has no lexical or propositional form. For poets like du Bouchet and Mus, words of everyday use, *blanc, mot, vent, mur, jour, pierre*, are a source of inexhaustible novelty as they combine and recombine in shifting contexts which reveal the complexity of their connotational fields.[138] These technical developments, inaugurated by Rimbaud, Laforgue and Mallarmé, have moved French poetry away from explicit reference to the world of shared experience towards a lively and almost exclusive preoccupation with the properties of language itself. Just as a straightforward paraphrase of 'Toujours là' is clearly out of the question, so is any attempt to describe it satisfactorily in the formal terms we have been using. Alternation of accent in our text from Reverdy tells us that it is not prose, but in it, syllabic equivalence between line-units occurs only once.

Such equivalence together with alternation of accent are defining attributes of the couplings we have located, which is not to say that such couplings are the only way of creating non-paraphrasable meaning. The heterosyllabism of La Fontaine shows that this can be achieved through the correlation of accentual and semantic values alone. Though La Fontaine's metres are historically derived, his heterosyllabism does find echoes in twentieth-century lineation.[139] The poetry of the French twentieth century confronts its readers with an apparent break with that of previous centuries, but, despite discontinuities, the poetic potential of accent is still being exploited. Critics who love today's poetry will, while not forgetting its debts to forerunners, look to semiotic theory for new ways of thinking about the 'misuse of language', which is what poetry has always been about.

Notes to Chapter 2

1. Verrier, *Le Vers français*, II, 5.
2. For analysis of the colloquial register see Pensom, *Accent and Metre in French*, pp. 127–34, and Appendix IV, pp. 157–72.
3. If both passages are marked also for countertonic accent, the verse then shows thirteen runs of more than two atonic syllables of which three have more than three, while the prose shows thirty-six of which ten have more than three.
4. Paul Éluard, 'Blason des fleurs et des fruits', in *Poèmes choisis*, ed. by Pierre Garbarra and Rouben Melik (Paris: Temps Actuels, 1982), pp. 46–50. The equivalence between '[*Pen*]s' and the accented 'im[*men*]se' suggests that the poet accents the first syllable of *pensée*. Compare Lote's recording of *ma pensée entraînée* in n. 57 of the Introduction.
5. For further biographical and thematic comment see John Fox, *A Literary History of France: The Middle Ages* (London: Benn, 1974), pp. 180–83. More detailed consideration of this poetry is given in Roger Pensom, 'On the Prosody of the Decasyllabic Lyrics of the Roi de Navarre', *French Studies*, 39 (1985), 257–75.
6. The accent on *qui* marks a minor syntactic boundary, the inverted direct object of *prendra* separating subject and verb.
7. The accent on the otherwise high-frequency verb *a* marks a syntactic boundary, *en soi* being an adverbial insert.
8. Unlike modern French, the verb's distinctive first-person morphology would normally make the presence of the personal pronoun, *Je*, superfluous. Its function here is emphatic.
9. *Cil* is a demonstrative pronoun equivalent to *ceux-là*.
10. Thibaut de Champagne, 'Seigneurs, sachiez; qui or ne s'en ira', in *Anthologie poétique française*, ed. by A. Mary (Paris: Garnier-Flammarion, 1967), I, 360–61.

11. The translations given in this chapter are the author's own. They are limited to texts in Old and Middle French (thirteenth to sixteenth centuries), which might offer difficulties to readers of modern French.

12. The group-final accent is given further relief by the roughness of the hiatus of the neighbouring vowels 'a' + 'nasal □'.

13. The descriptive concept of 'coupling' was first formulated by Samuel R. Levin in *Linguistic Structures in Poetry*, Janua Linguarum XXIII (The Hague: Mouton, 1962). A coupling, essentially a 'relationship between relationships', is a powerful means of creating meaning at a level resistant to paraphrase.

14. A striking example of the flexibility of Old French syntax.

15. Luke 14:26–27.

16. Compare modern French 'joli chat', 'crayon vert'.

17. While phrase-internal countertonic accent juxtaposed to an oxytonic accent is deleted, the accents on *oignon* and *escalogne* are separated by a syntactical boundary.

18. 'Que # par amour # après # s'entrebaisoient | Et bouche et nez [...]'. *Que* (*Qui*), the relative pronoun for *le dru et la drue*, has a group-final accent being followed by a syntactic boundary. *Par amour* and *après* are intercalated adverbs, each carrying a group-final accent.

19. The accent on *Car* marks the syntactic boundary created by the leftward displacement of *jusque la*. Word-accent on *jusques la*, an adverb, implies normal countertonic accent.

20. *Moult* is a frequently occurring and hence atonic intensifying adverb.

21. Philippe de Vitry, 'Le Dit de Franc Gontier', in *Anthologie poétique française*, ed. by Mary, II, 126.

22. Contrast for example 'fr' in *fromage* and *fromagee*.

23. *Douz* is a high-frequency adjective (*douz sire, douce dame, douz amis, douz fils* etc.) and hence atonic.

24. The '?' notation indicates an attempt to name the semantic value produced by the interplay of semantic and formal structures.

25. *Ce* here a pronoun equivalent of *ceci*. The line means 'to launder that which covers back and belly'.

26. That is, the word-accent is given informational prominence by the inversion.

27. The coupling of the 'morally/humanly positive' with strikingly low accent-counts in ll. 28 and 30 irresistibly connotes 'modesty, humility'.

28. The syntactic boundary of this line separates what would otherwise be colliding accents. Compare ll. 647 and 670. Though the octosyllable is without cesura, poets who use it are aware of the possibilities offered by the 4 + 4 structure.

29. Of the six phrase-internal juxtaposed accents in this *ballade*, four occur in this already stylistically aberrant strophe.

30. François Villon, *Poésies complètes*, ed. by Claude Thiry, Livre de Poche (Paris: Librairie Générale Française, 1991), pp. 141–43. The pages which follow are a revised version of an accentual commentary which appeared in Roger Pensom, *Le Sens de la métrique de François Villon: Le Testament* (Oxford: Peter Lang, 2004), pp. 79–85. The whole of Villon's *Testament* is covered in this book.

31. 'Escrinnectes', i.e. little jewel boxes. This is found in only one manuscript. For Thiry it refers to woman's sexual parts. Most sources have 'chevaucheurs d'escouvectes' that is 'men who ride broomsticks'. This possible homosexual reference seems to have escaped Thiry's notice. Sodomy as well as sorcery were punished by burning.

32. E. Balmas and Y. Guiraud, *Littérature française: de Villon à Ronsard* (Paris: Flammarion, 1986), pp. 250–51.

33. Clément Marot, 'Preface', in *Oeuvres de Françoys Villon de Paris revues et remises en leur entier par Clément Marot valet de chambre du Roy*, quoted by Emmanuèle Baumgartner, *Poésies de François Villon* (Paris: Gallimard, 1998), p. 180.

34. Bearing in mind the correlation between accentual frequency and informational density, a verse-line with lower accent-frequency may be perceived as 'quicker' than a line with higher accent-frequency. Compare ll. 625 and 626: 'Pour ce, amez tant que voudrez | Suyvez assemblees et festes', where the latter is perceived as 'lighter and quicker' than the former.

35. [vu.dre] ≠ [mə.nə.trj□r]. The rhyme implies the silencing of the final [r] of *menestrier*, a feature of Villon's popular Parisian speech. It is only with the recurrence of the rhyme-scheme that the listener realises that he or she is in a *ballade*.

36. Unlike *murtrier/Chien* where the accent is displaced to the radical morpheme, its displacement here would site it on a syllable which a fifteenth-century francophone would identify as a *prefix* to the radical morpheme. With this extremely awkward preposing of the adjective, the poet sets a trap for the unwary reader aloud.

37. See Introduction, n. 2.

38. The tonic *sont* results from the syntactical inversion. Compare *Luy sont plus doulces que civetes*.* 00010010.

39. For the origins of the French sonnet see André Gendre, *Evolution du sonnet français* (Paris: PUF, 1996).

40. Joachim du Bellay, *L'Olive*, in *Poems*, ed. by H. W. Lawton (Oxford: Basil Blackwell, 1972), p. 18.

41. 'Il n'est pas interdit de voir en Du Bellay un poète plus violent au fond de lui-même que sa "douceur angevine" le fait penser' (Gendre, *Evolution du sonnet français*, p. 64).

42. Joachim Du Bellay, *Regrets*, in *Poems*, ed. by Lawton, p. 82.

43. Leftward displacement of juxtaposed accent, cf. *crayon vert*.

44. Elsewhere this quatrain strikingly illustrates the role played by syntax in the distribution of accent. (See Chapter 1, n. 27). Though word-accent, functionally related to position and relative frequency of occurrence, constrains the poet, syntactic ordering, though linguistically constrained, permits some variation. Thus while in l. 8, for example, any rhythmic solution other than *En rares nouveautez une Afrique seconde* is illicit, the syntactic variants 'semblable a la grand'mer est ce Paris', 'ce Paris, sans pair, est semblable à la grand'mer' and 'sans pair, ce Paris est semblable a la grand'mer' are allowed. But not 'Est ce Paris semblable a la grand'mer sans pair'*. The verb may not come first.

45. The aspectual contrast 'imperfect' ≠ 'passé simple', that is, 'continuous' ≠ 'punctual', implies an 'emphatic' value (i.e accentual) for the latter. The transition from 'imperfect' to 'passé simple' implies a quasi-adverbial function for this latter, equivalent to 'suddenly', 'unexpectedly'. Compare the relative 'flatness' of the alternative reading *Print esbaissement*. Though the *fut* of l. 13 might well have been 'C'était', the aspectual value of the preterite reiterates the now exasperated 'astonishment' of the narrator.

46. See Maya Slater, *The Craft of La Fontaine* (London: Athlone, 2000), pp. 29, 36.

47. Blank, *Kleine Verskunde*, pp. 61–62, draws attention to the stylistic function of alternation of accent in the first twelve lines, though his criteria for accent are neither explicit nor consistent.

48. La Fontaine, 'Le Corbeau et le renard', in *Fables*, ed. by Bassy, p. 7. This analysis is a revised version of one given in Roger Pensom, 'Sense and Rhythm in La Fontaine's *Fables*', *French Studies*, 64 (2010), 396–409 (pp. 402–04). This article also analyses 'La Mort et le bucheron' (Book I, 16) and 'Le Vieux Chat et la jeune souris' (Book XII, 5).

49. Though our accentuation of ll. 6 and 9 violates our model, readers may agree that stylistic pressure is very marked here.

50. For a more detailed review of the occurrence and significance of such runs, see Pensom, 'Sense and Rhythm in La Fontaine's *Fables*', esp. pp. 398–401.

51. In the second hemistich, stylistic pressure is again marked: the hyperbole of the expression throws the negative particles into prominence. The juxtaposed accent at the 'cesura' marks the intensity of the Crow's delight. In this line's return of the narrative voice, the poor beast is the victim not only of the Fox's mockery but of that of the poet too.

52. Jean de La Fontaine, 'Les Grenouilles qui demandent un roi', in *Fables*, ed. by Bassy, pp. 124–25.

53. From the thirteenth-century interludes of *Aucassin et Nicolete* to the Romantic 'Rodrigue pendant la bataille' of Émile Deschamps, the heptasyllable has done service as a workaday narrative metre.

54. This coupling of register contrast with metrical contrast is also found in in the poetry of André Chénier, as shown below.

55. The colloquial intercalation of *tout* into the noun phrase brings with it an accent and a shift in register.
56. Whose rhythm is exactly that of the alexandrine of l. 4.
57. Not only is La Fontaine's poem a metrical and prosodic script for performance, it is also an eventful journey for the reader.
58. Our sense of 'acceleration' in this line, in contrast to l. 19, is due to: 1. syntactical unity; 2. absence of internal pause; 3. contrasting line-length; and 4. the dominance of accentually weaker 'anapests' (001001010). The 'anapestic' rhythm gives playfully emphatic relief to the countertonic accent on *fourmilière*, itself a wry metaphor.
59. How can you do that to an alexandrine?
60. Lesser accentual density implies a lesser informational density and hence a sensed distinction in tempo.
61. The former is the view of Gouvard, *La Versification*, p. 86.
62. For Chénier's biography and place in the history of French verse see Jean M. Goulemot and Jean-Jacques Tatin-Gourier, *André Chénier: poésie et politique* (Paris: Minerve, 2005). Essays on the relation between Chénier's biography and poetry and on his themes and influences are found in *Lectures d'André Chénier: 'Imitations et préludes poétiques', 'Art d'aimer', 'Élégies'*, ed. by Jean-Noël Pascal (Rennes: Presses Universitaires de Rennes, 2005).
63. André Chénier, 'L'Aveugle', in *Oeuvres poétiques*, ed. by Eugène Manuel (Paris: Flammarion, [n.d.]), pp. 28–29.
64. The increased 'density' of accentuation coincides with the semantic 'compression' created by the rhetorical device. The impact of the double accent is further overdetermined by the voiced *liaison*-consonant in 'bra.zivʀ', where the onset [z] shares the increased intensity of the accented vowel. Though Dominique Billy remarks that in Chénier's *Élégies* 'les juxtapositions d'accent sont assez rares', their effect in this passage is cumulative and significant (see Billy, 'La Versification d'André Chénier l'élégiaque', in *Lectures d'André Chénier*, ed. by Pascal, pp. 103–16 (p. 110, n. 14)).
65. Where the relation between syntactical unit and verse-unit is concerned, François-Charles Gaudard comments: 'Pour ce qui est de la versification *stricto sensu*, c'est vraisemblablement La Fontaine, inventeur de la première génération de ce que l'on a coutume d'appeler "le vers libre", qui a le plus influencé André Chénier' (see 'Poésie et versification dans les *Élégies* d'André Chénier', in *Lectures d'André Chénier*, ed. by Pascal, pp. 117–31 (p. 125)).
66. Where the numerals represent syllables and the + word-boundaries.
67. The prolonged resonance of the onset, the nasal 'double consonant' [m], augments emphasis on the vowel which is also lengthened by the group-accent. The 'prolonging' effect of final [ə], in contrast to the proclisis of 'tomb(ə)→ Et' of ll. 11–12, shows the poet's awareness of the creative potential in either coupling it with a semantic value or deleting it by proclisis.
68. André Chénier, 'Saint-Lazare', in *Oeuvres poétiques*, pp. 271–72.
69. The accent on normally atonic *sont* is due to the syntactical inversion.
70. This accent thus has increased values in intensity and pitch.
71. Beside the syntactical limit following *soudain*, the inversion of syntax creates a limit *before* the adverb. This causes a double break in phonation.
72. '[ə]' after 'a' as in '□wa' is not pronounced.
73. 'Que toujours dans vos vers le sens coupant les mots | Suspende l'hémistiche, en marque le repos' (Nicolas Boileau-Despréaux, 'L'Art poétique', in *Oeuvres poétiques*, ed. by Charles Louandre (Paris: Charpentier, 1865), Chant I, p. 290).
74. André Chénier, 'A Abel', *Elégies: livre premier, 2*, in *Oeuvres poétiques*, p. 94.
75. The IPA notation at relevant points will clarify the nature of the infractions.
76. Billy notes this extreme case, but the concentration of violations makes it difficult to accept, at least where 'L'Aveugle' is concerned, his judgement that 'Chénier nous a laissé une oeuvre assez conforme par bien des aspects aux goûts de son époque: l'alexandrin y domine, et il suit les règles en usage de son temps' ('La Versification d'André Chénier l'élégiaque', p. 103).
77. For a searching exploration of this neglected sonnet see David Mus, *Le Sonneur de cloches:*

Villon, Shakespeare, Baudelaire, Mallarmé, Reverdy — et nous autres (Seyssel: Champ Vallon, 1991), pp. 62–133.

78. Charles Baudelaire, 'Bohémiens en voyage', in *Oeuvres complètes*, ed. by Claude Pichois, 2 vols, Bibliothèque de la Pléiade (Paris: Gallimard, 1975), I, 18.

79. The suddenly heavier accent-count of *mise en route* may give the reader the sense of a 'laboured stride?'.

80. Rhythm, unlike meaning, is felt in the body.

81. The semantic contrast is one of register: A is 'high', *La tribu prophétique aux prunelles ardentes* 001001 # 001001; and B 'low', *Hier s'est mise en route* 010101 #. And the formal contrast is X [001001] ≠ Y [010101]. Thus X is coupled with A and Y with B.

82. It is this semantic value which is 'le mot étranger à la langue', the meaning which finds no lexical or propositional equivalent.

83. In twelve out of the fourteen lines of this alexandrine sonnet, the mid-line accent/pause falls on/after the sixth syllable.

84. This boundary is marked by absence of *liaison* in [li.vRã. # a.] as opposed to [li.vRã. ta.]*.

85. These couplings are identifiable only if one assumes the linguistic reality of word-accent within the phrase.

86. These three hemistichs are also semantically equivalent with respect to the value 'laborious?'

87. In modern cartoons, 'zzzzzz' in a speech-bubble connotes 'sleepy'.

88. The poet conforms to the rule of cesural accent *only* if there is, as we claim, accent *within* the noun phrase.

89. Rhythmical 'similars' are coupled with semantic 'similars'. But these 'similarities' are themselves complex in that *couler ≠ rocher*, that is, rocks do not normally flow, and in *fleurir ≠ désert* the terms are normally antonymous.

90. See Frédéric Deloffre, *Le Vers français* (Paris: SEDES, 1973), p. 19.

91. The Miracle of Moses (Exodus 17:6)?

92. *Couler* ('euphoric') + *rocher* ('dysphoric') = *fleurir* ('euphoric') + *désert* ('dysphoric'). By now the 'anapestic' hemistich has itself been indelibly semantised as 'euphoric'.

93. Each hemistich consists of a noun phrase (noun + adjective) where *empire = ténèbres* and *familier = futures* in syllable count.

94. Charles Baudelaire, 'La Beauté', in *Oeuvres complètes*, ed. by Pichois, I, 21.

95. We note the semantic neutrality of formal oppositions: the 'euphoric' connotation of 001001 is unique to 'Bohémiens en voyage': here it may acquire a different value, or no value at all.

96. The dieresis [my.□] is required by the syllable-count.

97. Each of the accented vowels of *sein* and *meurtri* falls on position 3 in its hemistich, the symmetry again suggesting equivalence. The idea relates here to the etymological sense of *sphinx*, i.e σφιγγειν, 'compress', 'strangle', 'torture'. Is there a suggestion of algolagnia here?

98. While the 'weightier' accent-count of the first hemistich confirms the 'active' connotation of the transitive verb and the 'dysphoric' sense of its direct complement, the contrast presented by the 'lighter' accent-count of the second hemistich overdetermines the 'euphoric' quality of *la blancheur des cygnes*. The sense of *J'unis* is enacted in the *liaison* [□y.ni.zœ̃.kœR] and in the anaphora of tonic [œ] in *coeur* and *blancheur*.

99. A preposition is generally atonic: however, its function as a noun (*le devant de la maison*) or as adverb (*passer devant*) can trump its identity as a preposition. In principle, any word capable of standing before a full stop has word-accent in all its occurrences.

100. The possible *liaison* [zjøzo. klaR.te] would obscure the deliberate anaphora of [zjø].

101. His *Nouvelles Fleurs du Mal* were contributed to the first series of *Le Parnasse contemporain*. See Baudelaire, *Oeuvres complètes*, ed. by Pichois, I, 1103.

102. Jean-Michel Gouvard, 'Éléments pour une grammaire de la poésie moderne', *Poétique*, 129 (2002), 3–31 (p. 3).

103. [ə] of *gouttes* avoids the 'stop' caused by the collision of the unvoiced and voiced forms [t] and [d].

104. Jules Laforgue, 'L'Hiver qui vient', in *Derniers vers*, ed. by Michael Collie and J. M. L'Heureux (Toronto: University of Toronto Press, 1965), pp. 19–20. As usual, our semantically blind

scansion follows word-accent as we define it and syntactic accent where relevant.

105. Laforgue, *Derniers vers*, p. 12.

106. *Levant*: the mysterious East, the rising sun.

107. See for example Ernest Pulgram, 'Prosodic Systems: French', *Lingua*, 13 (1965), 125–44, and J. Klausenburger, *French Prosodics and Phonotactics* (Tübingen: Niemeyer, 1970), p. 18.

108. So far it has been avoided; in the vowel-group of *Messageri(es)* and by synaloepha in *Nouvell(e) Année*. Generally the opposition 'presence/absence of syllabic word-final [ə]' correlates with the opposition metrical verse/free verse. This is because, by the poet's time, this [ə] had disappeared from the standard spoken French to which free verse increasingly approximates. Nevertheless, it seems that, for Laforgue, the 'presence/absence' of word-final [ə] in his free verse is context-dependent in stylistically significant ways.

109. Milner reminds us of the frequency of such runs in everyday French in 'Accent de vers, et accent de langue dans l'alexandrin classique', pp. 42–43. He adds that such runs 'sont absolument exclues des vers classiques'.

110. Of the eighty-four lines of 'L'Hiver qui vient' eleven are unpunctuated. Of these, in only one other place does the return to the left-hand margin interrupt a syntactic unit; l. 80: [...] *l'autan/ Effiloche* [...].

111. Laforgue's stylistically motivated deployment of sustained alternating accent can be seen in the analysis of 'Le Mystère des trois cors', in Roger Pensom, 'Musique et rythme chez Laforgue', *Poétique*, 160 (2009), 485–93.

112. The mysterious operations of the poet's mind might have moved from the 'popular' *fichu* to the literary/funerary overtones of *gît* via the phonetic relation between [fi.□y] and [□i], where [□] is the voiced form of [□].

113. Jules Laforgue, *Oeuvres complètes*, ed. by Maryke de Courten and Jean-Louis Debauve, 3 vols (Lausanne: L'Age d'Homme, 1986–2000), II, 786.

114. 'Strong' means that density of accent correlates with density of information. The corollary of this is that rarity of accent correlates with low density. For example, in runs of atonic syllables as in 'Gît sur le flanc, *dans les ge*nêts, *sur son man*teau', the frequently occurring words might be guessed by a reader just as *Gît* and *flanc* would not.

115. This, from *Calligrammes*, is in forty-six lines of free verse, with a single octosyllabic quatrain towards the end.

116. Guillaume Apollinaire, 'Les Colchiques', in *Anthology of Modern French Poetry: From Baudelaire to the Present Day*, ed. by C. A. Hackett (Oxford: Basil Blackwell, 1976), p. 111. The text is given as printed, Apollinaire did not punctuate. 'Cesura' is marked where the line is clearly alexandrine.

117. The *liaison* in [le.va.□ə.zi.p□.sã.] defines *y paissant* as adjectival. The alternative, [le.va. □i. .p□. sã], would break the alexandrine and imply a reading of the whole text without word-final [ə].

118. As Apollinaire does not punctuate, we read '[...] qui **sont** [...] Filles de leurs filles [...]' with *comme des mères* as an intercalated phrase. **Sont** is thus tonic, lying on a boundary.

119. Though there is no syntactical boundary, the '#?' marks the lengthening of the vowel in *fleurs* in the context of the collision of accents.

120. Cf. *Et son pied bat le sol* (Chénier, 'L'Aveugle', l. 12).

121. Cf. *Le quadrupède Hélops fuit* (Chénier, 'L'Aveugle', l. 26).

122. At all events, the articulation of [t][t] in separate syllables gives rise spontaneously to [tə?t].

123. The alternative [lã.te. mœ.glã] obscures grammatical agreement with *les vaches*, the form [lã.te] not distinguishing masculine from feminine or singular from plural. [lã.tse.mœ.glã] is also ungrammatical.

124. This epenthetic [ə] is a consequence of the *liaison*.

125. The leftward displacement of the adverb foregrounds its accents, which emphasis produces an epenthetic [ə] between them.

126. The register may elicit [e. jwã. dlaʀ.m□.ni.ka].

127. The articulation of [t][t] in separate syllables gives rise spontaneously to [tə?t]. In l. 14, the [ə] in [lã.tə.ze.mœ.glã] and in [le.va.□ə.za,bã.don] is a consequence of the *liaison*.

128. Compare the rhyme-scheme of the free verse in Laforgue's 'Mystère des trois cors'. See n. 111 above.

129. The French of free verse is a French in which word-final [ə] has disappeared from the standard register.

130. Or nine lines if ll. 2 and 3 are an alexandrine.

131. In spite of the rogue post-'cesural' [ə] of l. 8 in version A.

132. The word-accent displaced leftward in *courants d'air* is maintained in juxtaposition to the accent on low-frequency *vifs* since *courant* is also a low-frequency word.

133. Pierre Reverdy, 'Toujours là', in *Anthology of Modern French Poetry*, ed. by Hackett, pp. 137–38.

134. Compare ll. 1, 7 and 15 of 'Les Colchiques'.

135. The line-initial capital letter does not imply a preceding full stop. For example, in a tight enjambement, the last word in l. 14 , *d'air*, qualifies the grammatical subject of *Vont* at the head of l. 15.

136. *Besoin, ne plus, oublier, crier, rien, seul, personne, détournent* and *lourde*.

137. The exploiting of the polysemy of ordinary words proves a rich resource for Reverdy's successors.

138. For example, André du Bouchet, *Dans la chaleur vacante* (Paris: Mercure de France, 1961), and David Mus, *Débet* (Dijon: Thierry Bouchard, 2000).

139. Compare for example the coupling ('froggy chaos' + 'rhythmic irregularity' in seven syllables) ≠ ('regal authority' + 'rhythmic regularity' in twelve syllables) in ll. 1–4 of 'Les Grenouilles qui demandent un roi', with ll. 5–7 of 'Toujours là' , where 001001 units connote 'euphoric' and 00101 connote 'dysphoric'.

CONCLUSION

The burden of our argument has been the defence and illustration of the constructive role of alternating accent in French verse in the face of the current consensus. The route has been circuitous: our previous work on texts from Old French down to the present day implied unsurprisingly that the accentual prosody of modern French, just like its grammar, syntax and phonology, took root in the Latin transformed by the speech-habits of fifth-century Germanic invaders. This prosody had clearly not arisen spontaneously with the beginnings of French. Tracing its evolution from Latin has consolidated our view of the crucial role of accent in the construction of French verse. Our journey through the data has come up with some surprises.

'Recurrence' being a defining property of verse, the 'mora', the basic unit whose recurrent count structured classical Latin verse, was replaced in Romance by the syllable, a linguistic unit defined not by duration but by form, the combination of vowel and consonant(s). Though the transition must have been gradual, Latin syllabic verse was being written in the fourth century by Saint Ambrose. But this syllabic verse was not simply syllabic:

(a)	a solis ortus cardine	— — ᵕ —	— — ᵕ —
	adusque terrae limitem	ᵕ — ᵕ —	— — ᵕ —
	Christum canamus principem	— — ᵕ —	— — ᵕ —
	natum Maria virgine	— — ᵕ —	— — ᵕ —
(b)	maior et enim solito	— ᵕ ᵕ ᵕ	— ᵕ ᵕ —
	apparuisti omnibus	— — ᵕ —	— — ᵕ —
	ut potestatis ordinem	— ᵕ — —	ᵕ — ᵕ —
	in lustri mente vinceres.[1]	— — — —	ᵕ — ᵕ —

Both these fifth-century quatrains are strictly octosyllabic. With the exception of *Christum* and *natum*, (a) maintains accentual iambic rhythm in what are also quantitatively regular iambic dimeters. In contrast, (b), whose accentual iambic rhythm also follows Latin word-accent, is, where quantity is concerned, chaotic. In (b), alternation of linguistic accent has become the sole means of measuring the eight syllables of the verse-line:

maior et enim solito	10010100
apparuisti **om**nibus	01010100
ut potestatis ordinem	01010100
in lustri mente vinceres.	01010100

As in French, the Latin accent is properly linguistic though its deployment is at the discretion of the poet. In both (a) and (b), iambic rhythm is subject to some variation, but the principle of alternating accent applies throughout, both juxtaposition of accents and runs of atonic syllables being avoided. Our review of Burger's analysis of the iambic dimeter in Saint Ambrose's hymns found, in this extensive corpus, a decisive predominance of such alternation.

But what reason do we have to suppose that this alternation was a feature of Old French verse? We found evidence of persistence of this alternation into French in the effectively hybrid 'Aeterne orbis conditor' where alternating Latin word-accent coexists with French oxytonic rhyme-accent.[2] This latter is entirely foreign to the rhythmic structure of Latin rhymed verse in which the rhyme-syllable is never line-final. It is only with the erosion of Latin post-tonic syllables, 'principem', 'dominum', 'angeli', that typically French oxytonic accent emerges.

So the striking feature of this hymn is the coexistence of two systems of accentuation: in it, the rhyme-words, e.g. *conditor, infima, viscerum,* combine the 'last but two' Latin accentuation of trisyllables with French oxytonic rhyme-accent.[3] This suggests a French-speaking poet for whom countertonic and oxytonic accent in polysyllables is the way his language works.[4] If indeed the oxytonic rhyme here points to general oxytonic word-accent within the verse-line, then the accentual rhythm of 'Aeterne orbis conditor' would be close to that of verse in Old French being written in the time of the anonymous author of our hymn. Though its words, grammar and syntax are Latin, its accentual structure is not; we sense here the character of the 'rusticam romanam linguam' whose use the Council of Tours recommended to its clergy in 813. It supplies a very early confirmation of Verrier's hypothesis concerning the defining presence of alternating accent in French verse.

Integral to our conception of rhythm in French verse is the linguistic status in French of the countertonic word-accent we find in our hymn. In modern French, this has generally been discounted as an *accent d'insistance*, a feature of *parole* rather than of language proper.[5] Indeed, 'accent within the phrase' and 'accent within the word' are controversial topics. For Pulgram and Klausenburger accent in French is uniquely phrase-final: it tells you when you have got to a full stop.[6] Any word-accent within the phrase thus is effaced. On the other hand, for Lusson and Roubaud, oxytonic word-accent within the phrase is a feature of the language but accent within the word is not.[7] Similarly, in her analysis of the dramatic alexandrine, Beaudouin marks only oxytonic word-accent within the phrase.[8] In contrast, the evidence of 'Eterne orbis conditor' is that countertonic accent has been a prosodic reality in French from its earliest days.

The more general question raised by our assertion of the role of countertonic accent is the following: is accent in French uniquely 'demarcative', that is, does it mark solely the limit of a word or unit of syntax? While for Pulgram it marks only a syntactic limit, for Beaudouin it also marks the final full vowel of words with a relatively low frequency of occurrence. For us, however, accent in French has an informational function. Firstly, oxytonic accent distinguishes words with low frequency of occurrence from those with high frequency of occurrence; secondly, countertonic accent distinguishes words with more than two full syllables from others. This function is not limited to French since countertonic accent is found in classical Latin. If the longer a word becomes, the more subject it becomes to information loss, then countertonic accent ensures the word's distinctiveness. For example, we have seen that the difference in vocalic structure between di- and trisyllabic forms in the same verb must be phonological. If word-accent is only oxytonic, why do we have [l□vəʀe] and not [ləvəʀe]*?[9] And why do speakers give us 'chaperon **rouge**' and not 'chaper**on** rouge*'? One explanation might be that 'French avoids a series of [ə]s and juxtaposed accents'. A more economical account would be that the standard forms minimise potential information loss: in the first case, by loss of distinctiveness through lax articulation and in the second, by interruption of phonation due to adjacent word-accents in a noun + adjective phrase.[10]

Though our argument runs counter to current French thinking, we can be encouraged by remembering the reluctance of earlier English theorists to accept the defining role of accent in their national verse. It may be that in earlier England as in modern France, eye has been more important than ear in perceiving what is really going on in verse. In agreement with the isosyllabic doctrine of Port-Royal,[11] to say nothing of Cornulier and Gouvard, George Puttenham's *The Arte of English Poesie* (1589) had already stated that 'This quantitie with them (the Greeks and Romans) consisteth in the number of their feete: with us in the number of sillables, which are comprehended in every verse, not regarding his feete'.[12] Even as late as the eighteenth century, Edward Bysshe's *The Art of English Poetry* (1702) affirmed that 'The Structure of our Verses, whether Blank, or in Rhyme, consists in a certain number of syllables'.[13] In spite of which Sir Philip Sidney in his *The Defence of Poesie* (1595) had already remarked that 'Now for Rime, though we doo not observe quantitie, yet wee observe the Accent verie precisely'.[14] The idea that English verse was accentually structured emerged only gradually. Since the accentual properties of English are self-evident to any native speaker, this reluctance must have been cultural, as it had been among composers setting French verse between 1300 and the late 1600s. Unlike that of English, the evolution of the prosodies of French had levelled the accentual profile of the language in a way that distinguished it from its Romance sisters. This 'levelling' makes it easy to believe today that nothing 'accentual' is happening within the phrase. Indeed, from the sixteenth century on, commentators observed that the 'word' had given way to the phrase as the basic unit of the sentence.[15] But the fact that the phonetic boundary of the word had been eroded by *liaison* and *enchaînement* does not imply the effacing of its prosodic markers. The informationally critical 'word' remains as a prosodically stable component of the phrase. It is this informational role that has been overlooked in the emphasis on its segmental identity.

That critics and performers, as opposed to poets, could remain unaware of, or indifferent to, rhythm in French verse was indeed something which worried Lote. Though no accentualist, he complained that the uniform flow of syllables in the declamation of serious verse had 'une allure lourde et pesante qui déplaisait à beaucoup et, à mesure que les années passaient, devait déplaire encore davantage'.[16] The picture is further confused by the relation between earlier verse and music: from Machaut in the fourteenth century to Mauduit in the sixteenth we find little or no correlation between rhythm in music and in verse. Though we have found that the verse these composers set shows alternating accentual structure, their settings pay little or no attention to it. For Machaut this is especially striking since he was both poet and composer.

We had to wait for the seventeenth century to resolve this puzzle. Lote thought that this resolution was due to a conscious reforming spirit abroad among dramatists and composers of the time. Whatever the truth of this notion, the evidence is there for all to see and hear. Lully's settings of Quinault's libretti show a clear and consistent correlation of musical rhythm with the intraphrasal accentual patterning of the verse. Once this crucial cultural shift had occurred, the reconciliation of musical rhythm with the accentual structure of the verse became the norm. From Rameau to Debussy, the resources of musical notation are placed at the service of the verse's accentual rhythm.

We have often felt baffled that influential critics from Port-Royal to the present have remained insensitive to those rhythmic qualities of French verse relished and acknowledged by our francophone composers. The possibility remains that these latter were mistaken in their reading of the verse they set, but if so, there is a remarkable consensus in their misapprehension. Could it be that our critics share the constitutional deafness to rhythm in verse that we have noted in pre-Lully stage-declamation and in composers from Machaut to Costeley?

The politics of culture are perhaps relevant here. As Lombez observes in a review of the work of Paul Verluyten: 'force est de reconnaître que de nos jours encore, les théories divergeant tant soit peu de l'isosyllabisme ont bien du mal à se faire entendre, sinon accepter'.[17] She adds that Jean-Louis Backès has also wondered about the origins of this 'resistance': 'Il y a d'intéressantes recherches à faire, pour un comparatiste, sur le jeu des idéologies dans une discipline apparemment aussi innocente que la poétique. La métrique elle-même n'est pas pure de toute politique, loin s'en faut'.[18] Does France, whose 'exceptionalism' in culture and politics are well known, require, even in metrical matters, a proof of its distinctiveness? Current insistence on a metric unique in Romance guarantees its immunity to the compromising Germanic accentualism which afflicts its Romance congeners.

Our argument has not only demonstrated the metrical function of alternating accent in measuring isosyllabic verse: it has also revealed the structuring presence of this alternation in the heterosyllabic verse which has always existed beside it.[19] Once the principle of alternation is accepted, Cornulier's difficulties with the heterosyllabic La Fontaine evaporate. And what is more, the transition to the free verse of modern times cannot be understood without reference to alternation of accent as an organising principle: we have shown its importance in the work of poets from Laforgue to Reverdy.

But the real value of these insights lies in understanding the role of this alternation in the creation of meaning. Problems arising in interpretation of the relation between 'rhythm' and 'meaning' have however left theorists who are sympathetic to the accentual thesis vulnerable to the fatal objection that their notion of accentual rhythm is circular: it relies on the very meaning it aims to account for. Gouvard cuts to the heart of the problem with his assertion that 'la métrique n'est pas sémantique'.[20] His detailed discussion of the thesis of Jean Mazaleyrat shows that the latter's identification of the syntactic unit and hence its accented boundary relies on stylistic criteria.[21] Gouvard finds also that Lusson and Roubaud are similarly influenced by semantic considerations in locating accented boundaries.[22]

So how do we get from Gouvard's outright 'la métrique n'est pas sémantique' to a conception of metre which, rather than relying on meaning, produces it? The first imperative is that any description of the accentual-metrical structure of a poem must be independent of any reference to meaning and formulated prior to any consideration of it. Only then will it be legitimate to look for significant interference between accentual structure and semantic values. We satisfy this proviso because our accentual model is derived solely from analysis of the distribution of a semantically empty prosodic marker in verse-texts in Late Latin and Old French.[23] Consequently each of our analyses of French verse-texts in Chapter Two is strictly experimental: once prior scansion of the text in accordance with our model has been completed, there is still no way of knowing what, if anything, its interaction with the thematic structure of the text will yield. Even if the theory we propose is the product of a disordered imagination, the proof of the pudding is in the eating. Our analyses of French poetry over seven centuries have shown a considerable body of instances in which accentual patterning is coupled with semantic values to create 'meanings?' whose *sui generis* nature finds no propositional equivalent. This 'body of instances' points to a sustained tradition in French verse. Though such 'meanings?' cannot be peculiar to French, the relationship between French verse and the accentual prosody of French must be. Such a relationship could not have existed without poets being aware of the possibilities it offered in 'going beyond language'.

Since Scoppa, the accentual thesis has repeatedly resurfaced, only to fall victim to the criticism of isosyllabists. This criticism identifies two weaknesses: firstly, though Scoppa's foot-based model was independent of 'meaning', it was, to cite only one deficiency, incompatible with French word-accent; secondly, the metrical models of Mazaleyrat and Lusson-Roubaud, though acknowledging a role for accent, did rely in varying degrees on stylistic considerations. Our attempt to avoid both Scylla and Charybdis has resulted in an algorithm whose application to any French verse-text is mechanical: anyone can do it.[24] If the correlation we have found in the coupling of accent-patterning and semantic values in French verse is not mere chance, further experiment by interested parties will confirm the heuristic value of our model.

Notes to the Conclusion

1. Repeated from Chapter 1 for the sake of clarity. Accented vowels in bold.
2. See Chapter 1.
3. See Chapter 1, n. 15. The evidence for oxytonic accent in Latin verse given in Chapter 1, n. 27, includes French musical notation giving 'Eterne rer**um** condi**tor**'. This in no way precludes the Latin iambic patterning of our hymn with its antepenultimate word-accent. Line-final word-accent is of course incompatible with a quantitative reading.
4. For Latin countertonic accent see Chapter 1, n. 7.
5. See for example A. Rigault, 'L'Accent secondaire de mot français: mythe ou réalité?', *Actele celui de-al XII-lea congres international de lingvistică si filologie romanică*, 2 vols (Bucharest: Editura Academiei Republicii Socialiste Romania, 1970–71), II, 285–90. The *Dictionnaire de linguistique et des sciences de langage*, ed. by Jean Dubois and others (Paris: Larousse, 1994), states that 'Dans les langues où l'accent est fixe, l'accent d'énergie a une *fonction démarcative*, il indique la fin du mot, comme en français, où il n'affecte que la dernière syllabe' (p. 3).
6. See Chapter 2, n. 107.
7. See Pierre Lusson and Jacques Roubaud, 'Sur la devise de *Noeu et de Feu*: un sonnet d'Etienne

Jodelle, essai de lecture rythmique', *Langue française*, 49 (1981), 49–67.

8. See Beaudouin, *Mètres et rythmes du vers classique*.

9. In Old French the verb-stem alternates between first persons *lief* and *levons*, where tonic accent has diphthongised the [□] of the singular. A sixteenth-century future form *lieveray* is attested (see Pope, *From Latin to Modern French*, p. 391). This suggests a relation between accent and [□] in modern French *lèverai*, that is, the presence of a countertonic accent which is phonological. Thus, in any word of more than two full syllables, alternation of accent is phonological: *lèverais*; *retournera*; *université*; *insupportablement*.

10. Such a phrase is a minimal unit of syntax not allowing interruption.

11. 'Nos vers ne consistent qu'en deux choses: en la structure et en la rime. La structure ne consiste qu'en un certain nombre de syllabes', Lancelot and others, *Nouvelle méthode pour apprendre facilement*, p. 487.

12. Cited by Gasparov in *A History of European Versification*, p. 185.

13. Ibid.

14. Ibid.

15. 'Nous joignons tellement nos mots ensemble par une mutuelle liaison [...] qu'il semble que chasque comma ("phrase") n'est qu'un mot', in Charles Turot, *De la prononciation française depuis le commencement du XVIe siècle* (Paris, 1881), cited by Pope, *From Latin to Modern French*, p. 82.

16. See Chapter 1, n. 94.

17. Lombez, *La Traduction de la poésie allemande en français*, p. 5.

18. J. L. Backès, 'Poétique comparée', in *Précis de littérature comparée*, ed. by Pierre Brunel (Paris: PUF, 1989), pp. 90–91.

19. At least from Colin Muset in the thirteenth century to Verlaine.

20. Gouvard, *Critique du vers*, p. 40.

21. Jean Mazaleyrat, *Éléments de métrique française* (Paris: Armand-Colin, 1974).

22. Gouvard, *Critique du vers*, p. 49.

23. That is, belonging strictly to the domain of *langue* rather than *parole*.

24. As a reminder of our model, MARK: 1. group-accent at syntactic boundaries (canonically at the cesura and at the rhyme); 2. Word-accent within the phrase on, in order of priority, (a) monosyllables of low frequency of occurrence and low-frequency disyllables oxytonic and paroxytonic, (b) countertonic syllable(s) of oxytones of more than two syllables and paroxytones of more than three syllables. DELETE: any accent within the phrase next to another in the order of priority given in 2 above, e.g. 'un chaperon rouge'* becomes 'un chaperon rouge'; 'un gros chaperon'* becomes 'un gros chaperon' Displacement rule: 'un joli chat'* becomes 'un joli chat'. Accent on low frequency monosyllables is exempt from deletion, even in juxtaposition, e.g. 'un coeur dur'.

BIBLIOGRAPHY

Primary Works

ANON., *La Chanson de Roland*, ed. by Frederick Whitehead (Oxford: Blackwell, 1962)

ANON., *The Life of St. Alexius in the Old French Version of the Hildesheim Manuscript*, ed. by Carl J. Odenkirchen (Brookline, MA, & Leiden: Classic Folio Editions, 1978)

ANON., *La Passion du Christ*, in Karl Bartsch, *Chrestomathie de l'ancien français* (Leipzig: Vogel, 1910)

ANON., *The Poem of the Cid*, ed. by Ian Michael, trans. by Rita Hamilton and Janet Perry (Harmondsworth: Penguin, 1975)

ANON., *Le Siège de Barbastre*, ed. by J. L. Perrier (Paris: Honoré Champion, 1926)

ANON., *Les Séquences de Sainte Eulalie*, ed. by Roger Berger and Annette Brasseur (Geneva: Droz, 2004)

APOLLINAIRE, GUILLAUME, 'Les Colchiques', in *Anthology of Modern French Poetry: From Baudelaire to the Present Day*, ed. by C. A. Hackett (Oxford: Basil Blackwell, 1976), p. 111

BARTSCH, KARL, *Chrestomathie de l'ancien français* (Leipzig: Vogel, 1910)

BAUDELAIRE, CHARLES, *Oeuvres complètes*, ed. by Claude Pichois, 2 vols, Bibliothèque de la Pléiade (Paris: Gallimard, 1975)

BECK, JEAN, ed., *Les Chansonniers des troubadours et des trouvères*, 2 vols (New York: Broude Bros., 1964)

BERLIOZ, HECTOR, *Les Troyens* (Paris: Choudens Fils, 1892)

BOILEAU-DESPRÉAUX, NICOLAS, *Oeuvres poétiques*, ed. by Charles Louandre (Paris: Charpentier, 1865)

CHÉNIER, ANDRÉ, *Oeuvres poétiques*, ed. by Eugène Manuel (Paris: Flammarion, [n.d.])

CORNEILLE, PIERRE, *Théâtre complet*, ed. by Georges Couton, 3 vols (Paris: Garnier, 1971–74)

DEBUSSY, CLAUDE, *Songs of Claude Debussy: A Critical Edition*, ed. by James R. Briscoe, 2 vols (Milwaukee, WI: Hal Leonard Corporation, 1993)

DU BELLAY, JOACHIM, *Poems*, ed. by H. W. Lawton (Oxford: Basil Blackwell, 1972)

DU BOUCHARD, ANDRÉ, *Dans la chaleur vacante* (Paris: Mercure de France, 1961)

ÉLUARD, PAUL, *Poèmes choisis*, ed. by Pierre Garbarra and Rouben Melik (Paris: Temps Actuels, 1982)

FAURÉ, GABRIEL, *An Album of Twenty Songs* ([n.p.]: Edward B. Marks Music Company, [n.d.])

GLUCK, CHRISTOPH WILLIBALD, *Alceste*, ed. by Hans Vogt (Kassel: Bärenreiter, 1957)

HOFFMANN, FRANÇOIS BENOÎT, *Le Secret, comédie* (Paris: Vente, 1796)

LA FONTAINE, JEAN DE, *Fables*, ed. by Alain-Marie Bassy (Paris: Flammarion, 1995)

LAFORGUE, JULES, *Derniers Vers*, ed. by Michael Collie and J. M. L'Heureux (Toronto: Toronto University Press, 1965)

——*Œuvres complètes*, ed. by Maryke de Courten and Jean-Louis Debauve, 3 vols (Lausanne: L'Age d'homme, 1986–2000)

LANCELOT, CLAUDE, ANTOINE ARNAULD and PIERRE NICOLE, *Nouvelle méthode pour app-rendre facilement et en peu de temps la langue latine, avec une brève instruction sur les règles de la poésie française* (Paris: Vitré, 1650)

LEOPARDI, GIACOMO, *Canti*, ed. by John Humphreys Whitfield (Manchester: Manchester University Press, 1967)

LULLY, JEAN-BAPTISTE, *Alceste,* ed. and arranged for piano and voice by Théodore de Lajarte (Paris: Théodore Michaelis, [n.d.])

——*Thésée*, ed. by Théodore de Lajarte (Paris: Théodore Michaelis, [n.d.])

MACHAUT, GUILLAUME DE, *Musikalische Werke*, ed. by Friedrich Ludwig, 4 vols (Leipzig: Breitkopf & Härtel, 1926), I

——*Oeuvres complètes*, ed. by Leo Schrade, 5 vols (Monaco: Éditions de l'Oiseau Lyre, 1977), III

MALHERBE, FRANÇOIS DE, *Poésies*, ed. by Jacques Lavaud, 2 vols (Paris: Droz, 1936–37)

MARY. A., ed., *Anthologie poétique française: moyen age,* 2 vols (Paris: Garnier-Flam-marion, 1967)

MUS, DAVID, *Débet* (Dijon: Thierry Bouchard, 2000)

MUSSET, ALFRED DE, *Poésies nouvelles*, ed. by Jacques Bony (Paris: Flammarion, 2000)

PALSGRAVE, JEAN, *L'Esclaircissement de la langue françoyse* (Paris: [n.pub.], 1530)

RACINE, JEAN, *Théâtre complet de Racine*, ed. by Maurice Rat (Paris: Garnier, 1950)

——*Hymnes traduites du Bréviaire Romain: Le Lundi à Matines*, in *Oxford Book of French Verse*, ed. by St. John Lucas (Oxford: Oxford University Press, 1951)

RAMEAU, JEAN-PHILIPPE, *Hippolyte et Aricie*, ed. by Sylvie Bouissou (Kassel: Bärenreiter, 2010)

RIMBAUD, ARTHUR, *Œuvres complètes*, ed. by Rolland de Renéville and Jules Mouquet (Paris: Gallimard, 1954)

——*Oeuvres complètes*, ed. by Steve Murphy, 2 vols (Paris: Champion, 1999)

RONSARD, PIERRE DE, *Poèmes*, ed. by André Barbier (Oxford: Basil Blackwell, 1946)

——*Art poétique*, in *Œuvres complètes*, ed. by Gustave Cohen, 2 vols (Paris : Gallimard, 1950), II

SHAKESPEARE, WILLIAM, 'Sonnet XVII', in *The New Oxford Book of English Verse*, ed. by Helen Gardner (Oxford: Oxford University Press, 1972), p. 145

SUETONIUS, *The Twelve Caesars*, trans. by Robert Graves (Harmondsworth: Penguin, 1960)

TROYES, CHRÉTIEN DE, *Erec et Enide*, ed. by Mario Roques (Paris: Champion, 1978)

VALÉRY, PAUL, 'Le Cimetière marin', in *The Penguin Book of French Verse 4: The Twentieth Century*, ed. by Anthony Hartley (Harmondsworth: Penguin, 1959), p. 64

VILLON, FRANÇOIS, *Oeuvres complètes*, ed. by Auguste Longnon, 4th edn, rev. by Lucien Foulet, CFMA (Paris: Champion, 1932)

——*Poésies complètes*, ed. by Claude Thiry, Livre de Poche (Paris: Librairie Générale Française, 1991)

VIRGIL, *Aeneidos, liber quartus*, ed. by H. M. Stephenson (Oxford: Clarendon Press, 1924)

WACKEN, ÉDOUARD, *Fleurs d'Allemagne et poésies diverses* (Brussels: Labroue, 1850)

WADDELL, HELEN, *Medieval Latin Lyrics* (Harmondsworth: Penguin, 1962)

Secondary Works

ANTHONY, JAMES, *French Baroque Music: From Beaujoyeulx to Rameau* (London: Batsford, 1974)

BACKÈS, JEAN-LOUIS, 'Poétique comparée', in *Précis de littérature comparée*, ed. by Pierre Brunel (Paris: PUF, 1989), pp. 90–91

BALMAS, E., and Y. GUIRAUD, *Littérature française: de Villon à Ronsard* (Paris: Flammarion, 1986)

BAUMGARTNER, EMMANUELLE, *Poésies de François Villon* (Paris: Gallimard, 1998)

BEAUDOUIN, VALÉRIE, *Mètres et rythmes du vers classique: Corneille et Racine* (Paris: Champion, 2002)

BERTHOZ, ALAIN, *Le Sens du movement* (Paris: Odile Jacob, 1997)

BILLY, DOMINIQUE, 'La Versification d'André Chénier l'élégiaque', in *Lectures d'André Chénier: 'Imitations et préludes poétiques', 'Art d'aimer', 'Élégies'*, ed. by Jean-Noël Pascal (Rennes: Presses Universitaires de Rennes, 2005), pp. 103–16

BLANK, HUGO, *Kleine Verskunde* (Heidelberg: Carl Winter, 1990)

BURGER, MICHEL, *Recherches sur la structure et l'origine des vers romans* (Geneva: Droz, 1957)

CHARLTON, DAVID, *Opera in the Age of Rousseau* (Cambridge: Cambridge University Press, 2015)

CHERRY, COLIN, *On Human Communication* (Cambridge, MA: MIT Press, 1966)

CHOMSKY, NOAM, *Syntactic Structures*, Janua Linguarum, series minor, 4 (The Hague: Mouton, 1957)

COHEN, J. M., ed., *The Penguin Book of Spanish Verse* (Harmondsworth: Penguin, 1956)

CORNULIER, BENOÎT DE, *Théorie du vers: Rimbaud, Verlaine, Mallarmé* (Paris: Seuil, 1982)

——*Art poëtique: notions et problèmes de métrique* (Lyon: Presses Universitaires de Lyon, 1995)

——*De la métrique à l'interprétation* (Paris: Garnier, 2009)

CURTIUS, ERNST ROBERT, *European Literature and the Latin Middle Ages*, trans. by Willard Trask (Princeton, NJ: Princeton University Press, 2013)

DELOFFRE, FRÉDÉRIC, *Le Vers français* (Paris: SEDES, 1973)

DINU, MIHAI, 'Structures accentuelles de l'alexandrin chez Racine', *Langue française*, 99 (1993), 63–74

DUBOIS, JEAN, and OTHERS, eds, *Dictionnaire de linguistique et des sciences de langage* (Paris: Larousse, 1994)

DUFFELL, MARTIN, *Modern Metrical Theory and the Verso de arte mayor* (London: Department of Spanish Studies, Queen Mary and Westfield College, 1999)

DUJARDIN, EDOUARD, *Les Premiers Poètes du vers libre* (Paris: Mercure de France, 1922)

DURON, JEAN, 'L'Instinct de M. de Lully', in *La Tragédie lyrique*, ed. by Patrick F. Van Dieren and Alain Durel (Paris: Cicero, 1991), pp. 65–119

FABB, NIGEL, and MORRIS HALLE, *Meter in Poetry* (Cambridge: Cambridge University Press, 2008)

FAUQUET, JOËL-MARIE, 'Berlioz and Gluck', in *The Cambridge Companion to Berlioz*, ed. by Peter Bloom (Cambridge: Cambridge University Press, 1999), pp. 119–210

FOX, JOHN, *A Literary History of France: The Middle Ages* (London: Benn, 1974)

GARDE, PAUL, *L'Accent* (Paris: PUF, 1968)

GASPAROV, M. L., *A History of European Versification*, ed. by G. S. Smith and L. Holford-Strevens, trans. by G. S. Smith and M. Tarlinskaja (Oxford: Clarendon Press, 1996)

GAUDARD, FRANÇOIS-CHARLES, 'Poésie et versification dans les *Élégies* d'André Chénier', in *Lectures d'André Chénier: 'Imitations et préludes poétiques', 'Art d'aimer', 'Élégies'*, ed. by Jean-Noël Pascal (Rennes: Presses Universitaires de Rennes, 2005), pp. 117–31

GENDRE, ANDRÉ, *Evolution du sonnet français* (Paris: PUF, 1996)

GOULEMOT, JEAN M., and ANDRÉ TATIN-GOURIER, *André Chénier: poésie et politique* (Paris: Minerve, 2005)

GOUVARD, JEAN-MICHEL, *La Versification* (Paris: PUF, 1999)

——*Critique du vers* (Paris: PUF, 2000)

——'Éléments pour une grammaire de la poésie moderne', *Poétique*, 129 (2002), 3–31

GROUT, DONALD JAY, *A History of Western Music* (London: Dent, 1962)

GUIRAUD, PIERRE, *La Versification* (Paris: PUF, 1970)

HAAR, JAMES, 'The Operas and the Dramatic Legends', in *The Cambridge Companion to Berlioz*, ed. by Peter Bloom (Cambridge: Cambridge University Press, 1999), pp. 81–95

HACKETT, C. A., ed., *An Anthology of Modern French Poetry: From Baudelaire to the Present Day* (Oxford: Basil Blackwell, 1976)

HURFORD, JOHN, *Language and Number: The Emergence of a Cognitive System* (Oxford: Blackwell, 1987)

KASTNER, LOUIS, *History of French Versification* (Oxford: Clarendon Press, 1906)

KLAUSENBURGER, J., *French Prosodics and Phonotactics* (Tübingen: Niemeyer, 1970)

KOSCHWITZ, E., *Les Parlers parisiens: anthologie phonétique* (Paris: [n.pub.], 1896)

LEACH, ELIZABETH EVA, *Guillaume de Machaut* (Ithaca, NY: Cornell University Press, 2011)

LEVIN, SAMUEL, *Linguistic Studies in Poetry*, Janua Linguarum XXIII (The Hague: Mouton, 1962)

LOMBEZ, CHRISTINE, *La Traduction de la poésie allemande en français dans la première moitié du XIXe siècle: réception et interaction poétique* (Paris: Niemeyer, 2009)

LOTE, GEORGES, *L'Alexandrin d'après la phonétique expérimentale*, 2nd edn, 3 vols (Paris: La Phalange, 1913–14)

——*Histoire du vers français*, 4 vols (Paris: Boivin et Cie; Aix-en-Provence: Université de Provence, 1949–88)

LUCAS, ST. JOHN, ed., *Oxford Book of French Verse* (Oxford: Clarendon Press, 1951)

LUSSON, PIERRE, and JACQUES ROUBAUD, 'Mètre et rythme de l'alexandrin ordinaire', *Langue française*, 23 (1974), 41–53

——'Sur la devise de *Noeu et de Feu*: un sonnet d'Etienne Jodelle, essai de lecture rythmique', *Langue française*, 49 (1981), 49–67

MAZALEYRAT, JEAN, *Éléments de métrique française* (Paris: Armand-Colin, 1974)

MILLER, G. A., 'The Magical Number Seven Plus or Minus Two', *Psychological Review*, 63 (1956), 81–97

MILNER, JEAN-CLAUDE, 'Accent de vers et accent de langue dans l'alexandrin classique', *Cahiers de poétique comparée*, 15 (1987), 33–77

MURPHY, STEVE, 'Effets et motivations: quelques excentricités de la versification baudelairienne', in *Baudelaire: une alchimie de la douleur: études sur les Fleurs du Mal*, ed. by Patrick Labarthe (Paris: Eurédit, 2003), pp. 281–86

MUS, DAVID, *Le Sonneur de cloches: Villon, Shakespeare, Baudelaire, Mallarmé, Reverdy — et nous autres* (Seyssel: Champ Vallon, 1991)

NUSSBAUM, G. B., *Vergil's Metre: A Practical Guide for Reading Latin Hexameter Poetry* (London: Bristol Classical Press, 2001)

PASCAL, JEAN-NOËL, ed., *Lectures d'André Chénier: 'Imitations et préludes poétiques', 'Art d'aimer', 'Élégies'* (Rennes: Presses Universitaires de Rennes, 2005)

PENSOM, ROGER, *The Literary Technique of the Chanson de Roland* (Geneva: Droz, 1982)

——'On the Prosody of the Decasyllabic Lyrics of the Roi de Navarre', *French Studies*, 39 (1985), 257–75

——'Performing the Medieval Lyric', *Performance Review*, 10 (1997), 212–23

——*Accent and Metre in French: A Theory of the Relation between Linguistic Accent and Metrical Practice, 1100–1900* (Bern: Peter Lang: 2000)

——*Le Sens de la métrique de François Villon: Le Testament* (Oxford: Peter Lang, 2004)

——'Accent et syllabe dans le vers français: une synthèse possible?', *French Language Studies*, 19 (2009), 335–61

—— 'Musique et rythme chez Laforgue', *Poétique*, 160 (2009), 485–95

—— 'Sense and Rhythm in La Fontaine's *Fables*', *French Studies*, 64 (2010), 395–409

—— 'Rythme et sens', *Poétique*, 167 (2011), 53–72

POPE, MILDRED, *From Latin to Modern French* (Manchester: Manchester University Press, 1966)

PULGRAM, ERNEST, 'Prosodic Systems: French', *Lingua*, 13 (1965), 125–44

QUICHERAT, LÉON, *Traité de versification française* (Paris: Hachette, 1838)

RAVEN, D. S., *Latin Metre* (London: Bristol Classical Press, 2001)

REESE, GUSTAVE, *Music in the Middle Ages* (London: Dent, 1941)

RICKARD, PETER, *A History of the French Language* (London: Hutchinson, 1974)

RIGAULT, A., 'L'Accent secondaire de mot français: mythe ou réalité?', in *Actele celui de-al XII-lea congres international de lingvistică si filologie romanică*, 2 vols (Bucharest: Editura Academiei Republicii Socialiste Romania, 1970–71), I, 285–90

SAMPSON, GEOFFREY, *Schools of Linguistics: Competition and Evolution* (London: Hutchinson, 1980)

SCOPPA, ANTONIO, *Les Vrais Principes de la versification développés par un examen comparatif entre la langue italienne et la langue française* (Paris: Courcier, 1814)

SLATER, MAYA, *The Craft of La Fontaine* (London: Athlone, 2000)

SNEYDERS DE VOGEL, K., *Syntaxe historique du français* (Groningen: Wolters, 1919)

SPIRE, ANDRÉ, *Plaisir poétique et plaisir musculaire* (Paris: Librairie José Corti, 1949)

TAYLOR, ANNA LISA, *Epic Lives and Monasticism in the Middle Ages: 800–1050* (Cambridge: Cambridge University Press, 2013)

THIEME, HUGO, *Essai sur l'histoire du vers français* (Paris: Champion, 1951)

VAN DIEREN, PATRICK F., and ALAIN DUREL, eds., *La Tragédie lyrique* (Paris: Cicero, 1991)

VAN HASSELT, ANDRÉ, *Le Livre des paraboles* (Namur: Wesmael-Charlier, 1872)

VERLUYTEN, PAUL, 'Recherches sur la prosodie et la métrique du français' (unpublished doctoral thesis, University of Antwerp, 1982)

VERRIER, PAUL, *Le Vers français*, 3 vols (Paris: Didier, 1932)

WALKER, D. P., *Music, Spirit and Language in the Renaissance* (London: Variorum Reprints, 1985)

WARTBURG, W. VON, *Evolution et structure de la langue française* (Bern: Francke, 1946)

ZIPF, GEORGE KINGSLEY, *Selected Studies of the Principle of Relative Frequency in Language* (Harvard: Harvard University Press, 1932)

Website

1000 Most Common French Words, <http://french.languagedaily.com/wordsandphrases/most-common-words> [accessed 19 February 2010]

Recordings

BRULÉ, GACE, 'De bien amer grant joie atent', performed by Gothic Voices in *The Spirits of England and France* 2, directed by Christopher Page (Hyperion CD A66 773, 1995)

FORCALQUIER, GARSENDA DE, 'Vos que.m semblatz del corals amadors', performed by Hesperion XXI in *Cansos de Trobairitz*, directed by Jordi Savall (Virgin Classics, remastering of 1978 recording no. 7243 5 61310 26)

INDEX

Lightning Source UK Ltd.
Milton Keynes UK
UKHW030636270223
417728UK00010B/905